Mr Hamilton's Elysium

Mr Hamilton's Elysium

THE GARDENS OF PAINSHILL

'I . . . sauntered through the elysium of Mr. Hamilton's gardens
till eight in the evening, like the first solitary man through Paradise.'
LETTER FROM JOHN WILKES TO HIS DAUGHTER, 9 JUNE 1772

Michael Symes

FRANCES LINCOLN LIMITED

PUBLISHERS

In memory of my father, who loved Painshill

Frances Lincoln Limited
4 Torriano Mews
Torriano Avenue
London NW5 2RZ
www.franceslincoln.com

Mr Hamilton's Elysium: The Gardens of Painshill
Copyright © Frances Lincoln Limited 2010
Text copyright © Michael Symes 2010
Illustrations © as listed on page 176
First Frances Lincoln edition 2010

A catalogue record for this book is available from the British Library.

ISBN 978-0-7112-3055-2

Printed and bound in China

1 2 3 4 5 6 7 8 9

Commissioned and edited by Jane Crawley
Designed by Anne Wilson

PAGE 1 The Gothic Temple by GF Prosser, 1828.
PAGE 2 The Turkish Tent.
PAGE 3 The Turkish Tent, drawing with colour wash by Henry
Keene, *c.*1760.
THIS PAGE The 'Chinese' Bridge.

Contents

ABOVE The Ruined Abbey and vineyard from across the lake.

MR HAMILTON'S ELYSIUM

The Gardens of Painshill

*M*ANY VISITORS OVER THE YEARS have found Painshill to be a special and magical place that lingers long in the memory. They may well find it difficult to put the experience into words, but the impact is clearly the result of several factors that reach deep. This appeal operates on a number of levels – eye, heart and mind are all engaged and stimulated. There is also the psychological effect of the visitor circuit, giving a sense of roundness and fulfilment. This book aims to provide not only an account of the gardens and their maker but an understanding of the elements and features of which they are or were composed, often using contemporary comments by visitors who responded to the gardens at the time of their creation.

Painshill was not blessed in its natural topography. The land consists basically of three geological levels – the 100-foot terrace of the Thames, capped by gravel, the 50-foot terrace of the Thames and the flood plain of the River Mole that flows around it, ten to fifteen foot above sea-level. The soil is mainly sand, a mixture of sandy clay and peaty sand with silt found in the Mole valley. It is stony, too, and more acid than alkaline, which determined what plantings would do well.

The park and gardens at Painshill may look naturalistic but in fact are the result of long planning and skilful design. Formed by the Hon. Charles Hamilton between 1738 and 1773, they present a landscape that is rich, subtle and varied. Painshill is of its time yet timeless, and in many respects it was original and ahead of contemporary fashion and practice. Above all it has a presence and an atmosphere that are intangible and hard to put into words but which have affected visitors ever since it was created. Beauty and charm are the unchanging attributes.

During the eighteenth century, the age of the naturalistic landscape garden, Painshill was always considered to be in the highest rank. It was seen as a 'natural' composition that hid the considerable art that lay behind it. Joseph Warton gave it first place among the gardens which he said best embodied Alexander Pope's dictum that nature should never be forgotten:

> The best comments that have been given on these sensible and striking precepts, are, *Painshill*, *Hagley*, the *Leasowes*, *Persefield*, *Woburn*, *Stourhead*, and *Blenheim*; all of them exquisite scenes in different styles, and fine examples of practical poetry.[1]

A poem in nature's materials is a good metaphor for Painshill. Some visitors appreciated that art had played a major, though invisible, part in the design: Elizabeth Montagu, Queen of the Blue-stockings, commented in 1755:

> Pray follow me to Mr. Hamilton's: I must tell you it beggars all description, the art of hiding art is here in such sweet perfection, that Mr. Hamilton cheats himself of praise, you thank Nature for all you see, tho' I am informed that all has been reformed by art.[2]

When Samuel Richardson updated and revised Daniel Defoe's popular travel guide *A Tour Through the Island of Great Britain*, he judged Painshill to be unequalled, due in good measure to what art had been able to do for nature:

> This creation of Mr. Hamilton…justifies the general opinion of his consummate taste and knowledge in garden and park improvements: for, from a barren heath, by availing himself of fortunate inequalities of ground, and by a judicious disposition of plantation, which is unparalleled, with the addition of water and elegant buildings, he has produced a place which contains more internal beauties than can be seen in any other park or garden in this kingdom. There may be scenes where nature has done more for herself, but in no place that I ever saw, so much has been done for nature as at Painshill. The beauty and unexpected variety of the scene, the happy situation, elegant structure and judicious form of his buildings; the flourishing state, uncommon diversity, and contrasted groupage of his trees, and the contrivance of this water, &c.&c. will not fail to awake the most pleasing sensations of pleasure and admiration in every beholder of taste and sensibility.[3]

There we have in a nutshell the appeal of Painshill to contemporary visitors and as it still holds sway, though the remark about the barren heath has to be qualified (see pages 20–22). The natural appearance, the plantings, the use of water, buildings and exploitation of the topography combine to create a spell-binding series of views and experiences. Hamilton was both an artist who designed with a keen eye and a lover of trees and shrubs, and the combination was ideal for the forming of this remarkable garden.

The Rev. Stephen Duck, curator of Merlin's Cave in Richmond Gardens and a minor poet who drowned himself in a fit of melancholy, described Hamilton in 1755 as one of nature's children, adorning the Thames valley and cheering the populace with the produce of his vineyard:

> An honour'd Briton, Hamilton his name,
> Shall nobly beautify that silent stream;
> Whose curious nymphs shall leave their native floods,
> To visit and admire the stately woods;
> Delighted to survey the chequer'd scene
> Of flow'ring lawns and groves for ever green;
> And vineyards pregnant with the gen'rous bowl,
> To chear the drooping heart, and warm the frozen soul.[4]

Variety and surprise are the essence of the design. Many commentators at the time and since have seen variety as the central quality, a range which did not however mean a haphazard juxtaposition of ill-assorted scenes or objects. Thomas Whately, writing in 1770 after a visit probably made a few years earlier, perceived a consistency that united mixtures and contrasts:

> But Painshill is all a new creation; and a boldness of design, and happiness of execution, attend the wonderful efforts which art has there made to rival nature…Throughout the illustrious scene consistency is preserved in the midst of variety; all the parts unite easily.[5]

So it was that at Painshill the visitor would find a spectrum of colours, perspectives, changes in level, different views of the lake, contrasts of light and shade, dense and thin woodland, a great range of species of shrub and tree, and several styles of landscape and architecture. Despite the overall feeling of natural scenery, there were still one or two semi-formal areas such as the amphitheatre and the walk from it to the Gothic Temple.

Hamilton was a man in whom the visual sense was highly developed. He loved art and studied it; he painted; and the design of his parks and gardens is above all determined by his artist's eye. The materials he used, of course, were nature's, and his love of trees, shrubs and flowers ensured that the results would appeal as much to admirers of plantings. Painshill was planned as a sequence of different visual scenes, a kaleidoscope where buildings and other objects came forward or receded and presented a new appearance or effect when reached. Views were all, whether close-up or distant, and vistas (for instance framed or controlled views) appeared unexpectedly to reveal an object in a fresh light. Land Use Consultants in a survey in the 1980s identified a hundred separate axial views, which is testament to Hamilton's consummate subtlety of design.

Painshill was designed as a circuit garden, that is to say that there was an established way of going round it (broadly clockwise), as contemporary visitors indicated. It is not the only way, and visitors then and now could and can roam freely and discover scenes and pleasures for themselves. But the set circuit ensures not only that the scenes and views are seen to optimum effect and are not missed, but that the experience of viewing them in sequence is cumulative. In particular, it was often important that a building should first be seen at a distance (e.g. the Hermitage, Temple of Bacchus, Turkish Tent and Gothic Tower) and then encountered much later in the circuit by an indirect route. As William Shenstone said, the foot should never travel to an object the same way that the eye has travelled: 'Lose the object, and draw nigh, obliquely.'[6]

The idea of composing a garden as a series of scenes or tableaux in a landscape setting was relatively new. William Kent explored its possibilities in the 1730s, and in such a garden as Rousham, Oxfordshire, we can still see the intricate way in which the circuit (if followed correctly) reveals one set piece or picture after another. A second example would be Esher Place, Surrey, close to Painshill: although it has vanished, we can tell from visitors' descriptions and from the vignettes on John Rocque's plan of the estate that the buildings, with water or a small lawn in front of them, each constituted a tableau.

In the middle of the century there were several gardens which were based on the pictorial and circuit approach. Stourhead, Wiltshire, is probably the best known of these,

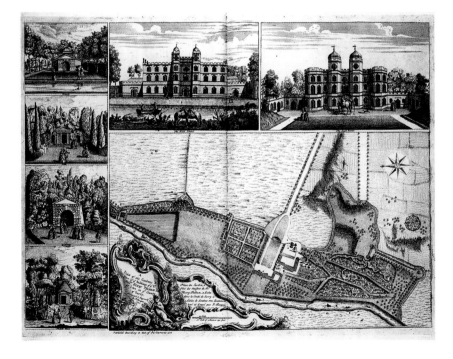

LEFT Plan of Esher Place by John Rocque, 1737.

with views across the lake ever changing as one goes round. The circuit was perhaps most pronounced at Shenstone's literary landscape of The Leasowes, Worcestershire (Shropshire at the time), where inscriptions marked the resting points so the visitor could savour the view and think the appropriate thoughts. The larger gardens, such as Stowe, Buckinghamshire, started to introduce guidebooks, and that in itself tended to suggest a set route. By 1770, when Whately's authoritative compilation of descriptions appeared, it was accepted that many sites had a preferred itinerary. Even in a small garden such as the eight-acre Woodhouse, Wombourne, West Midlands, the gardener was expected to conduct visitors round in the proper

sequence: to 'shew the wood and take People round the right way it being show'd wrong Distroys all the Effect'.[7] A circuit implied a journey, a path of discovery which led ultimately to a return to the start, completing a circle with a sense of fulfilment and purpose accomplished. In the case of Painshill, there was a final moment within the pleasure grounds before leaving across the park which provided a summing up and a remembrance of all that had gone before; this was the view from the Turkish Tent, which covered most of the features and provided a concluding and lasting snapshot and also a chance to reflect on what had been experienced (see page 64).

Hamilton's circuit was less obvious than most. If, as at many sites, the lake was the centrepiece, a path would go round, providing a simple viewing experience, mostly across the water. But at Painshill the path varies considerably – sometimes it proceeds alongside the water and sometimes it travels uphill and well away from the lake and into woodland or on to a clear plateau.

It is important to understand that Painshill was planned as a mixture of park and garden, with a distinct division. The highly-cultivated central area around the lake and on the amphitheatre was the garden, or pleasure ground as it was often called at the time. Beyond, including the wood to the west and the open land that stretched north to the house, was park, some of which was grazed by

ABOVE View of Stourhead.
LEFT Virgil's Grove, The Leasowes, engraving by James Mason after Thomas Smith, *c.*1752.
RIGHT Sketch of the grounds at Painshill by William Gilpin, 1772.

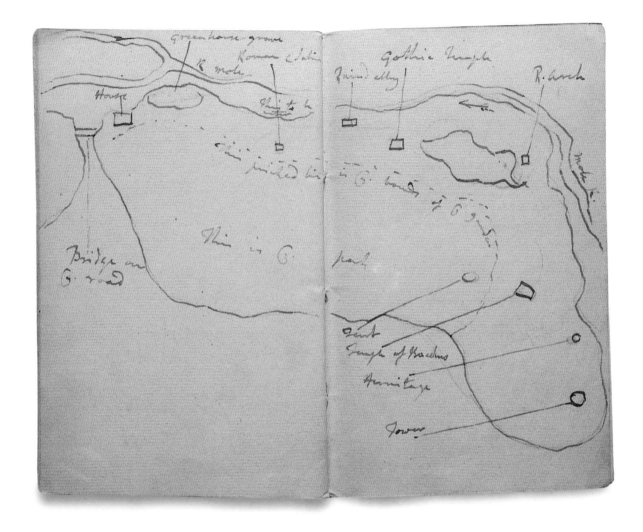

sheep. William Gilpin, in a rather scrappy sketch, makes the distinction and labels the two areas park and garden, even though he gets the proportions and spacing wrong. Where 'Capability' Brown would have used a ha-ha to denote the boundary between the two, Hamilton used blue mesh netting as a sort of invisible fence to keep the livestock out of the garden.

Painshill was also a garden independent of the house, which makes it a member of a very small group, including Stourhead and Rousham. Normally the house would be at the heart of an estate, whether a formal garden or a Brown park, but independence indicates the increasing status of the garden as an area of interest in its own right.

The circuit at Painshill was far from just visual. Apart from the interest of the plantings, the effects were emotional and associational, making the experience a voyage on many levels. In forming his contrasting scenes, Hamilton sought to alter the mood of his visitor, and this was achieved by a blend of buildings and plantings. Thus the Hermitage, a place for meditation and retreat from the world, was set at the edge of a dense, dark, damp forest, in order to engender gloom or melancholy. Immediately on leaving the wood one came upon a total contrast – the Temple of Bacchus, a light, cheerful building set in a lawn of colourful shrubs and flowers. The visitor's spirits were instantly lifted. The Mausoleum, too, had its own atmosphere: the ruined architecture was enhanced by the unkempt grass and the planting of yews around to give a feeling of solemnity and sadness at neglect, decay and the passing of former glories.

It is clear that many eighteenth-century thinkers were attracted to the idea that gardens should play upon the feelings of visitors. Shenstone considered that garden scenes could be categorised as sublime, beautiful or melancholy,[8] which he put into practice at The Leasowes, and the philosopher Lord Kames, writing in 1762, believed that individual areas within a garden could evoke particular moods and thoughts:

> Gardening, beside the emotions of beauty from regularity, order, proportion, colour, and utility, can raise emotions of grandeur, of sweetness, of gaiety, of melancholy, of wildness, and even of surprise or wonder.[9]

Kames thought that a good garden should inspire several emotions in turn:

> A ruin affording a sort of melancholy pleasure, ought not to be seen from a flower-parterre which is gay and cheerful. But to pass from an exhilarating object to a ruin, has a fine effect; for each of the emotions is the more sensibly felt by being contrasted with the other.[10]

It will be seen how readily these ideas were applied at Painshill. The emotional effect might come largely from what the eye saw – Kames actually called beauty an emotion, meaning that sight of it produced an emotion – but also from associations arising from (usually) a built object. The style of architecture would play a prominent part: thus, the classical buildings would suggest the world of ancient Rome, while the Gothic would evoke a British medieval past. The Turkish Tent would suggest something far away and exotic. Sculpture, too, would have various associations which the mind would make. So, while Painshill is in no sense a literary garden in the way that The Leasowes was, nor is the circuit allegorical, as it can be perceived to be at Stourhead, it is strongly an associationist garden.

A key principle in the design of Painshill is illusion. This particularly affects spatial awareness – the lake, because it changes shape and cannot be seen all at once, has often deceived visitors as to its actual size, as has the pine forest at the western end of the gardens. The open lawns were made to seem doubly large by cleverly placed plantings, again because they could not be seen in one view.[11] Buildings, too, could be deceptive, such as the Hermitage, which had a totally different back from its front and would be taken for another building when approached late in the circuit from the rear. Many of the buildings created illusion in being made of a different material from that which they appeared to be made from – the portico of the Temple of Bacchus and the Gothic Temple were of wood to resemble stone, and the Mausoleum, Gothic Tower and Ruined Abbey were of brick rendered to look like stone. The wooden five-arch bridge was often mistaken for stone. The grotto, again basically brick, was given a dressing of 'tufa' to look like a natural cave.

Illusion could extend to an entire area. The whole of Grotto Island was covered with 'tufa' constructions of various shapes and sizes as if to suggest an extensive outcrop of marine rock. Large boulders were strewn around the cascade to give the impression of mountainous terrain. The pine wood would suggest a forest.

There is something theatrical, too, in Hamilton's design. His control of illusion nods to the perspectives of a theatre as well as of a painting, and the buildings have sometimes been compared to a theatre or even a film set. The Kentian tableau, because it is of three dimensions, owes as much to the theatre as it does to art. And the amphitheatre, though so called because of the tiered nature of the plantings, suggests by name a link with the world of the theatre. In the eighteenth century the word 'theatre' could denote a place where things happened (compare the more modern 'theatre of war') as well as the more specific meaning of a place of performance; and a good many things happened at Painshill. The metaphor of the theatre occurred to Hamilton when describing in a letter the political turmoil of 'this theatrical Winter'.

Painshill may be seen as a garden with a political flavour in a broad sense of the word, inasmuch as the natural landscape look was being cultivated by the Whig Opposition, whose watchword was Liberty, expressed in gardening terms as freedom from geometrical constraints and from the authoritarian tyranny of design exemplified in Louis XIV's Versailles. As we shall see, Hamilton's work and social milieu brought him into the Opposition camp even though he himself was not politically active.

There was also a moral dimension to the gardens. Stephen Duck, in the poem quoted earlier, gives implicit approval to the vineyard as a source of giving pleasure, and Hamilton's transformation of the land from infertile to productive was very much in tune with the moral tenor of the times, although self-interest was permissible at the same time: 'were this sort of Husbandry practised in many other Parts of *England*, it would be of great Service to the Public, and amply increase the Value of the Lands to the Proprietor'.[12]

Painshill was not created in a vacuum, and Hamilton was well aware of contemporary developments in garden layout, some of which must have rubbed off on him. Writers such as Alexander Pope had been calling for a more natural approach much earlier in the century, though the relaxation of straight lines took time to

happen in practice. It was not until the 1730s that the more naturalistic look started to come in, and for some years geometry lingered on, often in conjunction with its opposite, especially in those gardens such as Stowe which had originally been constructed along bold formal lines. Even in William Kent's designs there are still straight lines. But the revolution had been started, and Hamilton can be seen as continuing and developing Kent's work in an ever richer and deeper way.

The date of 1738, when Hamilton commenced the creation of Painshill, was early in the history of the landscape garden, making him a pioneer. But a few gardens had been started, or begun to be re-shaped, by then, and several more grew up in the 1740s and 1750s when Hamilton was actively engaged in garden-making.

Some of those estates were close enough to have given Hamilton ideas, especially Claremont, Esher Place and Woburn Farm, all within a few miles of Painshill. Kent worked at the first two and advised Philip Southcote at Woburn.

At Claremont, more famed at the time than it is perhaps today, Kent had transformed Bridgeman's formal layout into something more natural and certainly more pictorial. It had a lake, an island with a building, a bridge and a belvedere by Vanbrugh that is a strong candidate for the inspiration behind Hamilton's Gothic Tower. The grotto by Stephen Wright (1750) could be a harbinger for the Painshill grotto, for it was cave-like in appearance and sited by the edge of the lake. Esher Place had a number of buildings in settings that showed them off, while Woburn Farm was the epitome of the *ferme ornée*, an estate where the decorations of a garden were brought into the agricultural parts. Shrubs and flowers were planted in profusion well away from the house, as at Painshill, and the walk to the belvedere, perched on top of a slope looking down on the River Bourne, resembled the straight walk from the amphitheatre to the Gothic Temple at Painshill, with its view down to the lake. The ruined chapel could well have been a contributory inspiration for Hamilton's abbey.

We do not know whether Hamilton knew Southcote, the owner of Woburn Farm, personally, but they had a mutual friend in Joseph Spence of Byfleet, and Hamilton appears to have followed several of Southcote's ideas on

TOP The Belvedere at Claremont.
ABOVE The grotto by Stephen Wright at Claremont.

design, as recorded by Spence. One was that the whole view of a garden should not be visible at once;[13] another that ''Tis best to look up to wood and down to water. Everyone must feel that 'tis more pleasing to see a hanging wood that one on a flat.'[14] In general, Southcote shared Hamilton's painterly approach to gardening: 'Perspective, prospect, distancing, and attracting, comprehend all that part of painting in gardening.'[15] Since both men were engaged at the same time (Southcote, with a slight head start, from about 1735), it is difficult to say that there was a definite influence one way or the other.

A fourth local garden, Oatlands, seat of the Earl of Lincoln, was known to Hamilton, but he may not have learned much from it. The grotto was the most obvious point of comparison, decorated by the Lanes, who constructed Painshill grotto, but their involvement was a decade later than at Painshill. Hamilton, in fact, disapproved of what Lincoln had done in the way of planting. In his only recorded thoughts on design he declared: 'At Oatlands they had done *just the contrary* to what they ought to have done: they had planted the low grounds close and left the hill quite naked.'[16] His own hanging wood, of course, demonstrates the reverse.

Slightly further afield lay Kew Gardens. Chambers's spate of buildings there postdates most of Hamilton's, but the Ruined Arch at Kew bears some resemblance to the Mausoleum at Painshill and may have been inspired by it. Contemporary with Hamilton in the service of the Prince of Wales, who owned Kew, was George Lyttelton of Hagley, Worcestershire. This estate, which may have been known to Hamilton at least by repute, **was** developed intensively in the late 1740s, and shared some of the qualities of Painshill – open landscape, buildings on eminences, a cascade and thick woodland.

As regards plantings, Hamilton cannot have been unaware of the Duke of Argyll's massive plantations and nursery at Whitton, near Hounslow Heath. Apart from his unparalleled collection of rare species from far away, Argyll placed lines of cedars on each side of his canal to magnificent effect, which could well have shown Hamilton the possibilities of this tree.

Hamilton knew the 2nd Duke of Richmond, so may well have been acquainted with his seat at Goodwood, Sussex, which became famous for its plantings, cedars in particular. From Hamilton's friendship with Richard Bateman he would probably have learned about, if he had not seen for himself, Bateman's flower-bedecked garden at Grove House, Old Windsor, which could have given him some ideas about ornamental planting. A more distant garden, which Hamilton saw in 1749, was Mount Edgcumbe, Cornwall. Although this expansive landscape, surrounded on three sides by sea, does not have much

something of it. Features which might possibly have impressed themselves on Hamilton included the Grecian Temple (compare the Temple of Bacchus), the cascade, the Gothic Temple and the grotto.

Perhaps the most significant comparison can be drawn with another Surrey garden, Virginia Water. There is no record of Hamilton making a visit, but circumstantial evidence points to a degree of familiarity. Virginia Water, at the time the largest artificial sheet of water in the country, was owned by William Cumberland, another son of George II, notorious as the 'Butcher of Culloden' for quelling the Jacobite rebellion in 1746. From that date there were a number of landscape developments that foreshadow similar elements at Painshill. One was the 'Chinese' bridge (actually Palladian) designed by Henry Flitcroft in about 1750. This massive single arch span made it the longest of all such bridges. The *chinoiserie* at Virginia Water was enhanced by a Chinese-style yacht built on the base of a hulk, which became known as 'The Mandarin', and a Chinese temple on an island. Other features which may have made their mark on Hamilton were the cascade and grotto. The rockwork cascade caused great trouble and later had to be replaced after flooding, but its appearance might well have influenced the Painshill cascade. The grotto nearby was also replaced, or relocated, much later but its rock construction might have planted a thought in Hamilton's mind.

in common with Painshill, it did have a ruined chapel, which might have been in Hamilton's mind when he constructed the Ruined Abbey twenty-three years later.

A central question is: did Hamilton ever visit Stowe? Through his connection with the Whig Opposition he would have been in contact with the men involved in its evolution as the greatest landscape garden of its time, and Richard Warner, writing many years later, seemed to think that Hamilton had encountered a building-filled garden which could well have been Stowe.[17] It would not actually have been necessary to visit Stowe: through guide books, prints and paintings it was the most recorded garden of all, and anyone interested in gardens would have known

All this is not to imply that Hamilton was a copyist. The combination of elements at Painshill makes it both original and unique, but Hamilton was inevitably of his time and sensitive to ideas and fashions swimming around him. Contemporary opinion set great store by his originality: George Mason, comparing the gardens with those at Hagley, wrote that 'Paine's Hill has every mark of *creative genius*, and Hagley of *correctest fancy*.'[18] In another such comparison, Arthur Young spent some time measuring Painshill (rather unfairly) against the spectacularly 'picturesque' landscape of Piercefield, Monmouthshire, concluding that '*Cobham* [Painshill] is the range of *beauty*; but *Persfield*, superiorly *sublime*.'[19]

Joseph Spence set out his theories of how a garden should be laid out in 1751, ideas which owe a great deal in turn to Pope. It will be seen how many of these ideas can be applied to Painshill, which implies that Hamilton and Spence, who knew each other well, had exchanged thoughts about the principles of design. Spence's rules were: (a) consult the Genius of the Place (its special character); (b) fix the principal viewpoint and any secondary points; (c) follow nature – no lines or angles; (d) assist or correct the general character of the ground if deficient or displeasing (e.g. add water or knolls); (e) correct or conceal a disagreeable object; (f) open a view to what is particularly agreeable; (g) 'manage your plantations in such a manner that you may be led to some striking object, or change, unexpectedly: in which case not only the change or object, but the surprise itself is pleasing'; (h) conceal the bounds (e.g. by fences, groves or ha-has); (i) unite the parts; (j) unite the outer parts with the countryside; (k) mix the useful with the ornamental; (l) draw distant objects nearer and hide the intermediate ground; (m) seek variety, inequality of surface, light and shade, different trees in groves; (n) place harmonious colours together; (o) provide overall light, to give joy. Spence concluded by saying that Pope summed it all up in one word, and it is a word that encapsulates Painshill – variety.[20]

BELOW Plan of Painshill Park today.
OPPOSITE View with the Gothic Temple in the distance.

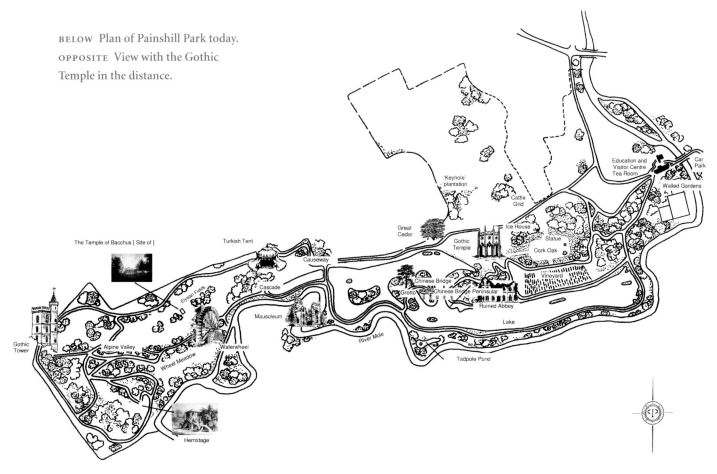

ABOVE View from the Hermitage across to the North Downs.

MR HAMILTON'S ELYSIUM

A Brief History of the Estate

HE HISTORY of the area known as Painshill Park is quite complex, both in terms of what happened chronologically and also in the matter of boundaries and ownership, which even required parliamentary intervention at one point to resolve the situation.[1] What emerges from looking at the early history is that the basis of the layout, the divisions of wood and open land, though much blurred by the time of Hamilton's arrival, gave him the broad lines of the design he was to create.

The name Painshill probably relates to an owner of part of the land. A Richard Payne (recorded c.1263) and a John Payn of Walton-on-Thames (1332) are candidates, but there is no conclusive evidence. The name itself – originally as 'The paynes hawe' or 'Painshill common field' – appears by the sixteenth century, referring to the land surrounding the present-day Pains Hill house. Other parts have other names.

Painshill was originally part of the Manor of Walton-on-Thames, though with close connections with Cobham, and by 1512 most of the land had been sold out of the manor. In 1511–12 part was conveyed to Richard Fox, Bishop of Winchester, who acquired the greater part of the property. As soon as 1516, however, he conveyed the whole of his land to Corpus Christi College, Oxford.

In 1539 Henry VIII established a new, enlarged Chase of Hampton Court which incorporated much land either side of the River Mole including Painshill. Freeholders within the Chase were allowed to remain but did not have hunting rights. A survey of the woods within the Chase (c.1540) indicates six groves within Painshill, including the forty-acre 'Greate grove', the three-acre 'hobbery', the two-acre 'paynes hawe' and the one-acre 'hale hill' that would in course of time be transformed into Grotto Island. The 'Greate grove' incorporated an area known as Redhill and the woodland to the west. The term 'grove' does not mean dense woodland, and open spaces could be found within the trees. Since 'the paynes hawe' and 'Painshill common field' (i.e. to be used as common land) were the same, the implication is that the space was pasture and herbage studded with trees.

After 1549, following the death of Henry VIII, the Crown land was leased out in separate plots. The two largest, known as the 'Tenement at Payneshill' (forty-nine and a half acres) and 'The Tenement at Coveham Bridge' (forty-eight and a half acres), were merged in 1570 as a single holding, the 'Tenement at Payneshill', thus establishing the nucleus of the future estate. By the terms

of the lease woodland was required to be managed, including coppicing and pollarding as well as felling at the appropriate time.

In March 1649 the Crown lands at Painshill were included in a survey by a parliamentary committee. Although there is some question as to whether the land described in this survey is identical to that of the lease a century earlier, the number of field names indicates that it was well farmed and also that the extent of woodland had become significantly reduced, the original named groves having all shrunk in respect of numbers of trees. Overall the land at this juncture comprised arable, pasture, meadow and woodland. It was farmed by a number of owners and tenants. Of the Crown lands the former Coveham (Cobham) Bridge holding included forty-five acres north of the Guildford (Portsmouth) road. This was the plot that was to become Hamilton's farm and which was already farmland.

Gabriel, Marquis du Quesne, son of a well-known French admiral, enters the scene in about 1717. In common with a number of his Huguenot countrymen he had fled France for the safety of England. He acquired

the freehold of two properties (Croft tenement and Lanshutts, part of the common field in the 1649 survey). He was ruined after the bursting of the South Sea Bubble in 1720, and had to mortgage the property the same year, but presumably remained until 1725, when it was acquired by William Bellamy of the Inner Temple, a Treasury barrister. To du Quesne are attributed the Vanbrugh-style house which Hamilton inherited, a barn, stable, granary, dovecote and gardens round the house, though Bellamy might have added to the house.

Parallel to the ownership by du Quesne was the holding of the Crown lease of the joint tenements of Painshill and Cobham Bridge by Robert Gavell from 1704, the year Hamilton was born. Gavell died in 1724, and Bellamy added the Crown lease to his freehold of the du Quesne property in 1725. The final parcel of land to be acquired by Hamilton, Redhill wood and farm, was a separate freehold, held from 1720 by Peter Cartwright.

Bellamy died in 1733, and Hamilton acquired the land, partly by purchase (of the freehold part) and partly by continuing the Crown lease. To meet the cost of the purchase Hamilton took out a mortgage of £3,000 from Henry Fox at the standard four per cent rate of interest. On 16 May 1737 Hamilton paid Fox £150, presumably in connection with the mortgage. Payment of interest would have amounted to £120 per annum.

The land when Hamilton took it over was in a meagre and unproductive state. Many eighteenth-century commentators considered the estate to have been largely or even entirely waste heathland. In theory this should not have been the case, as the various leases and surveys make clear, but in practice what might once have been farmland and woodland was very much in decline. The Crown lease, confirmed in 1738, spells out the division of half of Hamilton's land, totalling ninety-seven acres and three roods: sixty-eight and a quarter acres of arable, fourteen of meadow, seven and a quarter of pasture, thirty-two of woodland and four of waste. Of the former du Quesne holding of Lanshutts, approximately sixty acres, forty-five were 'coney warren', ten coppice and five meadow. Redhill wood and farm, purchased in about 1740, comprised forty to fifty acres. This all sounds varied and fertile, but the reality was very different, as Thomas Ruggles noted in 1786:

> a great proportion of the plantations there, are on very poor sandy soil; and by the taste of Mr Hamilton, now form a beautiful and profitable contrast to the poor and unproductive rabbit warren which it was when that gentleman, with his prophetic eye of taste, first viewed and purchased the land.[2]

Large tracts of the district around Cobham were bare heath, which contributed to the overall image. For example, Salmon's *Antiquities of Surrey* (1736) (of which Hamilton had a copy) describes Cobham as a 'large Parish with much heavy and woody land in it, and a great deal of barren Heath'.[3] The approach to Painshill from Cobham Heath emphasised the impression of 'dreary wild heath…called Cobham Heath, as barren and wild as a mountain'.[4] A French visitor observed that it was evident from the top of the tower that the gardens were set in the midst of arid heathland.[5] Painshill was considered to have originally been part of this scene by commentators such as Dodsley (1761), who declared that Hamilton had made great improvements 'by inclosing a large tract of barren land, which though so poor as to produce nothing but heath and broom, he has so well cultivated and adorned, that few places are equal to it'.[6]

It was generally acknowledged that Hamilton went to great lengths and considerable difficulty to transform the estate into his landscape garden. From waste, scrub and stony soil he created a landscape that was both ornamental

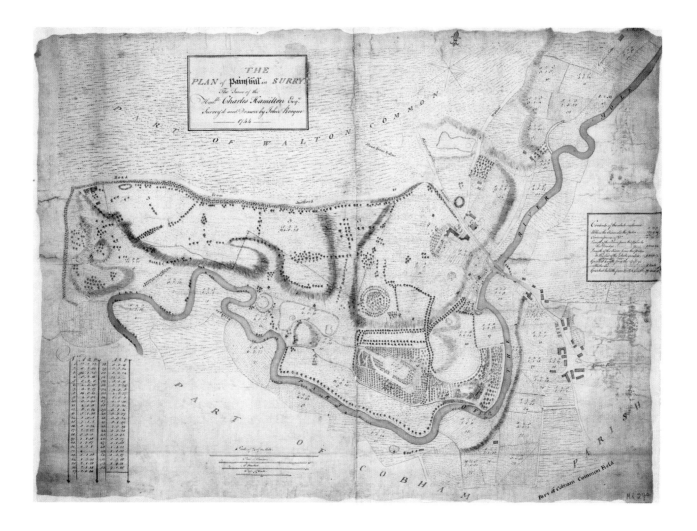

and productive. This made a deep impression on visitors, who continued to stress the earlier poor condition of the land. One such was Henry Skrine, who declared in 1801 that Hamilton had 'rescued it from a rude uninteresting common'.[7]

The length of the Crown lease was thirty-one years, the maximum duration permitted by statute at the time. This agreement had been revised, since the unexpired portion of the original lease to Gavell would have lasted for a further eighteen years only. The rent was £6 16s 4d per annum. Together the freehold and Crown areas totalled approximately 185 acres, with up to fifty further acres added by the acquisition of Redhill.

In the summer of 1761 a dispute arose over the land leased from the Crown, in particular a patch of two acres that Hamilton said was never his but had earlier fraudulently been taken from the Crown holdings. In order to resolve the situation Hamilton had to renew the lease for a further twenty-one and three-quarter years from the expiry of the existing lease in July 1769 at the same rental. However, Hamilton neglected to maintain the boundaries of the Crown land, and he was taken to task. In 1763 he agreed to make distinct boundaries as determined by the King's Surveyor-General. But that was not the end of the matter: after the death of Hamilton's successor, Benjamin Bond Hopkins, in 1794, there was further uncertainty and it became necessary for an Act of Parliament to be passed in 1795 so that the Crown could grant the appropriate land in fee-simple to Bond Hopkins's trustees before the estate could be sold.

What is difficult to determine is the state of any previous gardens or ornamental plantings when Hamilton arrived. The Marquis du Quesne (and/or Bellamy) had made gardens near the house, and there may well have been a line of trees to screen off the river to the south. A key piece of evidence is the plan drawn up by the surveyor and cartographer John Rocque (see opposite). Although dated 1744 it may relate to a survey conducted some years earlier, which would be consistent with Rocque's practice. So the question is, does the survey represent early Hamilton, the estate as he took it over, or a mixture of both?

On balance, and taking into account the state of the land as Hamilton acquired it, Rocque probably represents early Hamilton plantings. A perhaps surprising degree of formality is to be seen – the amphitheatre lawn on top of what was the scrub-covered Wood Hill and the large series of concentric circles constituting what has become known as the 'Keyhole'. Interestingly, both these formal features hark back to Renaissance and seventeenth-century Italian gardens which Hamilton may have known about. The amphitheatre has some similarities with the hippodromes at the Villa Mattei and the Villa Doria-Pamphili in Rome, while the 'Keyhole' could be derived from circular plantings such as at the Villa Ludovisi or the central grove of cypresses, myrtle and laurel at the Medicean villa of Castello. Its elaborate pattern consisted of seven circles, the innermost four of beech, the fifth of Scots pine and beech and the outer two of Scots pine. The outer circle has an extension including cedars, larch and juniper. Some of these trees have survived.

The survey illustrates the foundation on which Hamilton was to work for the next thirty years. The embryonic lake can be seen as a tight crescent; the water meadow below the site of the vineyard would become the final arm of the lake; the oak and birch in the western part, on Redhill, was to form the basis of his wild woodland. The concentration of planting was on the freehold land, which suggests Hamilton may have been initially reluctant to cultivate the Crown lease parts, perhaps through insufficient security of tenure.

Hamilton made full use of existing trees which related to the old field boundaries and which could be used as the basis of his sylvan plantings. These would, of course, have been native species, mostly oak and birch. Old paths, often relating to earlier divisions of the landscape, would be utilised, and pasture was regenerated for its proper purpose.

Much of the land had to be converted into fertile soil and lawn. The soil was often sandy or stony, and it was a considerable labour to produce acres of rich grass for pasture and for ornament. There is an account by Hamilton himself of the methods he used, which was sent to Lord Kildare of Carton House, Ireland in 1750. Kildare told Henry Fox that he was greatly obliged to Hamilton for it, having 'read it more than once, and shall

LEFT Plan of Painshill by John Rocque, 1744.

RIGHT Sheep grazing with the Turkish Tent beyond.

again and again'.[8] This no doubt laid the foundation for the superb landscape at Carton.

Hamilton starts his account by stating that the two principal objects are to cleanse the ground from weeds and to lay it down smooth. If any soil was particularly foul he would spend a whole year in cleansing it by ploughing four or five times and harrowing closely after each ploughing, first with an ox harrow and then with small harrows. All couch grass and weeds would thus be brought to the surface and then they were burned. If weeds grew up again the ploughing would be repeated. After these operations the soil was fine enough for wheat; if it was spring, he would sow it with grass seeds and barley, which would protect the young grass from the summer sun. If the soil was not ready until August, the grass would be sown by itself.

If by June in a given year the soil looked as if it needed further attention (as it usually did, Hamilton noted), he would sow it with turnips. Because the turnips required frequent hoeing, this would cleanse the soil thoroughly. After Christmas sheep would feed on the turnips, and their manure further improved the soil. After the turnips had gone, by March, the final ploughing and harrowing would follow, and after the weeds had been removed and burned, grass seeds and barley would be sown as above.

Hamilton said he sowed six English bushels of the cleanest hayseed he could find, together with ten pounds of fresh Dutch clover seed, to each acre. If a quantity of the clover seed was required, the best thing was to get it direct from Holland.

If the ground required levelling first, before sowing, the ridges were ploughed into the furrows, and harrowing across what was left of the ridges spread the loose soil into the furrows. However, complete evenness was impossible to attain, so a few men were set to batter the earth flat with spades and to fill any hollows. The earth was so fine by this time that it could be worked very easily. The difficulty was not the soil but getting labourers with a good enough eye for levelling perfectly. If it was not done properly the old lines of ridge and furrow would show up when the grass grew. Hamilton said it took very few men to give such a finish to the ground, covering more than twenty acres in a day.

Much later Hamilton was to claim that the best and cheapest way to improve bare moor or heath was to plant it thickly with firs and pull them up after twelve years. The surface soil could then be treated with a compost of lime and dung.[9]

Hamilton's methods were largely in accordance with the standard practice of the day, and were derived in part from practical books in his library. Philip Miller was the principal source, who himself owed much of his material to previous authors such as Gervase Markham. Hamilton had *Markhams Farwell to Husbandry* (1620), which instructed on the enrichment of barren and sterile ground. This set out methods of ploughing, harrowing, burning and sowing. It was widely recognised that manured turnips were an excellent preparation for later sowing, and the clover grass that Hamilton mentioned was strongly favoured at the time – one of the 'grand pillars of British agriculture' as Arthur Young called it in 1770 in a section extolling its virtues and uses.[10]

During the 1740s the emphasis was on the eastern half of the property, especially in terms of planting, and included the laying out of the first vineyard and the enlargement of the lake. Since the lake as finally formed was several feet higher than the level of the River Mole which fed it, a device (the water wheel) had to be put in place that would raise water. Horace Walpole reported in 1748 that Hamilton had 'really made a fine place out of a most cursed hill',[11] meaning that Wood Hill (the amphitheatre hill) had been transformed from most unpromising ground.

By 1754 the plantings were well under way and the wild wood to the west was also maturing as Hamilton

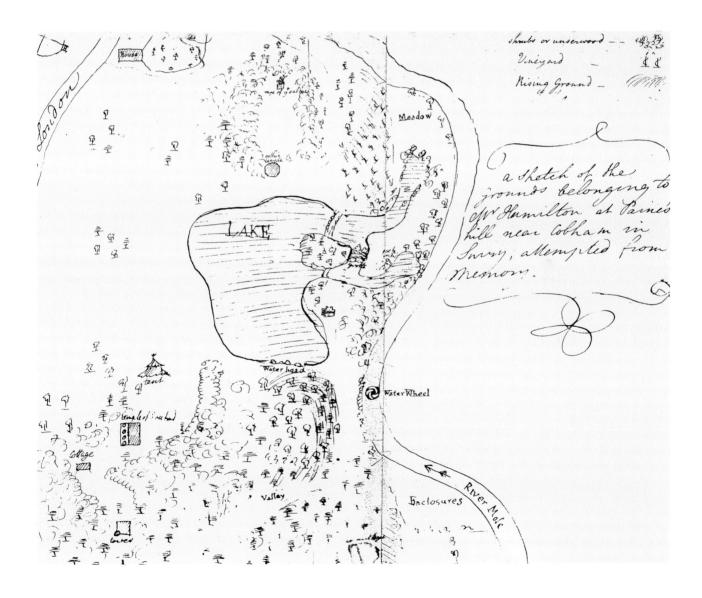

LEFT Portrait of Benjamin Bond
Hopkins by Francis Wheatley, *c.*1780.
RIGHT Plan of Painshill by Thomas
Crawter, 1797.

intended.[12] The second vineyard, over the road on the
north side, had been established. Oddly, John Parnell
describes the second vineyard as new in 1769, but it had
perhaps been replanted by then.[13] The walled gardens
were constructed in 1756, and towards the end of the
1750s buildings started to appear in the landscape, sited
mostly on a knoll or other prominent position so as both
to give a good view and to stand out in the view from a
distance. The building would often be complemented by
appropriate planting around it.

These follies were largely built by 1762, but the
greatest undertaking was still to come. In the early 1760s
work started on the grotto, a massive project which
involved linking two halves of an island by a rockwork
bridge and structural and ornamental operations on an
unprecedented scale. The 'tufa' cladding to the grotto
was carried on in outcrops all over the island. Work was
still continuing until at least the end of the decade.

Towards the end of the 1760s Hamilton tried to
provide bricks from his own resources and built a tile
and brick works on the site of what later became the
Ruined Abbey. After the financial failure of this enterprise

Hamilton effaced the works by covering them up and
constructing the Ruined Abbey in 1772 as the last built
feature from the time of his ownership. The purpose was
also to increase the sale value of the property.

Even the basic design of the landscape was altered right
up to Hamilton's departure. In front of the Ruined Abbey
and the vineyard the flat water meadow was converted
into a final arm of the lake, again to add to the value of
the place. Hamilton sold up in the spring of 1773, and
the estate was acquired by Benjamin Bond Hopkins, an
immensely wealthy man who owned several properties in
Surrey already, adding Wimbledon House in 1777. Under
Bond Hopkins there were 'several judicious alterations',[14]
and he is said to have spent a great deal of money on the
grounds in addition to building the large house (designed
by Richard Jupp, for thirty years surveyor to the East
India Company) that Hamilton had always wanted. He
thinned out the trees that had not done well, continued
Hamilton's policy of growing newly-introduced trees
and planted particularly on the terrace of the house and
on the slopes below. He constructed the Bath House near
what has become the giant cedar and a small island in the

lake in front of it. He also focused on the eastern arm of the lake, which Hamilton had not had time to beautify, and created the Solitary Bower and a boathouse at the end, together with the walk and screen planting on the south side opposite the vineyard.

Although Bond Hopkins died in 1794, the estate was not sold until 1797, partly because of the dispute over the Crown boundaries which had had to be referred to Parliament. The new owner, Robert Hibbert, and his successor, William Moffat, were both West Indies merchants who held the property for four years each. Under Bond Hopkins, visiting days to Painshill started as Tuesdays and Fridays, but changed to Mondays, Wednesdays and Fridays. As the *Universal British Directory* (*c.*1791) announced, however, 'Foreigners are admitted at any time'. In order to see the grotto at that period, a ticket

had to be obtained from Bond Hopkins in London.[15] Hibbert kept the same visiting days, but Moffat made himself unpopular by closing the gardens to the public.

In 1805 Henry Lawes Luttrell, 2nd Earl of Carhampton, who already lived at Cobham Park to the south of Painshill, purchased the estate from Moffat and stayed there till his death in 1821. His widow continued to live there till her own death in 1831. A single tree, the 'Carhampton oak', planted near the grotto, with an inscription to commemorate Wellington's victory at Waterloo, used to be his chief memorial, but Carhampton reshaped the plantings considerably. These included Scots pines to obliterate the derelict vineyard; oak and sweet chestnut near the wheel island; oak on Wood Hill and to the west of the walled gardens. The amphitheatre was planted over. Screen planting on the boundaries was

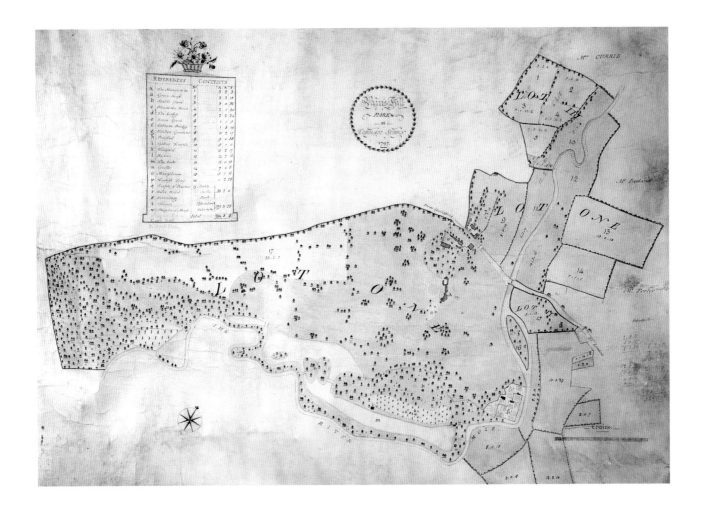

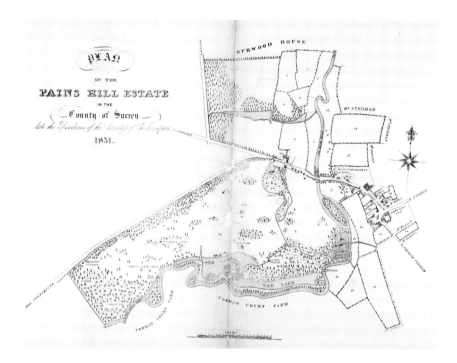

LEFT Sale plan of Painshill, 1831.
RIGHT Bath house and giant cedar
in 1937.

extensive: beech to the west, mixed with Scots pine and sweet chestnut, oak to shut off the Portsmouth road, yew and oak to exclude Cobham. In addition to, and partly to service, the new plantations, a series of new paths was constructed. The overall effect was to blunt and even distort some of Hamilton's design. The ice house is dated to the Carhamptons' time. The Countess of Carhampton, like Moffat before her, closed Painshill to the public after a renewed period of access.

In 1832 William Cooper, even wealthier than Bond Hopkins, took up residence, and the family was to remain until 1863. He brought in Decimus Burton to modify the house and build a conservatory, and installed the cast-iron water wheel by Bramah, who also replaced Hamilton's wooden bridge over the road with a suspension bridge in iron. The horse-pump by the large cedar also dates from those years. Cooper's main structural change to the landscape was a terrace walk from the road bridge to the southern end of the mansion. Cooper seems to have been almost as adventurous in planting introductions as Hamilton had been. To his period are attributed Wellingtonias (*Sequoiadendron giganteum*), Douglas fir (*Pseudotsuga menziesii*), coast redwood (*Sequoia*

sempervirens), Monterey pine (*Pinus radiata*), western red cedar (*Thuja plicata*) and deodar cedars (*Cedrus deodara*). He also planted well-established species such as cedars of Lebanon, sessile oaks (*Quercus petraea*), red oaks (*Q. rubra*), Corsican pines (*Pinus nigra maritima*) and robinias. Wood Hill was extensively planted (or replanted).

Harriet Cooper died in 1863, but because of legal disputes among her heirs the property was not sold until nine years later. Charles Leaf, a London dealer in silk and ribbon, was the new owner and brought in Norman Shaw to make alterations to the house. In turn he sold Painshill to Alexander Cushney in 1887. Cushney married in old age, and after his death in 1903 his young widow, a local beauty, married Charles Combe of Cobham Court south of the River Mole, thus uniting two large Cobham estates. Few changes were made in the Leaf/Cushney period, though some planting, including a larch plantation on the northern side of the park and one of Douglas fir near the Bath House, took place.

The Combes, however, were more ambitious. The slope of the vineyard was planted with flowers and marked by a rockery, with rustic steps formed by boulders taken from Hamilton's cascade. A terraced garden south

The Hon. Charles Hamilton

CHARLES HAMILTON came from a branch of the house of Hamilton which held the Abercorn earldom. By his time the family had established itself in Ireland, though originally the branch was Scottish, dating back to James Hamilton, 2nd Earl of Arran (1516–75). Although born into the Irish aristocracy, Hamilton spent most of his life in England. He was the fourteenth child, and the youngest son of nine, of James, the 6th Earl of Abercorn, who was a Protestant where his predecessors had supported the House of Stuart. James entered the Irish House of Lords in 1703 and became an Irish Privy Councillor to Queen Anne, George I and George II in turn. He died at the age of seventy-three in November 1734 and was buried in Westminster Abbey. His widow Elizabeth survived him by twenty years. Of Charles's brothers and sisters, James (who became the 7th Earl) was a Privy Councillor of England in 1738 and Ireland in 1739; George was an Irish MP from 1727 to 1780 and also MP for Wells 1747–54; and in 1719 or 1720 Jane married Lord Archibald Hamilton, son of the 3rd Duke of Hamilton, from the principal Scottish branch of the family. Lord and Lady Archibald figure in the story a little later on.

Born in 1704, Charles Hamilton was baptised at St Peter's in Dublin on 13 November of that year. Although he must have moved to England at an early age, he retained some financial interests in the Dublin property, as we shall see. In 1718 he went to Westminster School, where he would have studied Latin and Greek, and met fellow pupils who would become friends in adulthood, notably William Beckford, to be known as the Alderman and who acquired Fonthill; Henry Hoare, who would create Stourhead and become Hamilton's banker; and John Petty FitzMaurice, who would become 1st Earl of Shelburne and set in train the improvements to the grounds at Bowood.

After Westminster came Oxford, where he went up to Christ Church in 1720, gaining his BA in 1723. It was while he was up at Oxford that he met Henry and Stephen Fox, sired in old age by Sir Stephen Fox who indulged his own garden interests in a property adjoining Chiswick Villa. Both Fox brothers were to go on to achieve distinguished careers, particularly Henry, who was later created Baron Holland. Hamilton maintained constant touch with Henry until the latter's death in 1774.

LEFT Portrait of Charles Hamilton by Antonio David, 1732.

In 1725 Hamilton set off on the Grand Tour, almost obligatory for one in his position. In a letter to Horace Walpole written from Bath in January 1784 Hamilton corrected Walpole's account of the family history, particularly the French connections. Hamilton explained that his Grand Tour took him via the Academy in Lorraine, where he met some of his distant relations. He spent a week there 'most agreeably' and was shown 'the portraits of all my great uncles and aunts', including the Count and Countess of Grammont.[1] His knowledge of French was good, as the later correspondence with the Abbé Nolin demonstrates. Elizabeth Hamilton had married the reputedly dissolute Philibert, Comte de Grammont (1621–1707), who came over from France to claim her. On his return 'he was overtaken at Dover by her brothers Anthony and Richard, who asked him if he had forgotten anything in London. He replied: "I have forgotten to marry your sister", and turned back.'[2]

Hamilton reached Rome for the 'Jubilee', a year of festival in the Catholic calendar marked by the granting of indulgences. What he told Joseph Spence, who recorded the conversation as he did with many of his friends and contacts including the poet Pope, was corroborated personally in a letter in 1770, namely that he spent twenty-two months at a palace in the Corso in Rome and during that time associated with the best families in the country.[3] He is also listed in the Roman parish registers as living in the Strada Paolina, though as a staunch Protestant he was recorded as 'Carlo Amilton eretico'.[4] This tour was to make a lasting impression in a number of ways. First, it fostered his taste for the fine arts and acquainted him with the great works of antiquity and the Renaissance. His love of paintings and sculpture certainly grew from his exposure to Italy. Second, his collection of the *objets d'art* themselves would be a permanent physical reminder even if his memories of the places visited might dim. Whether consciously or unconsciously Italy would always be prompting him when he later started work on his great landscape.

It is likely that the bulk of Hamilton's collection (see following chapter), both paintings and sculpture, was acquired during this first visit, when he had time to cultivate acquaintances. Protective Papal edicts made it difficult to take some precious objects out of Italy, and Hamilton reported that he had had to buy the prize of his collection, the statue of Bacchus, from one of the noble families with a promise of secrecy.[5] This may have been to dramatise the situation – his reputed payment of up to £2,000 for the sculpture would have been way beyond his means.

While in Italy Hamilton travelled extensively. In March 1727 William Bentinck set off in company with Hamilton to Verona, though Hamilton left the party to go on to Munich.[6] Four days later he was back to join Bentinck in a trip to the University of Padua,[7] where he would have seen the old botanic garden. He also visited Vicenza and Naples, though the latter might have been on either of his tours. It may be that during his time in Italy he studied painting, as Uvedale Price and others seemed to think: there would have been no shortage of tutors.

On his return, Hamilton became MP for Strabane in Ireland in 1727, a position he held until 1760. Very much an absentee member, he does not appear to have devoted any time to constituency duties, and for six years of that time he was also an MP in England. The Strabane position was probably a sinecure obtained for him by his father the Earl. Between 1727 and 1730 he married his first wife, by whom he had two daughters, Jane and Sarah, who were close in age and born around 1730. Nothing is known of the first Mrs Hamilton – even her first name eludes us (possibly Jane?) – and it is quite likely that she died early, perhaps in childbirth.

It is not clear what Hamilton was doing professionally at this time, but he was around Court and he associated with the Fox brothers and Lord Hervey, who became Vice-Chamberlain at Court in 1730. There is a record of a visit by Henry Fox and Hamilton to a reception at Windsor where Hervey was officiating.[8] Hamilton was also a keen sportsman as a young man, and the portrait by Antonio David, showing him with two pointers and a gun (see page 30) is authentic as well as a conventional view of a British gentleman. He often went on shooting parties with Henry and Stephen Fox and other friends, but in 1731 his active participation ceased after some kind of accident to his hand at Redlynch, Somerset, a country seat belonging to Sir Stephen Fox which had passed to Stephen.[9] While the injury was healing, Hamilton attended Frederick, Prince of Wales, under whom he later took up an official post. But looking after the Prince when the latter was sick did not please Hamilton, who never cared much for him even though he occupied an important position in Frederick's household for several years.

Hamilton paid a second visit to Rome in 1732 to join Henry Fox, who had gone out the previous summer. The fact that Hamilton was on his own suggests that his wife had already died. Fox also had his portrait painted by David, forming a pair (see page 41). According to Joseph Spence, Hamilton mentioned having dined with Lord Middlesex at Sir John Collins's house in Rome,[10] but this encounter may have been a mixed blessing since Lord Middlesex, along with Sir Francis Dashwood, was reported seldom to have been sober during his time in Italy. Spence, who was Middlesex's tutor, listed a Mr 'Hambleton' among the people he met in Italy, but the name appears under Geneva for 1731, which is too early, although a second reference, under Florence, is for 1732 and could conceivably be a misspelling for Hamilton, since he was so spelled elsewhere.[11]

During this second stay, Hamilton may well have augmented his collections of art. He met the artist and dealer George Knapton, who encouraged him in his acquisitions and introduced him to the commercial art world, as will be discussed in the next chapter. A good many Italian books were also purchased, as the inventory of his library shows. These two lengthy spells in Italy had a profound effect on Hamilton as well as making him feel thoroughly comfortable: he later said he would be happy to spend the rest of his life there.[12] It is surprising that Hamilton never joined the Society of Dilettanti, founded in 1732 for the purpose of fostering interest in classical culture among those who had been on the Grand Tour, but the heavy emphasis on conviviality may not have appealed to him.

As Henry and Stephen Fox started to make their mark in politics on the side of the Whig administration, it is surprising to find Hamilton in the Opposition circle that began to build up particularly after 1733. The alignment of Government–Opposition was not simply Whig–Tory, however, and there was a Whig Opposition group of great strength (sometimes they joined forces with the Tories). It was to this group that Hamilton was attached while Henry Fox steadfastly supported the First Minister, Sir Robert Walpole. There were many thinkers and artists within the Whig Opposition who were connected with the landscape gardening movement, and Hamilton would have had the chance to absorb their ideas. One of these was William Pitt the Elder, whom Hamilton knew from about this time. Lord Cobham, who owned and planned Stowe, fell out with Walpole in 1733 and the Whig Opposition formed around him, basing its ideology on the defence of liberty and the Constitution.[13] Many of those who created the outstanding landscapes of the eighteenth century, which helped to express these ideals, were associated with each other through family or through their mutual membership of the Whig Opposition party.

In 1736 Stephen Fox married Elizabeth Strangways-Horner secretly because her father thought her too young and also objected to Stephen's politics. A second ceremony was conducted on 22 March, and Hamilton was one of the witnesses.[14] Both the Foxes' marriages were shrouded in secrecy, and there is some doubt as to whether Henry married legally (he eloped with Caroline, daughter of the 2nd Duke of Richmond). Notwithstanding political differences, Hamilton's friendship with the two brothers continued to be close, and they often referred playfully to him as 'Hammy'. The Fox connection brought Hamilton into the Richmond circle, which had significant gardening implications. Lady Caroline herself was very interested in plantings; the Duke was an avid plantsman; and Caroline's sister Emily married Lord Kildare and planned the gardens at Carton. We have seen Hamilton's advice to Lord Kildare in the previous chapter.

It was in 1737 that Hamilton started to acquire the lands at Painshill. The taking out of a mortgage from Henry Fox marked the start of a life of borrowing and debt: Hamilton was never in easy financial circumstances and had to borrow heavily from his bank in later years as well as from Fox. It was only through the eventual sale of Painshill that he could straighten out his finances. In the same year he was instrumental in securing for Stephen Fox the conditional promise of a peerage, which Stephen declined. This suggests that at this point Hamilton cannot have been without influence in high places, though such influence may have been through Lady Archibald, his sister, who exercised considerable power over the Prince of Wales.

At this time Hamilton was living in rented accommodation in Grosvenor Square (east side). In later years he would maintain a town residence in Welbeck Street.

The year 1738 marked a turning-point in Hamilton's life. He moved into Painshill and took up office in the Prince's household as 'Clerk Comptroller' (equivalent to the Comptroller of the Green Cloth in the King's household), a position he held for eight years. The appointment was made by warrant on 22 April. The post of Clerk Comptroller meant Hamilton was responsible for domestic arrangements under the Treasurer of the Household, Lord Scarborough. The job was essentially that of supervising and checking household accounts. The servants doing the domestic work were 'below' stairs, while those who attended the Prince and had ceremonial duties (and who were usually of good family) were 'above' stairs.[15] Principal among the Princess's own attendants was the Mistress of the Robes, and this post was given in 1736 to Lady Archibald, then at the crest of her favour with the Prince. Lord Archibald was surveyor and member of the Prince's council from 1738, and the family was so well represented in the Prince's household that it was said that if one were to meet a stranger there it would probably be appropriate to address him as Hamilton.

The influence exerted by Lady Archibald over the Prince is indicated by William, Earl of Shelburne (later 1st Marquess of Lansdowne), who was supplied by an elderly Hamilton with some contemptuous anecdotes, revealing how much Hamilton disliked his employer. According to Shelburne, the Prince promised to marry Lady Archibald as soon as her husband died, 'who, however, though old, lived longer than was convenient to his wife or to the Prince'.[16] Hamilton told Shelburne that once he had been summoned to attend the Prince and had had to miss the dinner he was about to sit down to, only to find that the business the Prince required him to conduct became forgotten as the Prince drew Hamilton in to play cricket with the page boys in a saloon in Norfolk House.[17] The third anecdote can be told in Shelburne's words:

The Prince gave Mr. Hamilton a full length picture of himself, his hand upon a Prayer Book, which was understood to have represented his solemn engagement to marry his sister. Mr. Hamilton has often told me that he despised the man so heartily, he could not endure to hang it up, and it lies ever since in a store-room.[18]

The dislike was almost certainly caused, or intensified, by the Prince's affair with Lady Archibald. Matters came to a head when the Prince wanted to make occasional use of Hamilton's town house for the purpose:

Mr. Hamilton refused it. The Prince taking him to task in Carlton House gardens, some strong expressions passed, and the Prince challenged him to fight him in the grove which makes part of the garden; but Lady Archibald took care to be near enough to interpose and save her hero from all harm.[19]

This sounds as if Hamilton would have been expected to have come off better, though it is of course Hamilton telling Shelburne the story.

Frederick embarked on his opposition to Walpole in 1737 as a result of various personal grievances, and by the time Hamilton entered his employ the Prince had become the focal point of the disaffected Whigs. His Secretary was George Lyttelton, cousin to Lord Cobham and later to be the improver of the park at Hagley, Worcestershire. Several of the household were MPs, and the number increased. The Government suffered considerable setbacks in the Cornish constituencies in 1741, thanks to the appointments made by the Prince within the Duchy. Hamilton was himself a beneficiary, for that year he was returned by Lord Falmouth for Truro and remained as MP for the borough until 1747. After 1742, and the fall of Walpole, Frederick gave support to the administration, but four years later returned to the Opposition. From then until his death in 1751 the Prince's household reflected his political patronage more clearly than before, and indeed many of the staff were given appointments only after affirming their political allegiance to him. Conversely he dismissed those who, like Lyttelton, were appointed to government posts.

All this affected Hamilton, who voted first for the Opposition until 1742 when, changing his colours to suit those of his master, he supported the Government in company with the other members of Frederick's household. His brief spell of opposition seems not to have debarred him from public office, however, for in May 1742 he was the only member of that party to be nominated in the ministerial list of members to serve on a proposed commission for examining the public accounts.

In October the new Prime Minister, Henry Pelham, owner of nearby Esher Place and associate of Henry Fox, listed Hamilton under 'Winnington' (Thomas Winnington, friend of the Foxes and government supporter) rather than 'The Prince of Wales', which suggests that by this time he was being drawn into active government involvement while nonetheless keeping his position in the Prince's retinue. In 1743 Pelham appointed him receiver-general of the King's Minorcan revenues, a post he held for fourteen years with a brief intermission. Minorca was a key strategic post in the seventeenth and eighteenth centuries, the object of Spanish, French and British interest, with fluctuating fortunes. Hamilton's appointment, probably not much more than a sinecure, though he had to record income and expenditure on Minorca, gained him a salary of £1,200 per annum, which while not a fortune gave him a necessary basis

for the task of transforming Painshill. The actual work of collecting Minorcan revenues and making payments to officials was conducted by an underling. The gross amounts passing through Hamilton's hands varied from about £3,000 to £7,000 per annum.

On 6 December 1743 Hamilton made his one recorded speech in the House, which seems to have been a family tradition – in the 1750s William Gerard Hamilton was known as 'single-speech Hamilton'. He spoke against dismissing the Hanoverian troops, which confirms his standing with the Government at a time when many of the former Whig Opposition had also come, or were about to come, into office. Hamilton was, however, neither very involved with politics nor politically influential.

The Prince was more than Hamilton's patron and employer. After Frederick's death the plant collector and botanist Peter Collinson spoke of him as 'the best friend of gardening and planting', for not only did the Prince visit many of the important estates of the day such as Pope's at Twickenham and Lord Cobham's at Stowe but was a gardener in his own right, practising the art of landscape in his grounds at Carlton House, Cliveden and Kew. He employed William Kent to assist in the layout at Carlton House and to design the White House at Kew. More than that, he associated for several years with the *avant garde* thinkers and writers on gardens, for example

LEFT Garden at Carlton House, London, engraving by William Woollett, 1760.

Samuel Molyneux, who had been his Secretary earlier and who, although before Hamilton's time, had been very interested in the new gardening. In the environment of Frederick's household Hamilton would have had the chance to become *au fait* with the stimulating new ideas about nature and landscape that were current particularly among the Whig Opposition.

According to Joseph Spence, Hamilton 'directed and oversaw all the operations, both in the buildings and gardens' at Painshill, adding that he 'would not have the same to go through again for all the world'.[20] Whether this is evidence of actual architectural input from Hamilton is unclear, but in 1745 we find the first indications of Hamilton the architect. His initial efforts were some interior work for Stephen Fox; chimney pieces for the parlour and saloon at Redlynch.[21] Stephen thought highly of Hamilton's draughtsmanship, and Henry seems to have shared this opinion. Henry and Hamilton intended to go to Greenwich together in February 1746 to see the original chimney piece by Inigo Jones on which the design for Stephen Fox had been based. The trip was postponed, however, because of Hamilton's illness, and they did not go until the end of the month. On 1 March Henry sent Stephen some revised sketches, and three days later wrote from Painshill to explain that Hamilton's advice and neatly-drawn plans were to arrive by the next post. In the same letter Henry described how he had just dined at Esher Place with Pelham, William Pitt and Lyttelton, a formidable trio representing the old and the new Whigs who had joined forces to overthrow the Secretary of State, Carteret, an *eminence grise* behind the throne.[22] Pitt would become Paymaster-General and Prime Minister in addition to advising on an array of landscape gardens. Hamilton had not been present, which is a fair indication that when it came to politics he was a trailing partner of little consequence. The talk would have been mainly political, but it is ironic that Hamilton was not there when landscape design was another topic shared by the diners. By 20 March Hamilton had written to Stephen Fox at Salisbury, and the matter of the chimney pieces had been settled.[23]

Hamilton's advice to Stephen raises the intriguing possibility that he may have had some hand in the laying out of the grounds at Redlynch. He was prominent in designing the gardens at Holland House for Henry Fox (see below), and having helped Stephen in some architectural matters he could well have advised on the grounds, which Stephen transformed from the late 1730s. There is no evidence of Hamilton's involvement, but the decorations at Redlynch included shrubberies, cascades, a lake, a temple, planted groves and a Chinese seat, all features with which Hamilton was familiar. Nearer at hand, however, was the ongoing work at Stourhead, where Henry Flitcroft was architect. Flitcroft was engaged to design a Gothic entrance to the west side of the park at Redlynch, while Stephen built a carriage drive from there to Stourhead, so perhaps he had input from both Henry Hoare and Hamilton.

On Sunday 9 June 1745 Hamilton received his first recorded visitor of note at Painshill, the 2nd Duke of Richmond, who came to lunch.[24] The significance of this is that the Duke was a known plantsman who had worked wonders at his own seat at Goodwood, West Sussex, and had obtained large stocks from the nurseries at Thorndon Hall, Essex, after Lord Petre's death in 1742. The Duke had also entered into the arrangement with Peter Collinson whereby boxes of seeds would be shipped to him from North America. Since Hamilton joined this scheme a couple of years later, it is reasonable to infer that the idea stemmed from discussion with Richmond.

Meanwhile his career stuttered somewhat. His receivership of the Minorcan revenues was in abeyance for a time, having been made inconsistent with a seat in Parliament, but was restored in 1746, a year before Hamilton ceased to be MP for Truro after failing to be renominated by Lord Falmouth. This illustrates the breach between Hamilton and the Prince: by 1746 Frederick had returned to Opposition, but Hamilton stayed with the Government. In March 1746 Henry Fox noted that Hamilton expected to be dismissed after voting with the Government,[25] and in November hinted to Stephen that Hamilton might be in some trouble, presumably with the Prince.[26]

The danger became reality the same month, when Hamilton 'recd a letter…to signify to him that it was his Royal Highnesses pleasure that he sh[d] no longer continue in his service'.[27] By February 1747 Lord Archibald had also been dismissed after voting for the Government. There was also the more personal matter of the Prince's affair with Lady Archibald, who herself had been dismissed in 1746 after falling out of favour. Hamilton tried to get back into the House as a government supporter for the constituency of Bishop's Castle, but was not elected and took up his old Minorcan post once more. He was now fully back in the 'Establishment' along with Henry Fox, who had been a Lord of the Treasury from 1743 and had just been appointed Privy Councillor and Secretary at War. During 1747 Hamilton opened an account at Hoare's Bank, already used by the Foxes. Apart from designing the gardens at Stourhead, Henry Hoare was familiar with Painshill and well known to Hamilton personally.

By this time considerable progress had been made in the gardens. Peter Collinson reported that the new Lord Petre had been staying at Woburn Farm and had seen various local properties, including Painshill: 'Mr Hambletons undertakeing I think is very great his situation being so very barren but Art one sees ther can do a great deal'.[28] Further visitors around then included the artist and writer George Vertue (August 1747), Horace Walpole (11 August 1748) and Lord and Lady Newdigate, who were on a tour of estates, a fortnight later. Daniel Defoe's topographical account of Britain was revised by Samuel Richardson to incorporate Painshill in that year as well.

In July 1748 Hamilton became involved in a legal matter for which his mother had sent for him. The details are not known, but there was a possibility of a lawsuit. The eagerness with which he hastened to attend his mother is indicative of the hopes he had of a large inheritance from her. In addition he was the youngest son and there may well have been a special fondness between them.

During the summer of 1749 Hamilton visited Redlynch again and was full of advice and schemes for the decoration of Stephen Fox's house. Fox noted wryly that hardly any of Hamilton's ideas would be put into effect, however.[29] Hamilton was also a constant visitor at Henry Fox's Kensington home, Holland House, which he had acquired in 1746.

That summer also saw a more extensive tour of the west country by Hamilton. In August he travelled from Redlynch to stay with Lord Poullet at Hinton St George, Somerset, and received the ultimate accolade in a letter from Poullet to Catherine Parker of Saltram, Devon, declaring that Hamilton '(now Mr Kent is dead) is certainly ye top man of taste in England'.[30] He goes on to say that Hamilton had been giving him advice and assistance in the laying out of his own grounds, which have survived as a park with a naturalistic lake. A few days later he commented that Hamilton had left behind a legacy that would always be remembered.[31] Hamilton seems, accordingly, to have 'arrived' as a recognised master designer, and Hinton St George was but the first of several estates on which he would advise. The tour continued to Mamhead (owned by Thomas Ball) and the Parker estate of Saltram itself, in both of which instances he may possibly have given advice too, as Poullet suggested he might. The next stop, and possibly the most significant, was Mount Edgcumbe, just inside the Cornish border. There Richard Edgcumbe, 2nd Baron Edgcumbe, entertained him for some time and commented in a letter to Henry Fox that the two had got on famously.[32] Whether that included any gardening advice from Hamilton is unknown, but the greater likelihood is that Mount Edgcumbe, a unique sea-girt landscape park with distant views and circuit drives, might well have made an impression on him. In particular, the

ABOVE The Ruined Chapel at Mount Edgcumbe.

Ruined Chapel, which had gone up in 1747, could have sown the seed of an idea that would lead to the Ruined Abbey at Painshill.

In May 1750 Hamilton's elder daughter Jane married a man nearly twenty years older, the writer Edward Moore. Among his works were *Fables for the Female Sex* (did Jane profit from them?), *Gil Blas* and *The Gamester*, a popular domestic tragedy first produced at Drury Lane in 1753. He edited the weekly journal *The World* for three years from 1753. It was a satirical publication that included landscape gardening among its targets. Jenny Hamilton seems to have been very fond of Moore, as a verse from a ballad by her shows:

As gay as I am, could I spend half my days
In dances and operas, Ridottos and plays,
Hard fate your poor Jenny with tears would implore
For alas! my dear Gill what are these without Moore.[33]

Moore was never well off, and died after only seven years of marriage, leaving their son Edward to be educated by Lord Chesterfield, famed for the sententious letters to his own son. Jane herself secured a minor post in the Queen's Court at St James's and subsequently obtained a small pension from the appointment. In her youth she was said to possess great charm and immense beauty, as Joseph Farington records in his diary for 9 May 1806, when a discussion arose at Lord Thomond's house concerning beautiful women. Lady Thomond said that the woman who had made the strongest impression of all on her uncle, Sir Joshua Reynolds, was Jane Hamilton, and that whenever he read a book in which he had to visualise a beautiful and interesting woman her image was always uppermost in his mind.[34] Reynolds did not paint her, surprisingly (and unfortunately). If the daughter had such striking looks, her mother, Hamilton's first wife, was likely also to have been of great beauty.

It is possible that Hamilton's other daughter, Sarah, married also in the summer of 1750, her husband being the architect Kenton Couse. However, there is some doubt, and the Sarah Hamilton who married Couse is likely to have come from a different branch of the Hamiltons.

At the mid point of the century Hamilton was well established, if not financially secure. He was forty-five, and the basic shaping of the gardens had been completed. Their fame, and his, were assured. Visitors flocked to visit Painshill from home and abroad, and it became a regular arrangement, with the gardener or *vigneron* showing visitors round and a system of pony chaises from the inn at Cobham being instituted for those who wished to be driven round. By now Hamilton had built up a great many contacts and was able to network: and because of his reputation at Painshill he was brought into various landscaping schemes. One such, which may well be apocryphal, is the Mansion at Leatherhead, a few miles away from Painshill, which had a lawn that sloped down to the river. A number of nineteenth-century commentators mention this, one getting the reference from another, but the earliest were Manning and Bray (1809), though William Bray had gone round Painshill in 1755 and might conceivably have been told something about the Leatherhead project then. But in the light of lack of evidence a question mark must remain over Hamilton's supposed hand in the design there.

What is definite, however, is Hamilton's part in transforming the grounds at Holland House for Henry Fox from about 1750. William Kent is said to have designed the terraces near the house, though that sounds too formal a concept for Kent's normal manner. Peter Collinson advised on particular species to plant and Hamilton planned the layout of the open parkland north of the house and the area to the west. Lady Caroline Fox also contributed to the design. Hamilton planted in groups and clumps, especially towards the north, and made the Green Walk the central feature, which was turfed on his advice. Thomas Faulkner spoke of Hamilton's input:

He introduced several American trees, and a vast variety of curious oaks, many of which are still flourishing in these grounds. The cedars planted under his direction are much admired, and one clump in particular, situated to the north-west, affords with its dark branches, a fine frame for the prospect, and the setting sun in a summer evening; but the greatest proof of his discernment and taste is to be found in a green walk, which, originally an open lane, was at his suggestion turfed, and ornamented by Lord Holland. It reaches very far towards the Uxbridge-road. Near the southern entrance into it are two noble oriental planes, remarkable for the size they have obtained in this climate.[35]

Hamilton's work had had a chance to mature by June 1765, when Mrs Elizabeth Montagu, 'Queen of the Bluestockings', visited Holland Park:

> Mr Hamilton of Cobham, who has the finest taste perhaps of any man in gardens, etc., laid out the grounds; wealth inexhaustible executed his plans with rapidity, and it is become within a short time the finest villa in England. There is an air of grandeur in it beyond what the extent should allow.[36]

The 'wealth inexhaustible' came, conveniently, from Fox's post as Paymaster-General, when (as would have been common practice) he appropriated government funds for his own purposes, and made further money out of them by loaning sums to his friends (including Hamilton) at four per cent interest. On 18 December 1750 Fox wrote to Collinson that arrangements were being made to dine with Hamilton: 'May I beg you to call on Mr Hamilton & make him come early on Saturday for he has a great deal to do.'[37] In the period 1755–6 there were further letters indicating that Collinson and Hamilton were working in partnership, which therefore covered a period of at least six years.

At Holland Park the limited space meant that Hamilton could not plan on a large scale, but he was skilled in giving character to small areas, and Mrs Montagu's comment that the place had more grandeur than its size ought to allow points to a favourite Hamilton device, the creation of illusion in the matter of apparent size.

During the early months of 1751 Hamilton's mother was seriously ill at her London home in Sackville Street and was not expected to live; Hamilton, in a letter of 2 April to Henry Fox, admitted mixed feelings: 'You will think me a great Hipocrite for what I'm going to say, which is that her Death whenever it happens will grieve me much, tho' at the same time I see my own Existence depends upon it.'[38] His mother gave him her will, which he thought to be in his favour although he claimed he did not need to have it. Had he read it at the time he would have been spared a future disappointment. The letter continues with an account of George II's interview with Princess Augusta, widow of the Prince of Wales, who had just died, in which the King assured her he would do all he could for their children. One of them, Prince George (to become George III nine years later), was so afraid of the King 'that he was forced to take something to keep up his Spirits, before he came into His Presence'. Hamilton concluded on a light note:

> You see all News except what relates to Royal Persons is below my Notice; I suppose there is a great deal

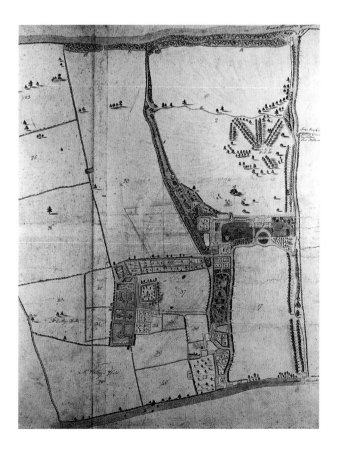

RIGHT Plan of Holland Park, surveyed by J Haynes, 1770.

stirring which may relate to You Demi-Gods, or second Order of Beings, if there is I know not one Tittle of it; I hate all News but the best and most genuine, which I never hear but when you now and then throw me out a Scrap.[39]

There is a domestic postscript which betrays an impatient or intolerant side to his nature: 'My Son of a Bitch of a Coachman forgot to grease the Chaise, tho' I gave him the strictest Charge about it to have it all ready, which I fear lost you a Q. of an Hour, and that of y^r Time is Something.'

Hamilton's financial worries surface in this letter, and from this time onwards a cloud of debts and mortgages hung over him, a situation he tried to alleviate from time to time by such measures as attempting to sell off his sculpture collection.

The year 1752 saw the return of Hamilton to the shooting parties at Redlynch and other places frequented by Stephen Fox. Stephen was an expert shot, but Henry lacked skill although it was his favourite pastime in the country. Hamilton reckoned they were too unevenly matched for either to take pleasure in competition together. He himself took up the gun not having touched it since the accident to his hand. Henry Fox noted in his diary for 5 October 1752:

> Weddington Farm, Chisenbury. *The Sportsman Redivivus*; or, *Hamilton has begun shooting again*, after 22 years intermission. *N.B.* He is older than Mr Fox.

> Kill'd by Ld Ilchester, 1 quail. By *Redivivus*, 1 quail. Lord Ilchester, Mr Fox, Mr Hamilton did not shoot at one partridge. Mr Fox did not let off his gun. Mr Digby [Edward Digby of Sherborne, Dorset, who married the Foxes' sister Charlotte] and Mr Hamilton shot at one partridge, and missed it.

> No one partridge was brought home – a thing not to be parallel'd in these records, nor to be believ'd by posterity.[40]

Four days later Fox recorded that Hamilton had killed five partridges from six shots.[41] The long lay-off had evidently not spoiled his accuracy.

In the autumn of 1753 Henry took advantage of a visit to Windsor to stop off and see Painshill at vintage time. Hamilton was still engaged in designing for Stephen at this period. In November he visited Wales briefly, but did not find it to his taste and left vowing never to return.

The following year brought several upheavals. On 19 March Hamilton's mother died at the age of eighty-six, having survived her husband by virtually twenty years. She died at Sackville Street and was buried in the Ormonde vault in Henry VII's chapel in Westminster Abbey. Hamilton's hopes of inheriting a substantial legacy from her were dashed, for the sum was disappointingly small. It is clear that at this time Hamilton still had some involvement with the Irish estates of the Abercorns, for we find him offering the Earl his Dublin furniture.[42] Hamilton claimed £1,000 on the York Street estates, but Abercorn thought this had been nullified by the £2,000 he had raised from the Strabane estate.[43] Also in 1754 he quarrelled with his master vine-grower, David Geneste, who had helped him produce a wine that had no equal in England.

In June Hamilton was engaged in designing a pair of gates for Stephen Fox, to whom he sent some wine with the comment:

> You are such an Infidel as to my Wine, I hardly expect to convert You, even when You taste it, but Lady Ilchester who liked my first so well, will be in Love with this; and I'll answer for't 'twill make Miss Cheek laugh and quicken her low Spirits.[44]

The Cheeks were neighbours and intimate acquaintances of the Ilchesters. Mr Cheek often joined the shooting parties. In the same letter Hamilton asked Stephen Fox's help in finding him an assistant for his old shepherd to look after the cows and the pigs. This would have been on the farm to the north of the Portsmouth Road.

At the beginning of 1755 the French nurseryman Abbé Nolin started a correspondence with Hamilton which will be described in the chapter on Hamilton's plantings. The letters are concerned principally with the exchange of seeds between the two collectors. In the autumn Hamilton was once more on his way down to see Stephen Fox; Henry informed him that Hamilton would give him 'the State of Domestick Politics'.[45]

In the early part of 1756 Hamilton was still helping Henry Fox with the gardens at Holland House, usually in tandem with Peter Collinson. For these visits Hamilton was generally based at his London residence in Welbeck Street, which he held for several years. On 13 May Hamilton wrote in desperation to Henry Fox, recounting his financial woes, caused partly by the imminent lapse of the Minorcan post, since Minorca itself was about to be lost to the French, and partly to the small inheritance from his mother. Hamilton told Fox he had only £800 *per annum* income and had in mind the idea of succeeding Sir James Gray as ambassador at Naples, or at Florence. He said that, if he had to live abroad, Italy would be the place to choose since he knew it and liked it, and indeed

he would not wish to remain in England except 'upon my own Plan', which was the fulfilment of his schemes at Painshill. Hamilton bestowed fulsome flattery on Fox, wishing that Fox were Prime Minister and in a position to cure the country's ills: he described Henry as the joy and comfort of his life from earliest youth.[46]

Henry Fox, who was by then Secretary of State, did not let him down. He tried to secure for Hamilton the Surveyorship of Woods, for which he would have been eminently suited by experience and inclination, but William Pitt, the Prime Minister, had reserved the post for his own brother John. A row ensued between Fox and the Duke of Devonshire over the matter, since Fox believed that he had obtained a promise from the Duke that Hamilton should succeed the present incumbent, Phillipson, a sick man.[47] Fox understood that no objection had been raised when the list of appointments had been submitted to the King, and informed Hamilton on 13 November that all was settled. Four days later he wrote to the same effect to Stephen, quoting the salary for the post as £1,200 *per annum*.[48] Phillipson died on 27 November, and John Pitt was given his position, the Prime Minister basing his claim on a previous agreement. Fox, who took the matter to heart, was furious and told the Duke of Devonshire on 30 November that Hamilton was the dearest to him 'of any person in question'.[49] In reply the Duke assured him that William Pitt was anxious to do something for Hamilton and proposed the Board of Green Cloth. Henry Fox was still angry but later made up the quarrel.

In the autumn of 1756 Fox was in line for the post of Chancellor. On 28 October Hamilton wrote to rejoice with him that the Duke of Newcastle had fallen from power.[50] The King asked Fox to form an administration with William Pitt: when the latter refused, the Duke of Devonshire formed one with Pitt. Hamilton made it clear in his letter that he regarded Pitt as an arrogant dictator.

On Fox's return to Holland House Hamilton visited him and wrote to the Duke of Argyll (a supporter of Fox as well as a fellow plant collector) that Fox would

LEFT Portrait of Henry Fox by Antonio David, 1732.

be Chancellor in the Pitt-Devonshire administration,[51] though in the event Fox accepted the lesser position of Paymaster-General. Fox continued to try to help, and on 5 January 1757 mentioned to Stephen in a postscript that he believed Hamilton would be his Deputy Paymaster.[52] This position would appear to correspond with the 'pension' of £1,200 a year which he thenceforth received from Fox. Hamilton was as lavish in his gratitude as he had been abject in his abasement earlier: 'A thousand thanks for the hopefull Scene You give me a Glympse of; indeed I have foreseen it wou'd be exhibited, from the first drawing up of the Curtain this theatrical Winter.'[53]

According to popular belief Fox used the revenue in his charge to expand his own private fortune as before, reputedly to the tune of £250,000. He remained Paymaster for the duration of the Seven Years War, and was then created Lord Holland in April 1763, his reward for successfully negotiating terms of peace with France and Spain. For two further years he retained the Paymastership.

The salary or pension which Hamilton now received justified him, he thought, in embarking on his building projects, though it was not enough to give him security. His plantings were given an impetus through the correspondence with the Abbé Nolin, and the buildings began to go up as the planting schemes reached their optimum.

Hamilton's financial difficulties continued to exercise Fox as well as Hamilton himself. In 1761 Fox suggested that he should contemplate selling Painshill to Lord Clive of India, a proposal vigorously rebutted by Hamilton, who protested that his accounts were in good order. He wrote on 15 May:

> You are a very pretty Gentleman to think I shou'd not find You out, after knowing You so well for above forty Years: and it is as extraordinary that in that Time You shou'd not have found me out enough to know all the Money in the Universe wou'd never tempt me to part with any thing I had set my Heart upon: cou'd You for a Moment suppose I wou'd exchange this Paradise upon which I have laid out all my Time, all my Thoughts, and all my Money for these twenty three Years, for some of the Nabobs dirty underground Trash which is not half so resplendent as what covers at this very hour every part of this delightfull Spot? No, the Nabobs whole Million shou'd not purchase it, nor wou'd I exchange it for the real Golonda Vispour, Morretta [Indian treasures] &c. &c. my only Way of measuring the Value of Money, is by the Happiness it procures, and I really don't think all the Money in the Universe cou'd procure me so much Happiness as this Place, ergo.[54]

Hamilton continued by justifying his expenses and by claiming that the cost of the buildings executed within the last three years had been within his income. He intended to complete his building in a year's time, and, after that, expense would be confined to maintaining the grounds. The exact expenses for four years were given; a total of £409 11s 8½d for maintaining the park, kitchen garden, flower garden and greenhouse. The farm made him self-sufficient, supplying plenty of beef and mutton, and he spent little on anything other than the gardens. He concluded by sending Fox a drawing and estimate for 'the Pavement of my Tent', which had been constructed two years earlier. Two days later Hamilton sent Henry Fox a further detailed statement, which showed the farm made a profit of £300 *per annum*.

At about this time Stephen Fox was altering the gardens at Melbury, Dorset, which he had acquired through marriage. He seems not to have been in touch with Hamilton by then, but the construction of a lake and a boulder grotto could have been inspired by what he knew of Painshill.

Even as late as 1763 Hamilton was open to ideas from others for improving his landscape. In August he wrote to Lord Bute, a great plantsman as well as a power in the land, to say he regretted that he had missed Bute's visit to Painshill the previous day. He combined flattery with a genuine wish to exchange thoughts with a leading botanist: 'Besides having the Honor he so much longed for, of waiting upon his Lords'p over his Grounds, he shou'd have profited by His Instructions, and begg'd His Opinion in some Knotty Points'.[55]

ABOVE The lake with the Turkish Tent in the distance.

During 1763 Hamilton was engaged in designing a castle as one of the follies at Henry Fox's (now Baron Holland) Kent retreat by the sea, Kingsgate. The 'castle' referred to in Hamilton's letter of 1 May applies specifically to Kingsgate and is not a term used for his own Gothic Tower as has sometimes been thought.[56] The letter says that Hamilton had just sent to Robert Whitfield, Lord Holland's agent, two packets of drawings for the four fronts of the castle and the plan.[57] Hamilton told Lord Holland that he had more or less cut himself off from the world in retirement ('I have long had an Antipathy to Courts and Politicks') and that he would like to have built a more comfortable house but would have to be content with the existing one. A letter of 5 October 1764 to Lord Holland blames his business affairs during the previous year for the decline in his fortunes, but he declared that he intended to live within his income, all his works now being at an end (this was not true, the most elaborate, the grotto, only just having been begun). For the first time the second Mrs Hamilton is mentioned, so it may be that he had only recently married her: '[I] find the Sweets of Domestick Happiness with a Wife who not only likes, but greatly assists me in, this prudent Scheme; I flatter myself I shall pass the Remainder of my Days not only in Quiet, but in Comfort'.[58] Agnes Hamilton was Scottish, daughter of David Cockburn, MD, of Ayr. She was thirty in 1764, just half Hamilton's age, but her life was to be cut short.

On 18 October Hamilton wrote to Lord Holland concerning plans he had drawn up, this time for a Mr Taylor. These architectural commissions lend weight to the supposition that Hamilton was at least part-architect for the buildings at Painshill. Hamilton admitted the drawings were poor and that it would be easier to draw afresh than 'to coble these into good ones; a Painter wou'd as soon work up a Sign into a good Picture'.[59] Although such commissions were essentially amateur, Hamilton took them seriously and said that far from being an amusement the real satisfaction for him lay in being of service to his friends. Hamilton paid Leoni, a stationer in Portland Street, seven shillings and sixpence a day for drawing a fair copy and supplying paper.[60] In the same month he surrendered the Burgership of Strabane to the Earl of Abercorn and wished him success in looking after it.[61]

About this time Hamilton considered selling his antique marbles, but the Duke of Richmond, writing to Peter Collinson on 27 November 1764, thought that the collection had been overpriced:

Last post I received your letter and shall be glad to have a list of Mr Hamilton's Statues & busts with the prices, tho' between you and I, you must know that friend Hamilton and I have often talked about them, & that I know he overvalues them at least ten times. His Bacchus I have heard him say was worth seven thousand pound. Now I dont think it worth above five hundred and I believe I was not wrong in my judgement. I love Hamilton and wish he may sell his things for what he thinks they are worth, but I cannot

be a purchaser on his notions. However there is no harm in having his prices. I would buy a bust or two if he is reasonable.[62]

The proposed sale developed into a raffle, which took Hamilton a year to devise. On 17 November 1765 he wrote to Lord Holland with an enclosed list of the collection, together with details of the proposed raffle or lottery. A number of subscribers would each contribute a sum of money, the item being given to the winner. Thus, a hundred people would subscribe forty guineas each for Bacchus, raising 4,000 guineas; the statues of Minerva and Flora would raise 800 guineas; and twenty-nine busts would raise a total of 1,200 guineas.[63] Hamilton was clearly asking a great deal of money, and soon realised it. By the next spring he was prepared to climb down and reduce the subscriptions so that more people might be encouraged to participate. Presumably the rates were still too high, for the scheme never materialised.

Hamilton continued to be, nominally at least and for the purpose of drawing income from that source, Deputy Paymaster-General to Lord Holland. When the latter relinquished the position in May 1765, Hamilton wrote to his successor, Charles Townshend, to ask whether he could continue as deputy. In a warm and courteous letter Townshend informed him that he could so continue, and a delighted Hamilton told Lord Holland the news. After some political gossip, Hamilton concluded with a mention of a weakness of eyesight which prevented him writing at greater length.[64]

Despite this renewed security of tenure and the fact that, apart from the grotto, the building work was complete (bar the late flourish of the Ruined Abbey), Hamilton continued to be in financial difficulties, probably through accumulated debts. During 1766 he took out a mortgage of £6,568 8s from Hoare's Bank,[65] having a year or two earlier borrowed a sum of £10,000 from Lord Holland at four per cent interest.

On 2 July 1766 Hamilton gave Lord Holland advice about a projected trip to Italy (the two had of course been in Rome together back in 1732). He recommended *grancii teneri* (tender crabs) as a delicacy from Civita Vecchia, where they were prepared by softening the shells.

Crab broth was reckoned to be the greatest 'Restorative and Sweetner' in the world, but Hamilton had never tasted it.[66]

In August Hamilton's post as Deputy Paymaster-General was confirmed once more after a further change of ministry, Lord North replacing Townshend as his superior. Hamilton wrote to Lord North's father, the Earl of Guilford (owner of the rococo landscape at Wroxton, Oxfordshire), whom he had known for many years, in flowery terms, and told Lord Holland of his appointment. This success came hand-in-hand with a bitter personal blow: Agnes miscarried, and was to bear no children.

Although Hamilton had previously not concealed his dislike of William Pitt, there were times when he had to repress his feelings and curry favour with him. In September 1766, when he was staying at Fonthill with Alderman Beckford, he wrote to Pitt 'to beg y.ʳ Ldps protection and assistance, for one who has had the Honor to be known to you above thirty years, and who for that whole Period has had the highest veneration & Regard for y.ʳ Ldˢp'.[67] Hamilton said that he had relinquished his entitlement of two-thirds of his pension of £1,200 upon the restoration of his Minorca post but that the pension had ceased altogether, and, further, his income had been reduced by almost £700 *per annum* by having half his Pay Office revenue stopped. He asked Pitt accordingly if the £400 *per annum* that should have been paid in respect of the pension could be restored. Pitt replied positively, and Hamilton's relief, in a letter of 2 November, is tangible: 'I feel myself so much honoured, and my vanity is so much flatter'd, by receiving so very Obliging a letter from the greatest Man of my Time, whom I look up to with a kind of enthusiastick Reverence.'[68]

From this time we do not know anything of Hamilton from his letters for four years, but the account books kept by Lord Holland tell their own story. The annual interest payable by Hamilton was £400, but he fell more and more behind with his payments. In the year ending 29 September 1767 Hamilton paid £245 17s 3d and the following year £310 10s 9d, but there was still a balance of £189 9s 3d outstanding. By 29 September 1769 nothing more had been paid, nor would be thenceforth. The sums due continued to be recorded, however, and the final

entry, for 31 March 1773, shows that the interest owing was £1,989 9s.[69] Lord Holland had, indeed, to suffer many bad debts, though Hamilton settled his finally by the sale of Painshill. Straitened circumstances did not prevent him, however, from contributing the largest amount, £30, in 1769 for the building of a workhouse in Walton.[70]

In 1770 Lord Clive, who had purchased the Claremont estate, walked round Painshill and was much taken by the statue of Bacchus. Hamilton, scenting a sale, wrote to the estate manager in the hope that Lord Clive might be willing to purchase some or all of the sculpture collection. It is ironic that financial difficulties forced Hamilton to swallow his former revulsion against Clive's wealth.

About this time Hamilton gave advice to Henry Hoare on the siting of his hermitage at Stourhead on a steep zigzag path up to the Temple of Apollo.[71] Hoare had already, whether through consultation with Hamilton or not, copied the idea and something of the appearance of the Turkish Tent in erecting one of his own.

Hamilton had always, since at least 1760, spent a great deal buying bricks and lime (for mortar) for his various building projects. He acquired both from the bricklaying family Field of Walton, who worked also at Oatlands. But, partly to save himself money and partly to generate income, he started his own tile and brick venture in about 1768 and by 1769 was supplying a wide range of people.[72]

Hamilton set out his financial affairs at some length in a letter of 19 January 1772 to Lord Holland. He said he was ashamed to be so much in arrears with the interest and he intended the sale of Painshill to cover both principal and interest. Hamilton referred to the tileworks into which he had sunk the money which should have paid Lord Holland back and which had given him hope of making enough profit to avoid selling up, but the project had proved a commercial disaster (and shown that Hamilton was no businessman):

general misinformation of the true selling Prices, Combinations to undersell me, Knavery of Workmen, bad Pay for some of what I sold, & the Expence of Land, Carriage, soon proved to me that the small profit I sh.[d] have, would not answer the continual pains and anxiety it cost me.[73]

The tileworks had created an eyesore in the grounds, and Hamilton was, as we know, to cover them up by the erection of the Ruined Abbey. Aware, furthermore, that his small house might not prove too attractive to a prospective buyer, he had drawn up plans for an additional suite of six rooms, costing under £1,000. He reckoned that, even if just the shell could be put up, the value of the house would rise in the eyes of 'the dullest purchaser'.

Hamilton considered that £400 *per annum* would set him on an even keel, particularly as his regular income had been reduced since his marriage. A further idea was to sell his marbles to the British Museum, but as usual this came to nothing. He concluded by saying that his sole object now, 'which I shall never quitt for the small Remnant of my life, is, to pay my Debts, to live quiet & retired, with the best of wives, and the few friends I have, and leave them in a comfortable & easy Situation'.[74] Following this wearied letter, tragedy struck in the autumn: on 18 October Agnes died at the early age of thirty-eight, and 'the best of wives' was buried in Cobham Church. The Painshill chapter in Hamilton's life was drawing to its close.

The year 1773 saw the melancholy business of the sale of Painshill. On 11-12 March Langford's auctioned off many of the paintings, and on 23 April Hamilton wrote to Lord Holland to confirm that the sale of the estate had raised £25,000, and that all he owed his old friend would be paid by midsummer.[75] Bond Hopkins, the purchaser, would move in immediately, but Hamilton had a month to remove his furniture and goods. The marbles remained at Painshill. He claimed he had undersold the estate, but as we have seen he was always inclined to overvalue his possessions. Indeed, had he not reduced the price considerably, Bond Hopkins would have purchased Hayes Place in Kent instead. [76] Disposing of Painshill was traumatic, and Hamilton suffered a 'swelled Face and feverishness'.[77] On 22 July repayment of his debt to Lord Holland was confirmed, two days after separate repayment to Hoare's Bank.

Hamilton moved to Bath at the end of July 1773, his furniture having preceded him, and after clearing all his debts he was left with about £5,000. He settled in the most fashionable part of the city, the Royal Crescent, where he occupied number 14, close to the centre, at a rent of £180 *per annum*. Although much of his collection had been sold off, there still remained a fine array of paintings with which to adorn his new home. His great-niece Mary visited in May 1774 and noted that it was 'fitted up in elegant style', with 'some capital Pictures'.[78] Nor was it to be a lonely old age: on 11 August 1774, within sight of his seventieth birthday, he married his third wife, Frances Calvert, at Walcot Church, Bath. Both husband and wife were recorded as being of Walcot Parish. They were married by the Rev. John Dibley, with Frederick Hamilton, Charles's nephew, who also had a house in the

ground at the back of his house with gravel walks. He had to ask the City Corporation for permission to take gravel from the common for the purpose in 1777, which was agreed.[81] In 1779 a further request was turned down, but in 1780 he was permitted 150 cart loads of gravel, and in 1781 twenty additional loads.[82] He also acquired a house on the hill in Lansdown Road, now known as Hope House. The collection of paintings went there with him, which made them inaccessible to those who had previously been able to admire them in the centre of town.[83] The grounds of Lansdown House were to win him acclaim as an exemplary town garden. The Rev. Richard Warner enthused over what Hamilton had managed to make of his ten-acre site:

> the little beautiful pleasure-ground attached to it [the house] was what chiefly marked the master touches of the man of refined taste; where, within limits extremely confined, variety and freedom displayed themselves; the agreeable wildness of Nature in the very lap of Art.[84]

Crescent, and Pat Calvert as witnesses. Mrs Calvert, the bride's mother, moved in with the Hamiltons. A pair of portraits of Charles and Frances (above) was painted by William Hoare to celebrate the wedding.

Kidney stone caused Hamilton great distress by the late 1770s. In December 1778 he wrote to the Earl of Abercorn to say he could not undertake a long coach journey because he was so full of stone and did not want to risk it being shaken up – 'il ne faut pas eviller le Chat qui Dort'. He had voided nearly a hundred large pieces of calculus by means of Adam's Solvent.[79] His nephew shortly afterwards said he was glad the stone had died down, but advised Hamilton not to use the solvent too much because it was abrasive and harmed the bladder.[80]

Retired Hamilton may have been in theory, but he was as active as ever in gardening. He laid out a pleasure

Hamilton's great-nephew William Beckford visited him in Bath on a number of occasions. Towards the end of July 1781 Beckford wrote to Lady Hamilton that his mother

> urges me without ceasing to visit our holy uncle at Bath, the everlasting C – H – who, it seems, is building a house to his garden and adding peach house to grape house and pinery to pinery on the slope of the crescent hill, which is already more than half embroidered with his vagaries.[85]

According to Beckford's biographer Cyrus Redding, Beckford discovered 'a thousand beauties' in Lansdown House garden.[86] Redding thought that the garden inspired Beckford as to the way in which his own

gardens at Fonthill might be improved. The ground included a variety of plantings in an irregular manner, open space, a walled kitchen garden to one side with hot-houses and pineapple pits, and a free-standing summer house. The inventory after Hamilton's death indicates a deal of gardening activity. In the pleasure ground there were six garden benches, ten Windsor chairs and twenty other chairs, together with a cast-iron roller, two of stone and one of wood. In the summer house there were six mahogany hair bottomed chairs and two 'elbow chairs'. The kitchen garden contained glass panes, seventeen melon frames, pots, eight wheelbarrows, a grindstone, watering-can, spades, scythes, hoes, rakes, stepladder, hand-cart, bill hook and hatchet *inter alia*.[87]

What direct influence Hamilton had on Beckford is difficult to assess. The large-scale romantic and wild landscape of Fonthill may have been coloured by conversations in Bath, given that Hamilton himself was said to be adopting a 'free and grand' manner in his later works, including Lansdown House.[88] Some of the elements of Painshill – the dark wood, the tower rising above the trees, the grotto, the American plantings, the lake – might well have made an impression on the young Beckford. Hamilton seems to have been fond of him: during the 1780s he wrote to him on such occasions as his coming of age and his marriage, and also to arrange a visit to Fonthill.[89]

If the connections with Fonthill remain shadowy, the same cannot be said of Bowood. Here Hamilton's input was considerable and dramatic. His links with the Shelburnes went back to university days, but the 1st Earl had died in 1761. Hamilton kept in touch with his son, the 2nd Earl, and in June 1765 gave him advice on erecting netting to protect young trees and plants from livestock.[90] This was at a time when Brown was in the process of landscaping the grounds. Post-Brown there was a large-scale planting of cedars of Lebanon in 1775:[91] Hamilton's name is not attached, but as it was a favourite tree of his he might possibly have had a hand in the scheme, being not far away by then. Correspondence between Hamilton and the 2nd Earl started up again in 1780, with Hamilton thanking him for the provision of game. Further letters concern Shelburne becoming Prime Minister, Hamilton asking him for the reinstatement of his pension and an unrealistic plea for getting Russia and Prussia to help retain America in the War of Independence.[92] Shelburne was responsible for the peace negotiations with America and became 1st Marquess of Lansdowne as a reward.

Hamilton was closely involved with designing the pleasure grounds at Bowood as a separate entity from about 1780. Although greatly afflicted by his kidney stone he was cheerful and enthusiastic and impressed Jeremy Bentham, who stayed for some time at Bowood in 1781, with the scope of his plans:

> Hamilton of Bath has been mentioned as another person whom I shall see, and that in a few days: it is he who was the creator of Payne's-Hill: he is the oracle for the gardening works that are carrying on here and been employ'd in undoing what Capability Brown had done.[93]

Hamilton assisted Shelburne in planting exotics as well as instigating considerable changes on the ground: ha has were established, walks made, fences put up, and earth levelled. Richard Warner rhapsodised about 'the superlative taste of Mr. Hamilton', which he claimed resulted in variety, simplicity and grandeur.[94] But the masterstroke was the design of the rockwork cascade and valley in about 1781, a project that encompassed a cascade, a Hermit's Cell further up the hill behind it, and the stream flowing from the cascade along a small valley, with a series of rock alcoves and niches of various shapes and sizes on each side. The cascade itself was a kind of grotto, with passages and apertures looking out through a curtain of the falling water. Implementation of Hamilton's design came four or five years later, mainly through the work of the mason Josiah Lane, who is the link between the grottoes at Painshill (possibly), Fonthill and Bowood.

In June 1782 the painter Edward Edwards was commissioned 'to paint three arabesque ceilings [in Lansdown House]…This was one of the greatest commissions he ever received, and occupied him till March 1783. Here his time passed very agreeably, owing to the politeness and liberality of Mr. Hamilton'.[95] This is one of the very few personal comments we have on Hamilton.

It was his love of gardening that brought Hamilton's end. Enthusiastic to the last, he planned an extension to his own garden, possibly to link the Royal Crescent house with Lansdown House, but a neighbour objected and the conflict may have brought about his death in September 1786. Horace Walpole recorded the sad event in a letter to the Countess of Upper Ossory on the 28th of that month:

> …I know no event but the death of Charles Hamilton, one of my patriarchs of modern gardening, who has been killed by Anstey, author of *The Bath Guide*.
>
> Mr Hamilton, who had built a house in the Crescent, was also at eighty-three [actually eighty-one] eager in planting a new garden, and wanted some acres, which Anstey, his neighbour, not so ancient, destined to the same use. Hamilton wrote a warm letter on their being refused; and Anstey, who does not hate a squabble in print, as he has more than once shown, discharged shaft upon shaft against the poor veteran, and…he died of the volley, as even a goose-quill will do the feat at eighty-three, and surely, since the *first* edition of *The Bath Guide*, never was a duller goose than Anstey![96]

Hamilton died at 6 a.m. on Monday 18 September in Lansdown House and was buried in the choir of Bath Abbey a week later. In his will he left Frances £3,000 and household goods, his coach and a sedan chair; he left £100 to his nephew James Connell; and the residue went to his great-nephew John James Hamilton, who succeeded in 1789 as the 9th Earl of Abercorn. He also acted as Hamilton's executor and settled all matters relating to the disposal of the estate. The contents of the house in the Royal Crescent were put up for sale from 3 October, since the property was leased only for Hamilton's lifetime and accordingly had to be vacated quickly.

Hamilton the Collector

THE EIGHTEENTH CENTURY was the great age of collecting. As well as reflecting the tastes and interests of the collector, a collection was often a means of ostentatious display. Not infrequently the objects would include trophies from the Grand Tour – paintings and sculpture – which was certainly true in Hamilton's case. His passion for collecting was lifelong (he was adding to his library in the year of his death) and covered paintings, sculpture, books and plants.

Collecting became a more serious and scholarly business through the century for a number of reasons. One was an increased intellectual and aesthetic curiosity in what was being collected, which was linked to the sophistication of the schedules of the Grand Tour. Young men on the Tour met painters and experts in Rome, and would be taken round by a 'bear leader' or tutor, the role that Joseph Spence filled for the Earl of Lincoln who owned Oatlands. However much the Grand Tour was given over to drinking and other pleasures, the appreciation of art and architecture was high on the agenda, and what the young men saw created a lasting impression, often leading them to recreate something of Italy in their own houses and gardens. So, while bringing home souvenirs certainly had its exhibitionist side, most owners were knowledgeable about what they had acquired.

Collecting can also be seen in the context of a rise in antiquarianism and the study of the past. Just as the Grand Tour involved a degree of study of classical, Renaissance and also contemporary Rome, so at home there was an increase of interest in native antiquities, as shown by the studies of William Stukeley or by the portfolios of prints by Nathaniel and Samuel Buck. This interest can be seen as part of the growth in patriotism and national identity, a Whig concept that led the British to regard their own cultural history, especially as evinced in actual remains, as just as important as what they might find abroad from other civilisations. Antiquarianism sometimes prompted the re-creation of old architectural forms in gardens, for instance sham ruins, which might include genuine medieval fragments.

Another reason for the growing interest in collecting was the evolution of the Enlightenment. This covered many areas of thought and life, but it

RIGHT The re-creation of the Sabine statue group by Ivor Abrahams after Giambologna.

particularly fostered a spirit of inquiry, of examining the natural and artefactual world. This led in practical terms to medical and other scientific advances as well as to the technological achievements of the Industrial Revolution. But in intellectual terms it also meant a burgeoning of serious scholarship and a determination to improve historical knowledge. This could well manifest itself through collecting, which was often carried out on a massive scale. Sir Hans Sloane's collection formed the basis of the British Museum (founded 1753), while Elias Ashmole, who had acquired the Tradescants' collection, founded the Ashmolean in Oxford.

Some collections were specialised, for instance the 'Arundel marbles', sculptural antiquities brought from Italy and other Mediterranean countries by Thomas Howard, Lord Arundel, in the mid seventeenth century, or the eighteenth-century sculpture collection of Charles Towneley now housed in the British Museum. Others were more general, and often included a library. This was regarded not so much as an accessory but a necessity for

any aristocrat or gentleman – for some of the hunting and shooting set it may well have been for show and to improve their image, but often it would indicate serious study. Hamilton's would be a good case in point: while a small number of volumes had (and still have) their pages uncut and evidently were not read, the vast majority were for intellectual interest and in some instances for practical purposes.

Having a collection came to be regarded as an important mark of taste. While criteria for taste changed during the century, as did fashions and indeed styles of laying out gardens, there were certain elements that demonstrated permanent, unchanging taste. One was the classical world: it would always be a sign of taste to own real antique marbles. The contents of a library, too, would have to embrace the 'classics', meaning both the (literal) classics of Greece and Rome but also the works of past poets and authors, particularly British. Such was the confidence in contemporary British literature, with Fielding pioneering the novel in its modern form, that many eighteenth-century authors were rapidly accepted into the canon. And in the field of painting, the landscape works of Claude and Poussin from the seventeenth century found acceptance at a level previously enjoyed only by religious, history or portrait paintings.

In order to build up a collection, an agent was often called in to arrange the purchase and transport of art. One such was the entrepreneurial Arthur Pond, a neglected figure until Louise Lippincott researched his story and published her findings in 1983.[1] Pond knew, or learned, the ways of maximising income from the art world and the sometimes gullible clients who inhabited it. His varied career included portrait painting, acting as an agent, dealing and printselling. He was a pioneer in commercialising the processes of buying and selling art, but was also a scholar, a connoisseur in the matter of provenance and attribution. This scholarship itself contributed greatly to the academic reputation of the art world and made the business of forming a collection a serious pursuit.

Pond spread his net widely to find clients, and although he was never employed directly by Frederick, Prince of Wales, he had dealings with several of the Prince's circle.[2] These included Hamilton, who, according to Pond's accounts book, gave him commissions from 1734 to 1740. Hamilton had heard of Pond while he was in Italy, through George Knapton, whose career was somewhat similar to Pond's, being at various times a book illustrator, portrait painter and art dealer. Knapton encouraged Grand Tourists like Hamilton to make use of Pond as a receiving agent for their purchases abroad, arranging storage, Customs clearance and transport.[3]

Hamilton used Pond mainly as a shipping agent, and although the accounts do not specify which paintings Hamilton acquired, there are numerous references to their carriage. In one case only is a painting named, a copy of a Cupid by Correggio, but that was being sold by Hamilton to General Dormer of Rousham.[4] Otherwise there are mentions of stretching frames for paintings and the assembling of a harpsichord.[5] In the autumn of 1739, seven years after his second trip to Italy, Hamilton obtained four marble busts shipped on *The Golden Eagle*.[6] Intriguingly, there was a sale in May 1740 of a painting from Hamilton to Lord Archibald Hamilton that was described as 'Mr Hamilton's picture'[7] – is this a lost portrait of Hamilton?

Pond was a much more astute man of business than Hamilton, for he did very well financially at Hamilton's expense. Louise Lippincott calculated that on one occasion Pond charged £64 3s 6d for services worth about £10 plus some Customs duties, while in a later transaction Hamilton paid twelve guineas for services costing Pond half that sum in connection with a painting that had itself cost no more than £9.[8] Again we see Hamilton's naivety in business matters and his consequent liability to be exploited or duped.

Hamilton's collection of paintings was considerable, and although his house was small there was one room that was fitted up as a gallery. Richard Pococke, visiting in 1754, was impressed by the gallery and praised two paintings by Paolo Panini in particular.[9] These are identifiable with two Paninis later described by Uvedale Price as having passed back into the Abercorn family, both architectural paintings, one showing the interior of St Paul's. Many paintings were acquired from his time in Rome, and included work by the finest Italian masters, but there was also a significant number of non-Italian canvases. A complete list does not exist, but on 11 and 12 March 1773, shortly before Hamilton left Painshill, the auctioneers Langford's put up for sale some eighty of his paintings, not all of which reached the reserve price. As a result some works remained with Hamilton and moved with him to Bath, where after his death an inventory of seventy-two paintings and sixteen prints was compiled.

From the list of the Langford's sale, two things emerge. One is the number of big 'names', such as Poussin (4), Rubens (6), Van Dyck, Holbein, Brill (2), Carracci, Domenichino (2), Salvator Rosa (2), Guercino, Parmigianino (2), Correggio and even Michelangelo, though perhaps today some of these might be considered copies or otherwise questioned or re-attributed. The prize piece was Correggio's 'most capital picture of Venus, Cupid and a Satyr', the painting of which a copy had been sold to General Dormer back in 1738. The second significant feature is the number of landscape paintings – thirty-one plus two views of monuments in Rome. This speaks loudly for Hamilton's taste and shows that when he came to design his own landscape it was through the filter of his knowledge of, and love for, the compositions of the masters of landscape painting.

The Bath inventory presents the same findings. Twenty-seven out of the seventy-two works are specifically landscapes and several others, mostly views of Rome or sea ports, could be classed as such. Hamilton evidently had an abiding love for the Roman views, reminding him of his time there, as well as for the landscapes generally. But most tantalising in the list are the twelve paintings of Painshill, only a couple of which are likely to have survived or be known today. Eight (unidentified) of these hung in Mrs Hamilton's bedroom; one in the drawing room (possibly the View from the Turkish Tent, see page 64); the Temple of Bacchus (possibly the Hannan, see page 128 top right) in the West Room; and two views of the grotto in the same room.

The 1774 portrait of Hamilton (see page 47) shows him holding a bulky volume entitled 'Views of Painshill'. As these were bound in book form, they were presumably additional to the framed and hung views mentioned, and could even be sketches or paintings by Hamilton himself. Taken together with the hung paintings they attest to the way in which the gardens Hamilton had created continued to reverberate in his years of retirement.

In addition to his paintings, Hamilton had an exceptional collection of sculpture, nearly all classical antiques, though supplemented in the 1760s by copies of four classical figures and by the purchase of two lead pieces from John Cheere. The antique marbles came as a result of his prolonged stays in Italy and from the years following his return home. The collection, unlike the paintings, was on public display, for it was dispersed in three locations around the grounds – in and around the Mausoleum, within the Temple of Bacchus and inside the Gothic Tower. The complete collection was listed in an enclosure with a letter of 17 November 1765 to Henry Fox,[10] in which Hamilton proposed the sale of the marbles by means of a lottery, but as we have seen the scheme fell through, as did the attempt to sell the marbles to Lord Clive five years later.

Hamilton's own list is corroborated by visitors, who mentioned many of the marbles. There were three full figure statues – a 7 ft 4 in supposedly Grecian statue of Bacchus (of which more later); a 4 ft 4 in representation of Minerva, also said to be Grecian; and a lifesize Roman figure of Flora, lacking arms but with elegant drapery. Bacchus was of course housed in the temple created for him, and the other two were in the Gothic Tower.

The Temple of Bacchus also contained what Hamilton claimed was a unique set of twelve busts of Roman emperors. However, in the sale of 1797, one bust, that of Antoninus Pius, was listed separately from the set although he was an emperor. Hamilton did not list the emperors as such, but in his full list of busts there are actually thirteen candidates for inclusion in the Temple: Julius Caesar, Augustus, Brutus, Caligula, Trajan, Hadrian, Commodus, Pertinax, Geta, Lucius Verus, Albinus, Antoninus Pius and Septimus Severus. Julius Caesar was never actually emperor, however, and Albinus was a Roman usurper proclaimed emperor by the legions in Britain and Spain and who gave himself the title but had no legitimacy. The one obvious anomaly is Brutus, whose exclusion would leave twelve emperors (and quasi-emperors), but his bust was definitely in the temple and regarded as particularly fine by Gilpin.[11]

The female busts included Antonia, Matidia, Domilia (Domitian's empress), Plotina (Trajan's empress), Sabina (Hadrian's empress), Faustina (Antoninus Pius' empress), Lucilla (Lucius Verus' empress), Crispina (Commodus' empress), Julia (Septimius Severus' empress) and Plautilla (Caracalla's empress). Finally Hamilton listed three unknown heads and two small heads of Jupiter

and Venus. Hamilton admitted that the identification of Sabina and Crispina were doubtful, and modern scholarship might question others. However, with the exception of Bacchus, the present whereabouts of all the marbles is unknown.

One or two busts, plus various funeral urns, a vase, a small sarcophagus and a Roman altar, could be seen in or close to the Mausoleum. The overall effect would have been to enhance the apparent authenticity of the two classical buildings, the Temple of Bacchus and the Mausoleum, but to make of the Gothic Tower a museum or showcase for the other pieces. In addition there were busts of the four seasons on pedestals outside the greenhouse in the parterre gardens near the house, but details are lacking and it is not known how old they were. They could conceivably be the four marble busts shipped over from Italy in 1739 as mentioned above.

Once the temple had gone up, it was necessary to augment the collection by new pieces, or copies rather, to adorn the niches in the main front of the building. Hamilton accordingly placed four plaster casts, two on each side of the entrance, of well-known figures from antiquity – the Apollo Belvedere, the Venus de Medici, the Venus Marina and Mercury. Although these were standard productions of the lead yards, Hamilton may have preferred to obtain plaster casts as they would have been cheaper. But he did purchase two free-standing lead works from John Cheere in 1763, with payments of £25 and £12 7s to Cheere the following year.[12] These were the Sabine group, after Giambologna's original created for the Loggia dei Lanzi in Florence, and an elaborate vase which was placed on the terrace at the top of the hill near Hamilton's house but now resides in an open arbour at Alnwick, Northumberland (see page 56). This vase is exquisitely modelled, with monkey supporters, a frieze of playful putti on the main body of the piece, heads of the four seasons above and on the top a basket of fruit, gourds and foliage. A fox surveys the scene on top of all. Lead casting was accomplished in individual units, so details could vary from one cast to another, which explains why the original copy of the vase, at Melbourne Hall, Derbyshire, lacks the fox.

The Sabine group consists of three figures cleverly poised on a base that would comfortably accommodate

MR HAMILTON'S ELYSIUM

only one, comprising the aged father crouching and the Roman soldier straddling him and bearing off the hapless girl. Interestingly, Giambologna's original was not described as portraying the Sabine story until some time after its installation. Cheere had inherited casts and models from the yard of John Van Nost at the beginning of the century: Nost offered 'A Sabine rape' for £90 in 1700, while the Melbourne Hall vase cost £100 in 1705, which is very early for the appearance of *singerie* in the form of the monkey supporters. The Sabine group survived in the amphitheatre area until 1952, when it was sold for its lead.

The story of Bacchus is particularly fascinating. Thanks to the assiduous researches principally of Jan Clark, Norman Kitz and Alastair Laing, it is now possible to trace most of the history of this figure up to its recent identification at the National Trust property of Anglesey Abbey, Cambridgeshire, and the subsequent taking of casts from the original to display copies at the locations associated with it, including Painshill itself. The history is not complete, however, and some questions remain.

Hamilton is said to have obtained Bacchus while in Rome in 1727. Joseph Spence related that he 'Bought his noble Bacchus of one of them [the Italian nobility] with a promise of secrecy.'[13] It was commonly reported that the statue had cost £2,000, probably the equivalent of £2,000,000 today, but Hamilton may have inflated the price to make his prize seem more valuable – he was inordinately proud of it. He boasted that it was the finest Grecian statue to be brought to England – but it is hard to believe that he did not realise that what he had acquired was a patchwork of pieces, very few of which were likely to have been originally Greek. Recent examination by archaeologist Andreas Kropp has shown that probably only the head and feet are ancient, together with the paws of the accompanying animal and the lower part of

FAR LEFT Vase at Painshill in 1904.

LEFT ABOVE Vase now at Alnwick.

LEFT BELOW Similar vase at Melbourne Hall.

RIGHT The Sabine statue in 1904.

the vine trunk. The head, moreover, is almost certainly a woman's reshaped as a man's.

The practice of assembling bits and pieces of genuine sculpture, and supplying the missing parts, was widespread in eighteenth-century Italy, as the Italian sculpture yards learned how to exploit milord on his Grand Tour. Allan Cunningham's account may serve for what happened to Hamilton:

> …a practice common in Italy – that of patching up and repairing old fragments for the collections of those rich and travelled persons whose pleasure it was to purchase them. In this kind of jugglery the Italians excel all mankind – they gather together the crushed and mutilated members of two or three old marbles, and by means of a little skill of hand, good cement, and sleight in colouring, raise up a complete figure, on which they confer the name of some lost statue, and as such sell it to those whose pockets are better furnished than their heads – especially our English *cognoscenti*. It is indeed wonderful with what neatness and elegance those practised impostors make up a work for sale; all fractures and patches and joints are concealed under a coat of yellowish colouring, which seems the natural result of time – and the rejoicing virtuoso treasures up in his gallery another legitimate specimen of the wonderful genius of Greece![14]

The pose of Bacchus, with one hand on top of the head, is common to other known images of the god, such as those at Versailles and in Madrid. The creature by the side of Bacchus looks more like a dog (and was usually described as such) than the panther with which the classical Bacchus was associated. It is easy to see why a dog should have appealed more to a sportsman such as Hamilton, and the canny Italian sculptor surely guessed that.

The question of authenticity divided contemporary visitors. Most, such as Parnell (1763), Gilpin (1765), Whately (1770) and Arthur Young (1772), accepted Hamilton's estimation of it as a magnificent and noble antiquity.[15] But others saw the joins and recognised it as a heavily-restored work. In 1801 Richard Warner thought the arms and left foot were modern, and John

TOP Hamilton's Bacchus at Anglesey Abbey.

ABOVE The copy of Bacchus being moved into position at Painshill.

RIGHT The copy of Bacchus unveiled at Painshill.

Britton in the same year described the arms and part of the torso as restored.[16] Scorn, though, was reserved to a French visitor, Jacques Cambry, who in 1788 disparaged the workmanship and the mixing of ancient and modern marble with the lines all too evident.[17]

Bacchus stayed in his temple until the sale of 1797, following the death of Bond Hopkins, when he was offered up at auction along with all the other marbles. The purchaser was Hamilton's great-nephew William Beckford, advised by Joseph Nollekens, the contemporary sculptor, who recognised that the head and trunk might be the only original parts and who himself would not have given ninety guineas for it.[18] In the event the extravagantly monied Beckford bought it for £400, using his furnisher Foxhall to do the bidding. At Fonthill the statue was placed in a dove-coloured marble niche in the dining room of the large Palladian house (Fonthill Splendens) built by his father in the 1750s. When Beckford came to demolish the house in favour of the monumental but ill-fated Fonthill Abbey he sold off many of the contents, including the Bacchus, which presumably would not have fitted in with the Gothic scheme of the Abbey. So it was that in the summer of 1807 Bacchus passed to Thomas Johnes of Hafod, Cardiganshire.[19] The price had declined to 210 guineas, showing that Beckford had paid more than the market value.

Hafod was a remote picturesque and romantic estate in the middle of Wales, to the east of Aberystwyth. It was dogged by more ill luck than Fonthill, including a devastating fire in March 1807. So it was probably to help furnish the rebuilt house that Johnes acquired Bacchus and placed it in the entrance. Although he died in 1816, the estate was not purchased until 1832, by the 4th Duke of Newcastle, whose principal seat was at Clumber, Nottinghamshire. From here the story becomes a little hazy. Apparently arrangements were made to ship Bacchus by canal to Christie's for sale in London in 1839, but Christie's have no record of it.

The trail breaks off until Bacchus appears at the Brownlow estate of Ashridge, Hertfordshire, later in the nineteenth century, where it remained while the family wealth was steadily dissipated. In 1928 house and contents were put on the market, and an anonymous large marble statue, identifiable as Bacchus, fetched a paltry £13. The purchaser was the 1st Lord Fairhaven of Anglesey Abbey, Cambridgeshire, who was amassing an astonishing collection of statuary in the grounds at a time when old sculpture was still available and inexpensive. Bacchus was placed against a hedge at the end of a long, straight path, but eluded identification for decades. Lanning Roper, presumably on the basis of its similarity to the well-known representation of Apollino, called it Apollo, but although by 1997 the Anglesey Abbey guidebook recognised it as Bacchus with a dog, the provenance was given as eighteenth-century Italian.[20] In view of the heavy restoration, this may largely be true, but the association with Hamilton was still to come.

The statue had weathered badly at Anglesey Abbey, and the original is now housed indoors. It was a focal piece in the exhibition 'The Return of the Gods: Neoclassical Sculpture in Britain' at Tate Britain in 2008, and cast copies were subsequently made, the Painshill copy being unveiled in August of that year, with the intention that it should eventually be displayed in the rebuilt Temple of Bacchus.

Hamilton's library encompassed a range of volumes from the cultural and scholarly to the distinctly practical, particularly in matters of horticulture and agriculture. He had a large number of books on British and European history, quite a few on health and medicine, and several works in Italian, no doubt the fruit of his two stays there. On husbandry in general, he had the classic Gervase Markham text *Markhams Farwell* (sic) to *Husbandry* (1620), *Duhamel's Husbandry* (1759) and Richard Bradley's six-volume work (1728), while on agriculture and farming he possessed Arthur Young's *A Course of Experimental Agriculture* (two vols, 1770), Bradley's *Agriculture* (1721) and John Worlidge's *Systema Agriculturae* (4th edition, 1697). There were also one or two books specifically on viticulture.

But most of the practical books were on gardening. Philip Miller's *The Gardeners Dictionary* (Hamilton's edition was 1739) was essential reading for anyone concerned with making a garden, and Hamilton also had his *Gardeners Calendar* (1770 edition). Several of the seventeenth-century classics were in his library: John

Evelyn's *Sylva* (3rd edition, 1679), *Kalendarium Hortense* (1691 edition) and *A Discourse of Sallets* (1699); Nehemiah Grew's *Anatomy of Plants* (1682); John Parkinson's *Paradisi in Sole Paradisus Terrestris* (1620); John Ray's *Historia Plantarum* (three vols, 1686–1704); Joannes Bauhinus's *Historia Plantarum Universalis* (three vols, no date, orig. 1650–1); Jakob Breyn's *History of Plants* (two vols, 1674); Clusius's *Rariorum Plantarum Historia* (no date, orig. 1601); and other texts by Alpini, Theophrastus, Buccone and James Sutherland. In view of his later prominent use of American plants, it is significant that he had Charles Plumier's *Plantes de l'Amerique* (1693). Another classic text was René Rapin's poem *Of Gardens* (originally in Latin, 1665).

Contemporary eighteenth-century works or editions of earlier works included Bradley's *New Improvements of Planting and Gardening* (1726 edition), *The Flower Garden Display'd* (1734 edition), Herman Boerhaave's *Historia Plantarum* (two vols, 1738), Thomas Hill's *Treatise of Fruit Trees* (1768 edition), *The Gardener's Practical Surveying Improved* (1737), Arthur Young's two tours of the British Isles (1768 and 1770), Jean de la Quintinie's *Instructions pour les Jardins* (two vols, 1730 edition), Sir John Hill's *British Herbal* (1756), Jacques Delille's *Les Jardins* (1782 edition), De Combles's *L'Ecole du Jardin Potager* (two vols, 1752); *Culture des Pechers* (1750) and *Praedium Rusticum* (1742). It will be seen from the titles alone that Hamilton could have obtained a great deal of advice and information from these books.

There were several books on architecture, as one might have expected of someone who engaged in a considerable amount of building, in some cases probably to his own designs. Works by Roger Morris (1734) and Sir William Chambers (his *Views of Kew Gardens*, 1763) reveal a following of contemporary fashions in building, and Hamilton subscribed to Isaac Ware's 1738 edition of Palladio's *Four Books of Architecture*, which was manifestly a source of ideas to him. He was sufficiently up-to-date to have the first book on Greek architecture, Stuart and Revett's *The Antiquities of Athens* (1762), followed by Robert Adam's return to the Roman Empire in *The Ruins of the Palace of Diocletian* (1764). He had books of designs by James Gibbs (1728) and Inigo Jones (two vols, 1737). Both Vitruvius and Campbell's tribute to him, *Vitruvius Britannicus* (three vols, 1715), were included.

Hamilton's colleague George Lyttelton was represented by his *History of Henry II* (1767) and *Dialogues* (1760). Burke's *Sublime and the Beautiful* (1757) shows his interest in aesthetic theory which led him towards the Picturesque (see page 134ff), while Shenstone's *Works* (1764) suggests an interest in the literary landscape of The Leasowes as much as in his poetry. Salmon's *Antiquities of Surrey* (1736) indicates a wish to understand the locality at the time he moved to Painshill.

Another facet of Hamilton the collector shows in his plantings. These will be considered later, but although the main thrust of Hamilton's acquisitions was botanical, together with aesthetic concern in planting design, the collecting urge cannot be disentangled from these interests. It is apparent that he was eager to possess the latest available tree or shrub, especially from distant parts. Hamilton's zeal for collecting covered both the living and the inanimate.

ABOVE Charles Hamilton's bookplate, showing the Abercorn family crest.

The Lake

HERE IS NO QUESTION that the lake at Painshill is at the heart of the design. It is in itself ingeniously devised to furnish variety, illusion and surprise, and shows that Hamilton was well aware of the effects of images reflected in the water. It was always recognised as a masterstroke: Count Frederick Kielmansegge, going round the gardens in October 1761, declared: 'The finest part of this Hamilton garden is the lake',[1] while John Adam, brother of Robert, on a visit in summer 1759, singled out for praise 'a piece of water in the shape of a natural lake with islands in it'.[2] George Mason set it in the context of paradise: 'Primeval beauty at his lake HAMILTON well knew for its properest investment – within a Garden of Eden.'[3]

Several commentators have remarked that Hamilton's control of distance and perspective, combined with the windings of the water, which can never be absorbed in one view, create an illusion of greater size than is in fact the case. As Whately put it, 'the whole of this lake is never seen at once; but by its form, by the disposition of some islands, and by the trees in them and on the banks, it always seems to be larger than it is'.[4] Sometimes the lake appeared as a broad sheet of water, sometimes as the slim arm of a river. The size of the lake has deceived topographers as much as its illusive appearance did visitors. The lake was popularly supposed to have been about thirty acres in area, and Brayley claimed that its exact measurement was 31 acres 1 rood 26 poles.[5] Recent surveys, however, have shown that the real size is about seventeen acres, and the OS 6in map gives a figure of 14.854 acres for the water excluding the islands.

The shape of the Painshill lake is unusual, and far from conventional at the time. It could be seen from different distances and heights, and buildings around or near it, such as the Gothic Temple, would appear and reappear far and near during the circuit.

Water was recognised by critics as being crucial to a landscape garden. Whately, in a general section on water in his *Observations on Modern Gardening*, asserted that it is

the most interesting object in a landscape, and the happiest circumstance in a retired recess; captivates the eye at a distance; invites approach, and is delightful when near; it refreshes an open exposure; it animates a shade; chears the dreariness of a waste, and enriches the most crowded view...it may spread in a calm expanse to soothe the tranquillity of a peaceful scene;

ABOVE The lake, with the 'Chinese' bridge in the distance.

THE LAKE

or hurrying along a devious course, add splendour to a gay, and extravagance to a romantic, situation.[6]

Kielmansegge concurred, concluding that 'an Englishman thinks nothing of a garden without water'.[7]

In general, the irregular curving of Hamilton's lake accorded with the theories of the new generation of garden pundits, schooled to believe in what Hogarth promoted as the serpentine line of beauty. The variety of effect sought by Whately was acknowledged by him to find best expression at Painshill in the view from the Turkish Tent (see below), which looked down on much (though not all) of the lake:

> …[the water] is seen to greater advantage from this point than from any other; its broadest expanse is at the foot of the hill; from that it spreads in several directions, sometimes under the plantations, sometimes into the midst of them, and other times winding behind them; the principal bridge of five arches is just below; at a distance, deep in the wood, is another, a single arch, thrown over a stream which is lost a little beyond it…the banks also of the lake are infinitely diversified; they are open in one place, and in another covered with plantations, which sometimes come down to the brink of the water.[8]

John Trusler, who visited Painshill (and indeed lived only a mile away), also mused in his *Elements of Modern Gardening* (1784) on the importance of water, considering that a river was never seen to better effect than when lost in a wood or retreating behind a hill, 'nor better situated, than when running under the side of a wood, and affording a delightful walk on its banks, under the shade of trees reaching to the water's edge'.[9] Although he was talking in general terms, and about a river rather

than a lake, it can be seen how applicable his words were to Painshill. Another of his dicta recalls the view across the lake to the Gothic Temple or the Turkish Tent: 'The more a lake spreads, the handsomer it is, and nothing has a finer effect, than a very large piece of water, with the shore on the further side rising from it in wood, and decorated with a building.'[10]

The lake was excavated and developed over a period of years. It seems to have been made from a small pond at most and probably from gravel pits providing hollows on which to base the work. Rocque's map of Surrey, published by his widow in 1762, may be assumed to be the product of a much earlier period, possibly the late 1730s, when Rocque was also engaged in surveying the grounds at Esher Place and Claremont. The map shows an area of water shaped somewhat like a slim bow-tie, with the western side larger than the eastern. No islands are visible, and the shape bears little resemblance to that of the present lake. The assumption must be, therefore, that Rocque saw the lake in the early stages of its formation. His detailed map of 1744 (see page 22) corroborates the small early size of the lake.

The lake was lined with puddled clay, as was the eighteenth-century practice. The islands could possibly have been created from the spoil thrown up by excavating the lake, but could also have been simply land left standing above water level when the lower hollows were flooded. The lake was some fifteen feet above the level of the River Mole, and water had to be drawn up from the river by means of various devices described below. The lake seems to have been more or less complete by about 1750, though the final arm, below the Ruined Abbey and vineyard, was not formed until 1772. It was created by flooding a flat water meadow.

Hamilton constructed three, possibly four, bridges of different kinds for varied visual and associative effect. One was the bridge on the south-western side of Grotto Island, a single-span structure of wood clearly depicted

in the foreground of Woollett's engraving (see page 68). It does not survive, but was a close copy of Palladio's Plate 3 in Book 3 of his *Four Books of Architecture*, originally published in Venice in 1570 but known in Britain through Isaac Ware's edition of 1738, to which Hamilton was a subscriber. This bridge probably did not last long – perhaps it was too flimsy or even too dangerous.

The bridge seen in the background in Woollett was described as a 'Chinese' bridge, though it is in fact no such thing. It is taken from Plate 5 in Palladio (see page 68), and is claimed to be of the architect's own invention. Unfortunately the criss-cross lattice design caused such bridges, of which there were a considerable number in English gardens, to be designated Chinese, particularly at a time when the vogue for *chinoiserie* in gardens was at its height. By 1765 or even earlier Hamilton had replaced it with a five-arch bridge. The 'Chinese' bridge may have been dismantled and re-erected to replace the Palladian bridge across to Grotto Island – some traces of brick foundations can be seen not far from where the Palladian bridge was placed by Woollett. The 'Chinese' bridge is clearly depicted in the painting of the view from the Turkish Tent of about 1770 (see opposite), though the pitch seems steeper than that of the distant bridge in Woollett. Steep curves on 'Chinese' bridges were not uncommon, and one that is almost unclimbable has been reconstructed at Wotton in Buckinghamshire. Hamilton may well have been acquainted with the 'Great Bridge' at Virginia Water, built *c*.1750, with its 165 ft span. William Gilpin scathingly described the Painshill bridge in 1765 as a glaring object and a spot [blot] in the view, presumably in its relocated position.[11]

The bridge that has survived, though repaired or rebuilt more than once, is known today as the 'Chinese Bridge', though it owes more to Palladio than to China. But, as with the curved arch type of bridge, it was considered to be Chinese at the time. Before its recent repair there were the remains of hinges on the bridge, suggesting that a gate controlled the passage of visitors across to Grotto Island. Parnell, on his visit in 1763, mentions two Chinese bridges, presumably the present one and the steep curved one on the other side of the island.[12]

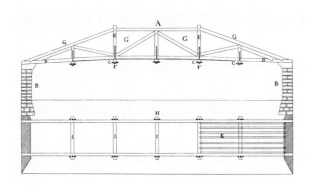

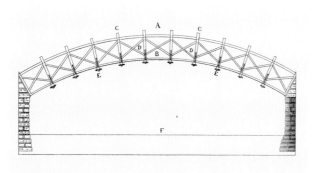

The principal bridge, however, crossed the arm of the lake that leads to the cascade. This was the five-arch structure which replaced the bridge in the background in Woollett. It was mentioned by Whately in his account of his visit to Painshill in the middle to late 1760s, where he says that the bridge was made of stone.[13] However, later descriptions make clear the bridge (or its successor) was made of wood to resemble stone. Since Whately did not actually cross the bridge on his circuit, perhaps he did not go close enough to discover the deception. Gilpin sketched the bridge in its five-arch form in 1772 (see page 87), and this may be the same bridge depicted by Prosser in 1828 (see opposite), though perhaps with some modifications or refurbishment by then.

The boat depicted in Woollett was real, not an artist's fancy. It was described by Robert FitzGerald, *c*.1755, as a paddle-boat, with the wheel, composed of four broad blades, situated under the rear of the boat. A person turned the wheel by hand by operating a crankshaft while his feet controlled the rudder.[14] The Surrey historian William Bray described using the same boat in May 1755, adding that it was invented by Hamilton.[15] This reminds us that, although visitors' descriptions are confined to the paths and walks on

OPPOSITE ABOVE Detail of the bridge
and boat in Woollett's engraving of
1760.

OPPOSITE BELOW Plates 3 and 5 from
Book 3 of Palladio's *Four Books of
Architecture*, Isaac Ware edition, 1738.

ABOVE The lake and island in 1937,
crossed by a nineteenth-century
bridge.

RIGHT The five-arched bridge and the
Gothic Temple by GF Prosser, 1828.

dry land, a different perspective would be provided by seeing the gardens from the lake. The presence of the pleasure boat suggests that, despite the lack of descriptions, this mode of experiencing Painshill was a regular occurrence.

Replenishing the lake and keeping the water in circulation required considerable hydraulic ingenuity. The problem of raising water from the river gave Hamilton the opportunity both to exercise his practical creativity and to design a machine that would fit in with the appearance of the garden and be a prominent visitor attraction. There have been five devices in all, and Hamilton was responsible for the first two and possibly the third.

The first device was a thirty-six feet in diameter vertical wheel which may have been based on designs found in an edition of Vitruvius's *De Architectura* (1522), which would have given the wheel the authority and authenticity that Hamilton had sought and found in Palladio for his bridges. In Hamilton's library there were several relevant volumes: Dezagulier's *Treatise of Hydrostatics* (1718), the Vitruvius, *Architecture Hydraulique* (three vols, 1737) and *Architectura De Vitruvio* (1684). In addition Hamilton may have been acquainted with Stephen Switzer's *An Introduction to a General System of Hydrostaticks and Hydraulicks* (1729), which includes methods for raising and conducting water, together with descriptions of wheels. Hamilton's first wheel must have been installed by 1750, since the lake was dependent on it, and there are various descriptions of it which, taken together, provide a reasonably clear picture. The working is summarised thus by Dodsley in 1761:

> Every time it turns round it takes up the water and conveys it through a spiral pipe from the circumference of the wheel to the center of it, from whence it is discharged into a trough, and from thence through pipes into the gardens, where by the joint assistance of nature and art, it is formed into a fine winding lake.[16]

This description was taken as standard and was reproduced verbatim or nearly so for a good many years, despite the fact that the original wheel had long since been superseded. Richard Pococke, who went round the gardens in 1754, provides the additional information that the first wheel was invented by Hamilton himself, based

presumably on the ideas he would have got from his reading.[17] That Hamilton had a scientific and inventive bent could be confirmed by a document among his correspondence in the Holland House papers describing a perpetual motion instrument, a pendulum that swings between alternate magnets.[18] There is no signature, however, so it is not definitely by Hamilton.

Robert FitzGerald sketched the wheel and gave the following written description, which amplifies Dodsley and Pococke:

> the water is raised by a large Wheell turn'd by the Mole and contrived as they told us by Mr Hamilton – its curious Enough & therefore I will give a description of it [:] as the broad boards turn the wheell round the spirall tubes receive the water at their openings and as those openings are Elevated the water is compress'd into the Narrower parts of the tubes and Discharges itself into the hollow axle tree & from whence it proceeds by pipes, it raising about 4 hogsheads of water in a minute.[19]

Writing in about 1752, Spence provides us with further details of its size and capacity:

> The wheel can fling up 30,000 hogsheads in 24 hours: the great machine at Marly [devised for Louis XIV] only 21,000 in the same time. Near four revolutions in a minute when it works the fastest. The diameter of the wheel is 37 feet. The bore where the four collected streams are delivered into the trough is eight or nine inches in diameter. (This raises the water but 17 feet, that above [i.e. Marly] above 200.)[20]

Count Kielmansegge confirms the size of the wheel (36 feet) closely enough to Spence, and tells us that the four pipes leading from the circumference to the centre were made of leather.[21] It operated somewhat jerkily.

The wheel lasted till about 1770, after functioning for some twenty years. At that date Hamilton erected posts and gates in the river to pen a head of water two feet in height to feed the wheel. Unfortunately Hamilton and the man who lived on the opposite side of the river, a Mr Wood, were not on good terms, and Wood was so annoyed by the enterprise that he arranged with Nathaniel Keene of Cobham Court to dig a ditch on his own land to divert the water from Hamilton's dam. The wheel was then abandoned.[22]

Since the lake could not function without some means of raising water, the first wheel was speedily replaced. Hamilton took the opportunity to experiment with a very different kind of machine, a horizontal device worked by a horse yoked to an arm which operated the lifting mechanism as the horse proceeded round in a circle. The horse-engine was invented by an agricultural engineer, Cuthbert Clarke, and is described in the *Gentleman's Magazine* for February 1771 with an illustration and explanatory text. The engine is shown in section below. The description is as follows, the numbers relating to those on the illustration.

> FIGURE (1,) represents the shaft, which is supported by a pedestal, (19) with a box to hold oil, in which the pivot (20) turns very freely, and the upper end, or spindle of the shaft being sheathed with steel, passes through a collar of hard brass, and with a square tenon fixes into a mortice in the start, or leaver (7) very securely by a crank of iron, which is screwed upon the

start, and clasps a cock of iron which is sunk about three feet into the shaft, nearly in the manner as a mill-stone is connected to its spindle. The cog-weel which is erected upon the six arms of this wheel, turns a trundle (2) (2) of twelve rounds, which is fixed upon an iron axle-tree that has the waller (3) (3) likewise fixed upon it; this waller is about three feet diameter, and stuck with pikes of iron at convenient distances, to fall into the links of the chain (5) (5) which carries six buckets, (6) (6) (6) (6) placed at equal distances along the chain, holding each about 24 gallons of water, which are discharged at (15) by means of a trigger placed on each bucket, and a fork fixed in a frame contiguous thereto, which tips up the bukets [sic] as they revolve round the waller, in a very natural, easy manner, without loss of time or water. From this point the buckets descend empty to the surface of the water in the well at (14) where they turn their mouths down, being made of a proper figure for that purpose, with a contrivance to let the air escape the buckets; they then pass under the axle-tree of the under waller (4) (4) and emerge out of the water with their mouths up, quite full of water, and ascend with a velocity of about one hundred feet per

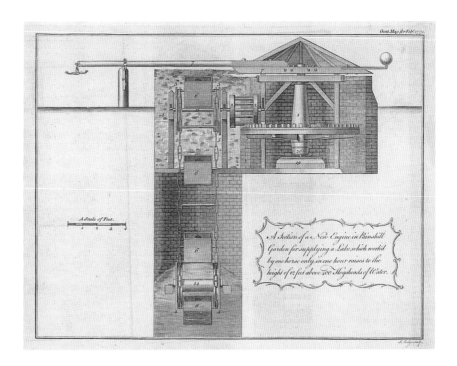

RIGHT Section of Cuthbert Clarke's horse-engine, for the *Gentleman's Magazine*, February 1771.

minute. The radius of the start being sixteen feet, the horse journeys on at the rate of two miles and a half per hour to occasion this velocity, which he performs without inconvenience to any of the machinery, or oppression to himself, and lifts, abating for all waste, above four hundred hogsheads of water per hour to the height of twelve feet. A quantity so vastly superior to that raised (with a similar force) by any pump or engine yet invented, that we know of, and the whole contrivance so simple and ingenious, that we thought a drawing and description of it could not fail of proving acceptable to our readers, and beneficial to the public in general.[23]

Although it has been queried whether the horse-engine was put into practice, there are records of three payments to Cuthbert Clarke which suggest remuneration for the design and then the implementation of the machine. Payments of £28 and £25 were made on 7 August and 15 August 1770 respectively, with a final payment of £17 13s 0d on 22 March 1771.[24] Furthermore, the heading to the above description states specifically that the device was executed, under Clarke's direction. Matthew Boulton's visit in 1772 seems to corroborate the use of the horse-engine since he refers to buckets (though containing 16 gallons each rather than 24), which were not used for the other wheels.[25] However, it does not seem to have lasted long, and was soon replaced by a vertical wheel somewhat similar to the first: in fact it may have been the first one refurbished. Again, there cannot have been a gap between the operation of one device and the next, which suggests that the new wheel was installed towards the end of Hamilton's time.

This new wheel was sketched by the French artist FJ Bélanger, probably after 1774 although he refers **to** Hamilton as the owner. It appears to resemble the first one in its diameter (given as thirty-six feet) and in its general description and functioning, except that it shows seven rather than four pipes: 'The wheel turns on an axle, and is set in motion by the current of a stream. – It takes up the water into spiral pipes which lead to a trough in the centre.'[26]

This wheel was examined by the Swedish architect Fredrik Magnus Pyper on his visit in 1779/80. Pyper made

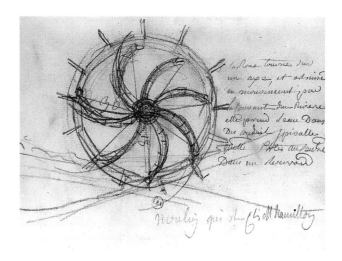

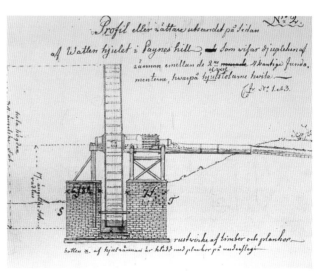

detailed drawings and measurements on fourteen sheets – but although the overall description tallies with Bélanger, and indeed with the original wheel, there is one problem, namely that the number of spiral pipes has been reduced from seven to four (as with the first wheel). Pyper's account is so meticulous that he cannot have been wrong: does this mean, then, that between the time of installing the wheel (*c*.1772) and Pyper's visit three pipes had been

TOP Water wheel sketched by FJ Bélanger, *c*.1775.
ABOVE Water wheel sketched by FM Pyper, 1779.
RIGHT Bramah's water wheel restored.

removed, presumably for practical reasons? The pipes were ten inches in diameter, according to Pyper, widening to thirteen inches where they took in the water.

The wheel probably lasted until not long into the 1780s, for in 1795, William Robertson described and sketched a fourth device. This consisted of a multiple wheel – a large wheel about twenty-four feet in diameter and two smaller ones. Its operation was also different from that of its predecessors:

> The Simplicity of this Engine struck me – & its disposition was different from any I had seen the draft of – so that I took particular Notice of it – the great wheel (for there were two, Seem'd about 24 feet in diameter – & its Spokes were all Hollow & curved. but not discharge that water at the Axletree, but in the verge of a Small wheel about 4 or 5 foot diameter which was also hollow discharged the water into a trough elevated just as near as its inside edge as would permit the wheell to clear it – from this trough the water ran to another wheel placed at right Angles to the great one & about 7 or 8 feet diameter – instead of Fans, there was ladles like those of an Over shot wheel which received the water at the height of the Semidiameter of the Wheel – on the Axis of this was two cranks which worked to [sic] forceing pumps & forced the water up to a small wooden reservoir on the top of the Hill thro' a pipe of two Inches bore, the height said 100 foot above the river & this reservoir is above the level of the top of the House to which the water is conveyed by leaden pipes of the Same diameter as mention'd while the water that turns the forceing wheel passes under it & Supplies the Lake – the float boards of this engine are of a particular form being bent in the middle in this manner ∧ from the Stream, I suppose to prevent the water from acting on them with full force – when

I saw it the wheel move slowly – which attribute to the great diameter of the wheel – the crooked spokes I observed were not in a right line between the verge & axis but inclined out at head.[27]

This multiple wheel was probably commissioned by Benjamin Bond Hopkins as a means of supplying his new house with water. The fifth device was the wheel that has been refurbished and operates today, the cast-iron giant by the firm of Bramah, dating from the 1830s. The designs are to be found in the Science Museum. The wheel is back to the size of Hamilton's first wheel but functions quite differently, as described by Brayley:

> The new wheel was manufactured by Bramah at the cost of about £800, and the works, put into motion by a small stream of water acting upon the floats, are fed by a short canal issuing from a part of the river crossed by a dam. It is 32 feet in diameter: from the central shaft twelve double ribs extend to the periphery, or outer circle, to which forty-eight floats are attached, each being 3 feet 2 inches long, and 2 feet 6 inches wide. The shaft is connected with two sets of cog-wheels applied to work six lift-pumps, three in a set; the smaller set aided by a stand-pipe, &., supplies the house, and the larger set the lake, which necessarily requires a constant stream of water to keep it in motion and preserve its clearness. The entire height to which the water is raised for domestic use is between 90 and 100 feet.[28]

The cascade formed one of the most admired set pieces of the gardens. It was an artful cluster of rockwork to disguise the conduit which brought the water from the wheel to the head of the lake. There are no records of its existence before 1760, though the descriptions of it from then onwards suggest that it would have been mentioned earlier if it had been there. The supposition must be, therefore, that the lake and wheel functioned for up to a decade with a pipe simply discharging into the lake. Then, in the late 1750s, Hamilton conceived the idea of building up an artificial cascade by means of rocks, with some stones scattered nearby to enhance the flavour of the area. To this end he employed Joseph Pickford, the

stonemason who had built the rock grotto at Claremont in 1750: Pickford received payment from Hamilton of £30 14s in April 1759.[29] He had been receiving payment for mason's work at Oatlands during the period 1756-8, but that predated the grotto there, and since there was little stonework going on at Oatlands at that time Pickford was then free to come to Painshill.[30] His experience at Claremont would have made him the perfect candidate for assembling the cascade.

Arthur Young thought the cascade was

> in a very just taste. The water gushes in five or six streams, out of tufts of weeds growing in the rock; over it bends the trunk of an old oak, from side to side, which has an exceeding good effect; and the trees rising to a great height above all, finish the scene very completely.[31]

The front-on view of the cascade, described by Gilpin in 1765 as 'natural and romantic', has been preserved in a drawing by Pyper (see above), which shows an elaborate construction of branches and stone, with water issuing from crevices in the rocks. The rocks appear to be stacked in a not too disorderly fashion in the Pyper drawing, but

Kielmansegge assures us they were set irregularly.[32] As time went by, and the cascade required refurbishing, it may have looked somewhat regular to some eyes, as in the case of Robertson in 1795, who described the water as bursting out

> from between the roots of old trees that over hang & stones amongst them, which if not placed quite so regularly would have had a very natural appearance. Here is entrance to the wild, neglected scene, described by Whately – Large fragments of rude rock are strewed Around to strengthen the idea.[33]

Cascades of this sort were still uncommon in 1760, though a famous example which Hamilton may have known about was at Stowe. At Virginia Water there was a cascade in place, accompanied by a grotto, by 1753–4 (see page 15), which was relocated and rebuilt in the 1780s following a flood. This is a further instance of Hamilton possibly getting an idea, or some inspiration, from that garden. The second cascade there survives with rockwork, though in a surprisingly regular formation. 'Capability' Brown designed a number of cascades, for instance at Blenheim, but they were later. Mostly cascades had been in semi-formal arch form, such as the triple-arch configuration beloved by William Kent (Claremont, pre-Wright, and Chiswick). The dispersal of boulders in proximity to the cascade may have led to the more extensive use of secondary and related rockwork on Grotto Island. The cascade concept was elaborated substantially by Hamilton himself in the rockwork valley at Bowood in the 1780s (see page 49).

OPPOSITE The cascade, sketch by FM Pyper, 1779.
BELOW The cascade today.

The Buildings

*T*HERE IS A CONSIDERABLE DIFFERENCE between Painshill and the more abstract naturalistic parks of 'Capability' Brown, although Hamilton's garden-making was contemporary with Brown's and indeed he survived Brown by three years although he was born twelve years before. If Painshill is to be considered as a pictorial garden, much of that effect derives from the careful placing of buildings in the landscape. Seen from a distance they draw the eye and lead the visitor onwards in the hope of coming across them at closer quarters later in the tour. Seen close-up they reveal a wide range of architectural styles. Not great architecture, perhaps, but the Temple of Bacchus had a classical purity while the grotto could lay claim to be the most astonishing of its kind.

Hamilton employed no regular architect in the way that Henry Hoare, for example, engaged Henry Flitcroft at Stourhead. As we have seen earlier he may well have been his own architect in some cases, though the position is far from clear, and others may have been involved. As was often the case, wooden models of some of the features were produced: the sale catalogue of 1797 mentions the water wheel, 'the great water engine', the tower, the Gothic Temple, the five-arch bridge (called the stone bridge) and 'various others'. All were sold for £1, but have since disappeared.

For the purposes of this chapter the buildings will be loosely grouped under three heads, classical, Gothic and rustic. A fourth category, the exotic and oriental, will be treated separately in the next chapter. In general, buildings had been appearing in gardens during the first part of the century with some frequency. Vanbrugh had early appreciated the positioning and appearance of buildings in the landscape, while William Kent often sketched them on top of a knoll with a sloping lawn in front: the buildings would be backed by trees that then also bounded the lawn. The taste for classical buildings in particular spread, with Roman and Palladian forms being employed, augmented by the Greek Revival from 1758 at Hagley closely followed by the Temple of the Winds at West Wycombe. Vanbrugh himself may even have anticipated the Greek Revival, with his Rotunda at Stowe (1720) possibly being modelled on the Greek Temple of Venus at Cnidos.

RIGHT The Gothic Temple, approached from the amphitheatre.

Hamilton shared with many of his contemporaries a love of the classical world and tried to recreate scenes of a classical kind in his gardens. His was not the consciously literary approach of William Shenstone at The Leasowes but a borrowing of the classical mode to produce visual and emotional effects. In addition, his two classical buildings were designed to show his antique sculpture to best advantage. He had plenty of precedent to draw on, whether actual buildings or images in books. In his library he had copies of Ware's edition of Palladio, James Gibbs's designs (1728), William Kent's edition of Inigo Jones's designs (1727), Vitruvius in Italian and Campbell's English tribute to him. In addition he had several books on Italian architecture.

The Temple of Bacchus appeared in the early 1760s. Woollett does not portray it accurately in his engraving of 1760, which suggests it was intended but not yet built. It was certainly complete by October 1762. Designs by Robert Adam dated 1761 are to be found in the Soane Museum, including three alternative designs for the ceiling, of varying degrees of ornateness, one of which is reproduced below. We cannot be sure which one was actually used. Adam also designed a pedestal (one of twelve the same) to hold the busts of the emperors and others that Hamilton intended to display within the temple. On the strength of these sketches for interior decoration Adam has been canvassed as the architect for the whole temple, but there is no definite evidence. The architect is, indeed, unknown.

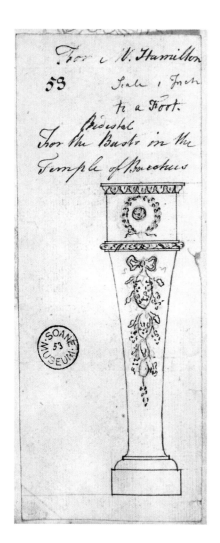

LEFT Design for a pedestal in the Temple of Bacchus by Robert Adam, 1761.
ABOVE Design for the ceiling of the Temple of Bacchus by Robert Adam, 1761.
RIGHT The Temple of Bacchus, sketch by FJ Bélanger, c.1775.

Adam's involvement at Painshill was early in his career, but on his return from Rome in 1758 he had rapidly been taken up by Nathaniel Curzon at Kedleston, Derbyshire, as designer of both house and grounds, including garden pavilions. His brother John went round Painshill in 1759 and admired it, so perhaps that visit led to Robert's engagement by Hamilton.

The temple was of the Doric order, a rectangular building with six columns supporting a pediment to form the front portico, and a rear portico with similar columns. What were usually described as half columns, but were probably three-quarter, were ranged along the sides and pilasters stood against the wall on each front. The temple had a brick core but the columns were of wood and the decorative scene in the pediment was of *papier mâché*, which lasted surprisingly until the late 1940s. The front portico was removed in 1925 for use in the east front of Pains Hill house; the *papier mâché* was removed in about 1950; and the temple fell down, or was pulled down, at the same period. The best depiction is the painting attributed to William Hannan (see page 128), but there were also three drawings dating from the 1770s, one by Gilpin (see page 80), one by Elias Martin (see page 24) and the third by FJ Bélanger, a French architect and garden designer (see below). There are no contemporary representations in prints.

The *papier mâché* pediment contained a group of the drunken Silenus (the foster-father of Bacchus) on an ass,

accompanied by bacchantes and satyrs, one of whom was being prodded in the rear by a goat. Two niches stood on each side of the entrance, occupied by the four figures in plaster previously noted among the sculpture: the Belvedere Apollo, the Venus de Medici, the Venus Marina and Mercury. Inside, the cella was dominated by the imposing statue of Bacchus, seen in profile as one entered. The motifs of vine and grapes on the sculpture were echoed in Adam's ceiling, described by William Robertson in 1795 as 'a Simple neat design a wreath Ornamented with four Eagles & grapes & vine leaves'.[1] The twelve busts sat on Adam's pedestals, which were of wood painted brown.

The temple had a door but no windows on the front, and a tall window or windows at the rear which looked out on a pleasing prospect southwards. It was set on a plateau planted with clumps of flowering shrubs and broad walks winding in between. The colour and brightness of the plantings made for a cheerful effect to complement the temple – Whately describes them thus:

> …all the richness of which plantations are capable; the thickets of flowering shrubs; and the openings are embellished with little airy groupes of the most elegant trees, skirting or crossing the glades; but nothing is minute, or unworthy of the environs of the temple.[2]

Not only did the building and the surrounding plantings interact to produce feelings of pleasure and delight, but they formed a stark contrast to the heaviness of the dark wood that had preceded the plateau.

The temple was unanimously acclaimed for its beauty as architecture. It was, indeed, the only building in

England praised by Thomas Jefferson on his visit in 1786.[3] Whether or not it was designed by Adam the result was worthy of him. It resembles some models of classical architecture, but is not an exact copy, especially in its use of Doric, and it has something in common with a number of contemporary classical-style garden temples. Brayley reckoned that it was based on the design of the Maison Carrée at Nîmes, though with less floridity of decoration,[4] and Hamilton had images of the Maison Carrée in his copy of Ware's edition of Palladio. Henry Hoare, however, detected alternative possible sources: 'It is an oblong, the Form of the Temple of Fortuna Virilis or the Long Temple of Balbec.'[5] The Temple of Fortuna Virilis in Rome was a likely candidate, though that is Ionic and has only four columns in front. Hassell seemed to think it was directly modelled, in miniature, on a classical Temple of Bacchus without giving the exact source.[6]

In addition to possible antique precedent Hamilton could have been inspired by similar buildings in gardens. He would have known about Stowe, either directly or through illustrations, with its 'Grecian Temple' of 1748–9 commanding the Grecian Valley (later it was renamed the Temple of Concord and Victory). The Stowe temple was Ionic, owing something itself to the Maison Carrée, and although much more substantial than the Painshill structure it has some correspondence of form. Another similar building was William Pitt's Temple of Pan at Enfield Chase, Middlesex. To dedicate a temple to Bacchus was not in itself unknown: Vanbrugh built one at Stowe which survived till 1914, though it was very different in appearance.

It would be good to think that the *papier mâché* on the temple and also on the Turkish Tent was created by the 'inventor' (self-styled) or rediscoverer of the medium, the Huguenot Joseph Duffour, who had worked for the Prince of Wales in the 1730s.[7] He was primarily a craftsman in wood, specialising in picture frames, and it may be in that capacity that Hamilton employed him

in 1752–4 (along with Charles Duffour, presumably his brother).[8] Unfortunately there are no records of payments to him thereafter, so he could not have been directly employed on either building. However, during his time with Hamilton he might well have discussed the possibilities of *papier mâché* with him.

The second classical building was the Mausoleum. It became known as the Mausoleum from an early date but is actually a representation of a ruined Roman arch, and was called such by Gilpin when he sketched it (see page 141). It resembled an arch of the sort Hamilton would have seen in Rome, most notably the Arch of Constantine. It consisted of two uprights with alcoves and niches and a connecting span with a panelled soffit on the underside. This was ornamented by octagonal coffers with roses. It probably dates from the late 1750s. There was a patterned tiled pavement, dismissed by Horace Walpole as unluckily resembling a painted oilcloth,[9] which the surviving tiles vigorously refute. Walpole called the Mausoleum a columbarium, by which he meant a niche with a funerary urn rather than the primary meaning of a dovecote. This was because the niches were filled with some of Hamilton's antique fragments, which included urns, and scattered round the Mausoleum were Roman altars and a sarcophagus. A good picture is given by Brayley:

> In a retired nook at the extremity of a woody glade near the head of the lake are the imitation ruins of

LEFT The Temple of Bacchus, sketch by William Gilpin, 1772.

RIGHT Restored paving of the Mausoleum.

a Roman mausoleum, to which a character of reality has been given by the various antique sculptures and sepulchral inscriptions placed there. Among them are several Roman altars, a small sarcophagus of alabaster, and a recumbent (but mutilated) figure of a youthful female on a mattress. The latter, about 4½ feet in length, in respect to style and posture bears no inconsiderable resemblance to some of those represented by Montfaucon on Etruscan tombs.[10]

Evidently these ancient pieces had escaped the sale of 1797, since Brayley was writing long afterwards. There would originally have been even more that had been sold off.

The effect of the ruin was amplified by weeds growing out of the cracks and by the unkempt grass and the sombre plantings of yew. The way in which the building and the scenery complement each other was remarked on by Arthur Young: 'Through the arch, the river appears winding in a proper manner; that is, dark and gloomy, around a rough piece of grass, which has a consistent appearance.'[11] However, it was difficult to sustain the effect since one could see cheerful scenes from the Mausoleum, which in Young's words 'by no means affect the spectator in unison with the ruin of Grecian architecture, and the gloomy objects around'.

The Mausoleum was never regarded as a memorable example of architecture, and its impact seems to have been largely emotional and evocative. Apart from its likely source in a Roman arch, its form resembles one of Batty Langley's designs, 'Ruins for the Termination of

Avenues', in his *New Principles of Gardening* (1728), 'after the old Roman manner'.[12] Hassell commented that the doorway was the only part still intact, and that was partly overgrown with ivy when he saw it in 1818.[13] A number of tablets bearing Latin inscriptions had been removed from the walls.

Bond Hopkins continued his predecessor's love for things classical by creating the now dismantled Roman Bath House on the site of a spring, probably about 1790, when mention was made of it in *The Topographer*. It was a circular building of brick with a wood-based thatched roof, as can be seen in the photograph below. There is another view (see page 29), showing the great cedar to its right. These photographs were taken in 1937 when the Bath House was still intact. Its fate was to be pulled down after the war and the bricks used by a farmer for his piggery. The bath itself was fourteen feet across and five feet deep and was entered by steps. A small changing cubicle was attached. By 1900 it was noted that it was

seldom used on account of the excessive coldness of the water. There was a lantern – the use of a skylight or oculus of some sort characterised the term 'Roman' when applied to bath houses – but in the 1904 sale particulars the light is described as containing most unclassical stained glass.

Hamilton had three prominent Gothic follies, which need to be put into context. The use of Gothic in gardens dates from about 1720 (the alcove at Shotover, Oxfordshire) and was widespread by the 1750s when Hamilton turned his thoughts in that direction. To use Gothic (neo-medieval architectural forms, characterised particularly by the pointed arch), was to proclaim the value and enduring qualities of native arts, and by extension to celebrate long-standing principles such as Liberty that were deemed to have accompanied the original creation of Gothic. The political implications of Gothic were spelled out in the Gothic Temple at Stowe at a time when Liberty was the rallying cry of the Whig Opposition. But after 1750 the political undertones subsided, leaving Gothic as just one of a number of architectural styles that could be employed in the garden, though it would remain a patriotic choice. It would also chime in with the antiquarianism that was so evident by mid century. Gothic forms became twisted and distorted (perhaps rococo-ised) in ways that would have been incomprehensible in medieval times, and they not infrequently merged into *chinoiserie*.

Hamilton's choice of Gothic was a mixture of decorative and romantic, but probably not political, even though he had once been in the Whig Opposition. With the Gothic Temple, the emphasis was on decoration, while the tower and the Ruined Abbey were more for emotional effect. For precedent Hamilton could turn either to actual Gothic pavilions or to the many authors of pattern books which covered Gothic designs, starting with Batty Langley, who in conjunction with his brother Thomas compiled two such books in 1742 and 1747, purporting to reveal the secrets of 'Ancient Saxon Architecture', which they claimed had been lost to the world for more than seven hundred years.

OPPOSITE The Mausoleum in snow.

LEFT The interior of the Bath House in 1937.

Gothic Architecture Improved gives designs for various Gothic orders, entablatures and frontispieces. It contains several plans for 'umbrellos', seats covered by a roof, that could terminate a walk in a garden, and from which a view could be obtained. Different types of pointed arches and finials are described, together with turreting, buttresses, windows in trefoil or quatrefoil patterns, and so on. Others in the Gothic design field were the ubiquitous Halfpenny brothers, William and John, who produced pattern books of all descriptions during the 1750s and 1760s, together with Charles Over, TC Overton and Thomas Wright, all of whom were active over the same period and, again, whose designs ranged over various styles.

The Gothic Temple has generally been applauded (except by the dyspeptic Horace Walpole), and was the architectural showpiece of the garden along with the Temple of Bacchus. It is sited at the end of a straight walk from the amphitheatre and commands a view down to the lake and across to the western part of the gardens. This is an exemplary location for a garden

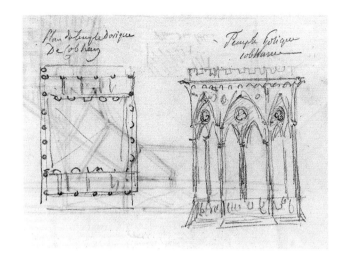

building, satisfying the dual criteria of terminating the view along a walk and of providing a vantage point from which the optimum views can be obtained. It is also the first building to be encountered on the circuit, and the showman in Hamilton knew how effective a piece of garden theatre it would prove to be.

The temple is a wooden construction, based on laths, plastered over and mounted on a stone platform. It is ten-sided, each side having a large pointed arch, with slender buttresses between each, rising to a pinnacle. Each arch contains a pendent, with cast-iron drops that represent an extremely early use of the material in gardens. Four of the arches are half-filled in with a screen. The fan vaulting has been repainted in its appropriate colours and the patterned floor restored. Originally it contained one or more elegant wooden seats, described as resembling 'contemporary petrified French sofas', two of which have been discovered and restored.[14]

The panorama from the temple is totally unexpected and constitutes one of the great experiences of the eighteenth-century garden. The view was extensive and distant yet contained mystery (the lake was partly cut off

LEFT Sketch of the Gothic Temple by John Parnell, 1769.
ABOVE Plan of the Temple of Bacchus and elevation of the Gothic Temple by FJ Bélanger, c.1775.
RIGHT Fan vaulting in the Gothic Temple.

by Grotto Island). William Gilpin had some reservations about one or two features that could be seen, but thought the temple itself was 'a desirable object', and by his second visit in 1772 was sufficiently impressed to revise his estimation and conclude 'rich view from it', which suggests that the plantations had improved in the intervening years.[15]

On 22 August 1761 Walpole visited Painshill to see in particular the Gothic Temple and the Mausoleum, and pontificated:

> The former is taken from Batty Langley's book (which does not contain a single design of true or good Gothic) & is made worse by pendent ornaments in the arches, & by being closed on two sides at bottom, with cheeks that have no relation to Gothic. The whole is an unmeaning edifice. In all Gothic designs, they should be made to imitate something that was of that time, a part of a church, a castle, a convent, or a mansion. The Goths never built summer-houses or temples in a garden. This at Mr. Hamilton's stands on the brow of a hill – there an imitation of a fort or watch-tower had been proper.[16]

To which the immediate reply is that the hill opposite was crowned with just such a tower, which was certainly there by the time of Walpole's visit, as Woollett's earlier print shows (see page 120).

Walpole's comments on the form of the temple betray his obsession with authentic Gothic style, though his own Strawberry Hill was as rococo-Gothick as the Gothic Temple. His reference to Batty Langley has led many to assume that the design for the temple was taken directly from one of Langley's pattern books. There is no single

LEFT Interior of the Gothic Temple in 1937.
RIGHT View from the Gothic Temple as sketched by William Gilpin, 1772.
OVERLEAF The heart of Painshill.

identical design, however, though *Gothic Architecture Improved* contains a number of germane elements in different illustrations, so that the temple as executed could represent a composite of various Langley designs. Those which bear some resemblance to the Gothic Temple – the four Plates LVI to LIX – contain arches of the same style, quatrefoil windows, small and narrow buttresses, and castellation. Langley's style was described by Thomas Gray as deriving from that of Kent, and although popular it was frowned on by many critics of the day. Langley's *Ancient Masonry* (1736) was dedicated to, among others, James, Earl of Abercorn (Hamilton's brother, who had succeeded their father to the title in 1734), just as Langley's earlier *Practical Geometry* had also been. There is a possibility, therefore, that Langley might have worked for the family and have been known personally to Hamilton. But the designer of the temple remains unknown: it could have been Hamilton himself, transmuting the standard designs of Langley into a *jeu d'esprit*, or even Henry Keene or Robert Adam, both of whom essayed Gothic.

During the course of the circuit the temple is seen from varying distances but keeps re-emerging right up to the final panorama obtained from the Turkish Tent. It is also mirrored in the waters of the lake although set back from it by more than a hundred yards. The temple faced west, and its appearance from that direction was marked by a spreading, sloping lawn in front, down to the lake, and a line of trees on each side, drawing the eye to it. This was a favourite device of Kent's, though his examples were generally for closer-range effects. Hamilton ensured that the temple could be seen from some way away, as for example in Elias Martin's oblique view from the rear of the Temple of Bacchus (see page 24).

Gilpin pointed to one of the effects in the view from the temple in his general sketch (see below). That was the *trompe l'oeil* appearance of the five-arch bridge, which looked as though it spanned a river flowing beyond it rather than just the short arm of the lake leading to the cascade.

The Gothic Tower commands a view from the highest, but also the most extreme, part of the grounds. The widening of the A3 (the old Portsmouth road) has meant that it has edged even closer to the boundary. It was intended to be seen from the Gothic Temple – one neomedieval building observing another – but tree growth shuts off that view except in winter. From the summit one could see (originally) St Paul's in one direction and Windsor Castle in another. Keane also mentioned Bagshot, Guildford, Box Hill and Blackheath,[17] while Hassell further lists, among others, Oatlands, Richmond Hill, Hampton Court, Cooper's Hill, Esher Place and Claremont, 'with the whole range of hills from Leatherhead to Guildford and Farnham'.[18] Whately, however, did not entirely approve of its siting:

From the tower on the top of the hill is another prospect, much more extensive, but not more beautiful; the objects are not so well selected, nor seen to so great advantage; some of them are too distant; some too much below the eye; and a large portion of the heath intervenes, which casts a cloud over the view.[19]

The tower is built in the style of a medieval watch-tower. It is made of brick, though originally rendered to make it appear stone. It is castellated and about sixty feet high. It has four rooms, one on each storey, and in one angle a staircase of 102 steps leading up to the roof, which has a viewing balcony, a round capped turret and a spire. It contained some of Hamilton's marbles, primarily Flora and Minerva, and Robertson in 1795 mentioned other busts as being Egyptian, though they could have been later additions.[20] The tower is a fitting companion-piece to Vanbrugh's Belvedere on a hill in the grounds at Claremont. Its effect is romantic – a fairy-tale castle rising out of thick woods (see opposite and on page 136). As with many buildings, it produces different effects when seen from varying distances – close-up it is framed by trees and creates an evocative picture (see Gilpin's sketch, page 139), while from afar it lends a note of mystery to the landscape (Gilpin again, see page 87).

Castellation links the tower to several other buildings of the time, mock castles having proliferated since the time of Stainborough Castle at Wentworth Castle, South Yorkshire (1731). Sanderson Miller made a speciality of ruined castles, as at Radway Grange, Hagley and Wimpole, and crenellation graced many a rococo Gothic seat such as that at Painswick. Vanbrugh, who considered that the house at Kimbolton, Cambridgeshire, should be given 'Something of the Castle Air' in 1707,[21] was famed for castellation, as at Castle Howard. The function of the tower, then, was to act as an eye-catcher, and its form invested the building with a chivalric medieval aura.

The third Gothic edifice with which Hamilton furnished his gardens was the Ruined Abbey. This was built in the early 1770s, partly to cover up the site of the tile and brickworks and partly to add to the sale value of the estate. Although for a long time now, and as restored, it is only a façade, originally it had side walls: the Barret painting (see page 146) gives a clear picture of Hamilton's conception. It did not form part of the circuit, and indeed requires a detour to take it in. Often viewed from the side (Barret, Gilpin or the anonymous painting on page 126), it also looked well from across the lake.

Being a ruin, it has something in common with the Mausoleum: the cult of ruins is discussed in the chapter on the Picturesque. Thoughts of old (genuine) abbeys would arise, such as the great derelict piles in Yorkshire – Fountains, Jervaulx, Rievaulx, Bolton. Nearer home there was the mock ruined chapel at Woburn Farm, which may have been making a religious point (Southcote was a Catholic).

A broad façade of two towers is joined by a wall with three tall arches, all in the pointed Gothic manner. It was built of brick but rendered to look like stone. The Barret painting indicates that the stone finish was scored or painted with lines to convey the impression of separate stones. Mock Gothic ruins were common in eighteenth-century parks, but actual designs are rare (unlike the spate of Gothic designs for complete buildings), and the only book with any plates of sham ruins, *Decorations for Parks and Gardens*, did not appear until about 1800.[22] Most ruins must therefore have been concocted locally,

ABOVE The Gothic Tower by Edward Hassell, 1827.
RIGHT The Gothic Tower amid the woods.

without any real design or proper architect's plans, and this may well have been true in the case here.

Hermitages were very fashionable in eighteenth-century gardens. Initially they may have been intended to signify a contemplative retreat from the world, but such serious purpose as they embodied tended to evaporate as the hermitage became not much more than a fanciful decoration. Not that associations were entirely lost, for the concept of a hermitage would survive even where the architecture veered towards the frivolous or the bizarre. Hermitages could be of various styles, but the characteristics were rustic materials and crude design: roots, branches, trunks, moss and straw were commonly used. An early famous example was William Kent's Hermitage in Richmond Gardens, a more formal structure in stone, which resembled his later essay at Stowe (which survives). Various other examples remain, though inevitably those built of roots and branches have tended to decay at an early date. The pattern books were full of designs, such as Thomas Wright's *Arbours and Grottos* and William Wrighte's *Grotesque Architecture*, which contains proposals for summer and winter hermitages, of varying degrees of warmth. The widespread eruption of these buildings prompted Horace Walpole to deride their supposed function: 'It is almost comical to set aside a quarter of one's garden to be melancholy in.'[23] But it is doubtful whether many hermitages would have had this effect on visitors.

BELOW The Abbey and Hermitage beyond, sketch by William Gilpin, 1772.
RIGHT The Abbey from across the lake.

The Hermitage at Painshill was a Janus-like building, very different in appearance from the front and the back. This was deliberate, to surprise the visitor, who would approach the rear after seeing the front at a distance from the Gothic Temple. From the front the Hermitage resembled a tree-house, as the sketch attributed to SH Grimm after FL von Sckell shows (see below). The back was composed of tree trunks used as pilasters, as depicted by Gilpin (see page 143). The main room had three large Gothic windows with shutters, overlooking the river and the downs to the south, and contained crude rustic furniture. A rear chamber served as a bedroom, and the space below the rooms formed a natural recess, as Spence laconically described: 'The room under it like a sandpit (and mistook for such lately by a fox'.[24] A secret door was thought to permit the hermit to disappear and change when visitors came. Table, bed and chairs were all primitive. There was a floor, and the roof was thatched with straw. Although composed of simple materials such as logs and roots it lasted until at least 1897, when a *Country Life* article speaks of it being in ruined form.

The Hermitage is first mentioned (by Spence) in about 1752, which makes it a very early building in Hamilton's

Painshill

landscape, second only to the Chinese Seat and possibly replacing it (see pages 102–3). An anonymous sketch of the rear (left) is paired with one of an alcove at Esher Place, described as 'Mr Pelham's', who died in 1754, which confirms the early date. Unlike the majority of contemporary hermitages, Hamilton's does seem to have retained the aura of a dark retreat, which was amplified by the approach to it from the pine wood, described by Whately:

about the hermitage it [the wood] is thickened with trees of the darkest greens; a narrow gloomy path, overhung with Scotch and spruce firs, under which the fern seems to have been killed, not cleared, and scarce a blade of grass can grow, leads to the cell…the design is as simple as the materials; and the furniture within is old and uncouth; all the circumstances which belong to the character [of a hermitage], are retained in the utmost purity, both in the approach and the entrance.[25]

It is clear that at least some visitors took the opportunity to meditate in the Hermitage: Spence commented that you proceeded to the front room 'after you have sat some time in the poor hermit's dark bed-chamber'.[26] And part of the atmosphere was engendered by the supposed inhabitant. Real hermits were employed in a few hermitages, but that tended to be a gimmick, and occupants at other places were sometimes simulated or replaced by wax or clockwork effigies. The fact that Spence considered one of the rooms to be the hermit's bedroom might appear to suggest that Hamilton engaged a hermit, but there is no contemporary evidence nor are there accounts by visitors. There is indeed a later story about such a being, but although it has been repeated numerous times the earliest record seems to be 1823, which is long after the event and which strongly suggests that the story is apocryphal.[27]

This probably mythical account sets out the hermit's terms and conditions, which were fairly standard. The stipulations were as follows: the hermit was to wear a camlet robe, and was not to cut his hair or nails; he was not to speak; food would be provided from the house; the hermit was free to walk in but not beyond the grounds; he would be given a Bible, optical glasses, a mat, a hassock and an hourglass. The recompense would be 700 guineas after completion of seven years' service, but nothing before. Another version mentions £700 *per annum*, which would have been a salary up to twenty times that of a labourer.[28]

Hamilton is said to have succeeded in attracting a hermit, but he lasted no more than three weeks. Various reasons have been put forward for his disappearance: it may have been that the Hermitage was cold and damp, or that the hermit had a weakness for beer and tobacco, or that he tired of visitors continually peering in at him. Most versions of the story end up with the hermit being caught as he slipped away to one of the inns at Cobham. Given the stringent conditions, it is hardly surprising, whether or not he had any previous fondness for the bottle, but, sadly, this is all almost certainly fiction.

OPPOSITE ABOVE Sketch of the Hermitage by an unknown artist, before 1754.
OPPOSITE BELOW Sketch of the Hermitage attributed to SH Grimm after FL von Sckell.
BELOW The front of the re-created Hermitage.

The Exotic and Oriental

*I*N ADDITION to the buildings mentioned in the previous chapter, there were others that showed a more fanciful architectural taste, exotic or oriental. The sheer range of styles to be encountered at Painshill indicates Hamilton's eclectic and catholic vision, and marks him out as maybe swayed by rococo fashion but also as open and experimental.

The grotto is a truly astonishing and imaginative creation. Among surviving grottoes of the period its only serious rival would be the slightly later construction at Ascot Place, Berkshire. Hamilton's grotto took several years to build and ornament, and has proved equally laborious to restore. It is located at the heart of the design, and for many visitors then and now it has been the focus of interest. The island on which it stands has an atmosphere of its own, providing an experience unlike any other on the visitor circuit.

The grotto was built up from a brick core on which spongestone, a porous limestone from the Gloucestershire region, commonly but incorrectly referred to as tufa, was used as dressing on the exterior. Work on the grotto probably began in 1762 or early 1763, for John Parnell in his account of a visit in the summer of that year spoke of the arch connecting both parts of the island and fragments of 'tufa' scattered around.[1] Hamilton might well have been his own designer, but he employed Joseph Lane of Tisbury as his master mason on the grotto. Knowledge of Lane's work almost certainly came from Fonthill, where Lane learned his stonecraft and where Hamilton often stayed with Alderman Beckford, his nephew by marriage. Lane lived on the Fonthill estate and doubtless endured a hard training in quarrying stone for Beckford's house, Fonthill Splendens, in the 1750s. The first recorded payment, of £43 2s 10d, was made to Lane on 16 January 1764, but as payment was often made well after the event it could refer to the initial work.[2] Further payments were made in the January of both 1765 and 1766, when the enterprise was at its height.[3] The next recorded payment, of £42 18s 10d, came on 1 July 1769,[4] which suggests a gap between the structural and external work, complete by the mid-1760s, and decoration of the main chamber – the painstaking additions of spar and stalactites. An Elisha Lane also features in the 1769 payments, likewise in 1770 and 1772:[5] Joseph is not known to have had a relative of that name, though his son Josiah was to become an even more illustrious grotto-maker than Joseph, and, though young at the time, could have

LEFT The exterior of the grotto.

helped his father at Painshill. Could one biblical name have been confused with another in the accounts, or did Elisha Lane have no connection with Joseph nor perhaps with the grotto at all? Joseph received his final payment, of £96 5s, in May 1772, which may suggest that all the decoration had been completed the previous year.[6] Hamilton did not have long, therefore, in which to enjoy the centrepiece of his landscape.

Many craftsmen and labourers of varying skills would have been involved in the construction of the grotto. One of the puzzling entries in the Drummonds Bank accounts is a series of three payments in 1768 and 1769 to the notorious Fuller White. White was a Surrey man, a carpenter who built bridges and was employed by Lord Lincoln at Oatlands from about 1750 before moving up to Clumber, Nottinghamshire, Lincoln's northern seat. There he acted as carpenter, paymaster and architect

before matters got totally out of hand, ending up in court, where White lodged bizarre and paranoid counterclaims against Lincoln. His employ at Clumber lasted from 1760 to 1767, when he was dismissed and returned to Surrey.[7] But what did he do for Hamilton? 1768–9 is too late for bridge construction, so one possibility is that he was engaged for late decoration of the grotto (the wooden laths for the stalactites?), though the timber beams must have been installed years earlier. Payments were made on 1 April 1768 (£20), 22 October 1768 (£31 8s 10d) and 28 June 1769 (£44 17s 6d).[8] The last is close to the date of payment to Lane. An alternative possibility is that White was brought in to repair or refurbish some of the wooden structures, such as the bridges or the Gothic Temple.

Hamilton may have been spurred on to create the grotto by rivalry with Lord Lincoln at Oatlands. The two-storey grotto there was under way from 1760 in terms of

materials being assembled, though construction did not begin until 1762, the likely start date of the Painshill grotto. In September 1762 Robert Parsons sent Lincoln 'rockified stone' from Bath, so Hamilton might have been alerted to a source of 'tufa'.[9] In the event Hamilton obtained his spongestone from three sources, Daglingworth, near Cirencester; Combe Down and Widcombe, outside Bath; and Bristol. But the two grottoes took very different directions, and Oatlands (substantively complete by 1767) was a surprisingly formal architectural structure, with spar and stalactite decoration by the Lanes carried out only during a makeover in 1774–8, inspired no doubt by their work at Painshill.

The grotto comprised a bridge/arch, a tunnel passageway and a main chamber thirty-six feet across. The core was brick, with the exterior surfaces mostly dressed with 'tufa', though variety was provided by the plain rockwork at the exit, which originally had the additions of brainstone and snake stone. The roof was timber, covered with lead, and a large central column provided support. Internal decoration consisted of a dazzling array of crystals – quartz, spar and Derbyshire 'bluejohn', with calcite, fluorite and gypsum being used in chips and flakes plastered on to pendent wooden laths to create stalactites. 'Bluejohn', a purple-banded variety of fluorspar, was often used for small ornaments, and Robert Adam had inlaid it in chimney pieces at Kedleston. The tunnel contained a niche with apertures looking out across the underside of the bridge, where its own crystals danced and winked in the reflection of light on the water. Entrance was by a lakeside path and also across stepping stones to a small iron gate leading to the tunnel. The main chamber contained some side niches for special water effects: water was drawn up from a sump beneath the floor to the height of the grotto by a pumping device in a separate room so that as it fell it trickled down the walls of the niches to a pool in the floor. The water fed a fountain in the central pillar before passing back into the sump and the lake. The flooring of the grotto consisted of sand with crushed sea shells, with some coral sticking through. A cave of fantasy from the entrance, the grotto became a natural rocky cave as one left it, with unadorned sarsens.

The effects of light were crucial to the impact of the grotto. The main opening faced west, so that late afternoon and early evening sun would give a particular iridescence to the interior of the chamber, with the sun bouncing off the water as well as entering direct.

When FM Pyper came to Painshill in 1779, he drew a number of sketches of the grotto, including a plan (see over). These give detail not only of what the grotto looked like at the time but how the water effects operated. Pyper also provided a commentary which is reproduced in English by Sirén. He describes the main chambers thus:

It consists of several vaults resting on pillars, and is on the inside ornamented with spars and stalactites, baldachins and chandeliers of all possible forms and shapes hanging from the vaults. From the floor, which is encompassed with a running stream, or rigole, one sees rather large and branchy corals growing up. In the interior of the grotto there are divers niches or depressions with small basins, where the water trickles down like a gentle rain from the strainers concealed in the vaults of the niches, and all this water finally runs down irregular little falls and cascades into the nearby artificial lake, from which the sunbeams are reflected through

LEFT ABOVE Plan of the grotto by FM Pyper, 1779.

LEFT BELOW Interior of the grotto, sketch by Elias Martin, *c*.1777.

ABOVE LEFT Exterior of the grotto in 1937.

ABOVE RIGHT 'Tufa' arch on Grotto Island in 1937.

RIGHT Interior of the grotto in 1937.

openings to the spars and crystallizations fixed in the vaults.[10]

In addition to Pyper's sketches, drawings were made by a fellow Swede, Elias Martin, *c.*1777. His brace of views of the interior of the main chamber (see pages 100, 130) substantiate the written description by Pyper.

The grotto is alone in the extent to which it is complemented by the 'tufa' outcrops, all relating to it, that appear as if naturally all over the island. Some are quite elaborate, such as the alcove on top of the bridge, or the arch which welcomes the visitor on to the island, while others are just small clumps or clusters of the material. In some later creations, such as at Bowood or Wardour (both executed by Josiah Lane), rockwork spreads far beyond the confines of the grotto, but the peculiar effect of the 'tufa' dressing renders Painshill unique.

The very first garden building to be erected by Hamilton was the short-lived Chinese Seat. It was mentioned by Lady Newdigate on a visit with Lord Newdigate on 25 August 1748, and does not feature in any other description of Painshill, so presumably disappeared soon afterwards. We are fortunate that Lady Newdigate sketched it (see opposite), as this is the only record we have of it. It is difficult to be sure where it was located, given that the description in the Newdigate diaries runs on without breaks in the sequence of the circuit taken. But the description – 'at ye foot of a high hill runs ye river Mole & upon it is an extreme pretty Chinese Building encompassed wth a fine plantation' – might well indicate a position with a drop down to the river, in other words where the Hermitage was subsequently put up.[11] It would make sense that Hamilton recognised that that was a good spot for a built feature, and that his growing taste for the Picturesque would lead him to replace the seat with the Hermitage by 1752. Alternatively, it may not have weathered well and had to be removed at an early date.

The illustration of the 'Seat a la Chinoise' indicates a box with fanciful decoration such as plumes, bells and curlicues, with the seat itself, six and a half feet high by eleven feet wide, contained inside. Rather theatrical in appearance, this seat was perhaps the most rococo of all Hamilton's structures, and its prettiness is slightly at

odds with the more solid and substantial buildings that followed. There are no exact parallels, but a Chinese Seat at Wroxton, Oxfordshire (1743–4), comprised an open pavilion with four corner columns and a three-fold seat within. Hamilton's friendship with 'Dickie' Bateman, however, might have led him to visiting the early *chinoiserie* garden at Old Windsor, and he may also have known of the Chinese House at Stowe. But examples of designs from the pattern books would have come too late for him.

A relevant contextual matter to consider in this chapter is the question of possible Chinese influence and presence. While arguments continue as to the impact of China on the English landscape garden in general, broadly speaking the most forceful commentators at the time in Britain denied Chinese influence, while their continental counterparts, especially in France, gave China considerable credit for what they dubbed '*le jardin anglo-chinois*'.[12] Some observations may be made here on Hamilton's possible perception of things Chinese.

There are two areas of confusion that beset any discussion of *anglo-chinois*. One is the distinction between individual garden artefacts (buildings, bridges) and the layout of part or whole of a garden: to have a pagoda or small pavilion with upswept eaves does not make an entire garden Chinese. The other is that several elements of what were felt to be indicative of Chinese gardens (most notably irregularity) were also to be found in landscape gardens – but that could be coincidence, with no implication of influence.

When Lord Macartney visited China in 1792–3 on a diplomatic and trade mission that ended fruitlessly, he was taken round the imperial gardens of Jehol. Perhaps surprisingly he recorded that the gardens reminded him of some well-known gardens at home – but conceded that there was no suggestion of influence despite the similarities:

Had China been accessible to Mr Brown or Mr Hamilton I should have sworn they had drawn their happiest ideas from the rich sources which I have tasted this day; for in the course of a few hours I have enjoyed such vicissitudes of rural delight, as I did not conceive could be felt out of England, being at different moments enchanted by scenes perfectly similar to those I had known there, to the magnificence of Stowe, the soft beauties of Woburn or the fairy-land of Painshill.[13]

The clear inference is that China had *not* been accessible to Brown and Hamilton, who had accordingly developed their ideas independently.

Chinoiserie as manifested in English gardens – usually a distinctly westernised version of real Chinese designs – took the form of buildings or bridges which proliferated in the middle years of the eighteenth century. They became so popular that pattern books with such titles as P Decker's *Chinese Architecture Civil and Ornamental* (1759) and the Halfpenny brothers' *Rural Architecture in the Chinese Taste* (from 1750) and *New Designs for Chinese Temples etc* (1750–2) provided ready-made designs if an architect could not be afforded. In the main such buildings were playful experiments in decorative architecture , and few aspired to authenticity, exceptions being Sir William Chambers's Pagoda at Kew, based on the Porcelain Pagoda at Nanjing, and the Chinese House at Shugborough, Staffordshire, taken from sketches made in China during the global expedition of Admiral Anson, brother of Shugborough's owner.

The larger question, of whether Chinese gardens, with their perceived irregularity, artifice based on natural forms and shapes, and buildings in a landscape, had any influence on the evolution of the English garden hinges not only on how much was known at the time about Chinese gardens in Britain but on whether the landscape garden would have come about anyway, China or no China. This seems highly likely – the causes and imperatives leading to the creation of the naturalistic garden were manifold and diverse, as well as mostly indigenous. Many factors propelled the garden in the direction of naturalism (and later to the Picturesque and romanticism):

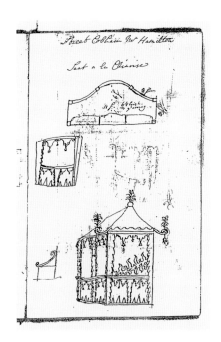

the philosophy of the Earl of Shaftesbury and others, glorifying nature; Whig politics which grew to equate political liberty with freedom of garden design; economics (a landscape garden was cheaper to maintain than a formal one); agricultural revolution (new methods were more efficient and placed more emphasis on productive use of land, so more fields in the view); the Grand Tour and the effect of paintings of the countryside round Rome – natural landscape with ruined classical buildings; and the Enlightenment generally, which encouraged progressive and less shackled thinking.

Hamilton's own knowledge of China and Chinese designs is not likely to have been extensive. He does not appear to have had pattern books that contained *chinoiserie* in his library, but he did possess J-B Du Halde's great four-volume work, *Description Geographique, Historique, Chronologique De L'Empire de la Chine, et de la Tartarie Chinoise*, published in Paris in 1735. Hamilton, who was fluent in French, did not acquire any of the English renderings which appeared soon afterwards. From Du Halde he would have learned very little about Chinese gardens, though there were one or two references to rockwork – a bridge of nine arches of massive stones, and a marble that had veins of different colours that sometimes took the shape of mountains, trees, flowers or rivers and that might be sculpted into tables or other ornaments.[14] He also owned Adam Brand's *A Journal of an Embassy from Muscovy into China, Over Land* (1698), but that contains no mention of rocks, gardens or landscapes.

The Painshill bridges have been considered earlier, so we have seen that the familiar 'Chinese' Bridge (see pages 4–5), although perceived as Chinese at the time and subsequently, echoes Palladio. Hamilton may therefore have been trying to get the

LEFT Sketch of the Chinese Seat by Lady Newdigate, 1748.

best of both worlds with a design based on the revered architect but with a resonance of the exotic.

There was a second bridge, depicted in the distance in Woollett's print (see page 120), which was taken more directly from Palladio, but which at the time was described as Chinese. John Parnell mentions both 'Chinese bridges' in his description of 1763, but William Gilpin shows in his sketch of 1772 (see page 87) that the second bridge had been superseded by a more solid five-arch design, in wood though resembling stone, which may be the same as that depicted in the early nineteenth century by Prosser (see page 69) and others, though it might well have been modified or even replaced by then. But the understanding of what constituted Chinese was changing as the century advanced, and William Robertson on his visit in 1795 describes the five-arch bridge itself more than once as Chinese.[15] Was this because to him something merely decorated in a fanciful way meant Chinese, or was it the references to the earlier bridge as Chinese that misled him?

This second bridge, as we have seen, may have been moved to replace the bridge in the foreground in Woollett's print, for the distinctive 'Chinese' (though actually Palladian) bridge forms an eye-catcher in the painting of the view from the Turkish Tent (see page 64). The overall impression, therefore, was that there were a number of 'Chinese' bridges, all in the vicinity of Grotto Island, thus enhancing the feeling that this was a special area with its own atmosphere of the magical and mysterious.

The paddle-boat in Woollett's print was described as Chinese by Barbara Jones, though she did not explain why she thought so.[16] Perhaps it was the decorative scalloping on the stern and the rear seat. But her opinion might echo a feeling at the time that it fitted into a scene with some Chinese flavour, where vessels reflected nearby architecture, as at Virginia Water.

Rockwork is one of the elements that are common to China and Painshill, as well as many other British gardens. The Chinese would often pile up rocks to form grotesque and awe-provoking structures, such as those described by Johan Nieuhof in the 1650s, published in English in 1669. He admired their gigantic rockwork recesses and illustrated an artificial 'mountain' that might have owed more to imagination than reality. Some of the rockwork

was so large that it contained chambers and was planted with trees. Much of what Nieuhof wrote was based on hearsay, but the book was popular and gave an idea (if exaggerated) of what was to be found in Chinese gardens to an enthralled Western audience.[17]

In the case of Painshill, rockwork is used in a number of ways for varying effect. Grotto Island is the most spectacular manifestation, where outcrops of supposedly marine rock erupt all over the island as well as apparently forming the grotto itself. It is all an illusion, of course. But that is not all. While the 'tufa' is confined to Grotto Island, to give it its special ambience and allure, granite and sandstone boulders were imported to build up the cascade and beyond it to create the feeling of a mountainous region.

Rockwork in Chinese gardens is undeniably a dominant feature, ranging from isolated stones to be admired and contemplated for their strange and tortuous shapes to artificial mountains. Some formations seem to resemble those on Grotto Island, both in shape and material, and also the cascade. Maggie Keswick's book on Chinese gardens has illustrations of some apparent similarities, though the conclusion must be that there were parallel but coincidental developments going on in both East and West.[18]

The use of 'tufa', or *pierre antidiluvienne* as it was sometimes called, was associated with China according to Pyper, who claimed, in relation to the grotto, that 'This species of stone resembles that used by the Chinese for their gardens.'[19] The idea that rockwork grottoes were identifiably Chinese was given impetus in France by Le Rouge, who captions them *grottes chinoises* in his engravings. But that is not to say that Hamilton was aware of the possible Chinese connections or intended to evoke a specifically Chinese feeling in his remarkable and original grotto. Indeed, he is much more likely to have found inspiration in Italian grottoes and sea caves from his extended visits to Italy, which included Naples and its coast. The grottoes of Capri could have furnished the idea of a waterside cave with stalactites, while several Italian Renaissance grottoes had naturalistic stonework within, together with decoration of *spugne*, a pumice-like stone of which 'tufa' might be deemed to be a counterpart. The grotto/nymphaeum at Villa Giulia in Rome, for example, had niches with trickling water.

There were, furthermore, contemporary English developments of which Hamilton must have been aware. At Stourhead, the grotto (1748), though architectural in layout, was composed of rocks, while Stephen Wright's grotto at Claremont (1750) was probably the first naturalistic cave grotto, which was decorated with shells and painted pebbles. Joseph Lane, moreover, created at least one rockwork grotto for Alderman Beckford at Fonthill. Nonetheless, despite all these sources at home and in Italy, the Painshill fantasy remains not only one of the most impressive of grottoes but extremely imaginative. It also exerted considerable influence on subsequent grottoes, such as the stalactite-filled marvels of Ascot Place, Oatlands and St Anne's Hill, Surrey, and 'tufa'-clad works such as the grotto at Croome Court, Worcestershire.

The last word may be left to Geoffrey and Susan Jellicoe, who saw Painshill not as in any way Chinese in respect of its artefacts but comparable to a Chinese work of art, with an effect as

poetic as the allegory at Stourhead: out of an unpromising scene to make an artificial landscape that would tell the story of past civilizations and their place in the great wilderness of nature. In contrast to Stourhead, he [Hamilton] made it linear – a study in time and movement as in a Chinese scroll. The symbolic objects were to be revealed in progression along a broad, sinuous and island-studded river apparently without beginning or end.[20]

Closely related to *chinoiserie*, and often conflated with it at the time, was *turquerie*, with its own oriental flavour. The

ABOVE The 'tufa' arch in snow.

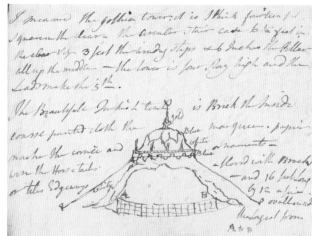

Turkish Tent can be considered, accordingly, as another facet of Hamilton's interest in exotic architecture. It was put up in 1759, and two good contemporary views exist: a pencil drawing with colour wash attributed to Henry Keene (see page 130), which may either be the design for it or a depiction after completion, and an ink drawing by FM Pyper in 1779, 'The Tent at Paynes-hill' (above). It was an appealing concoction in blue and white. At the core was an oval brick drum, with the painted canvas creating a broader oval in ground plan. A herringbone pattern was formed by bricks laid on edge to constitute the flooring. The canopy of the tent was adorned with a *papier mâché* cornice and copper wire plumes. All was surmounted by a Turkish crescent moon on a slender gilded stem from which a pennant flew. The roof was leaded on a timber frame.

Unlike some garden tents, the Painshill model was permanent and not able to be seasonally dismantled. It lasted until at least 1870, though shorn of its canvas and with some of the bricks recycled. It was copied, in a version reckoned to be inferior, at Stourhead. The idea of Turkish Tents probably came from the tents pitched

ABOVE LEFT The Turkish Tent by FM Pyper, 1779.
ABOVE RIGHT A sketch of the Turkish Tent by John Parnell, 1769.
RIGHT The restored Turkish Tent.
OPPOSITE The Turkish Tent reflected in the lake.

during campaigns by the Ottoman armies, and indeed the military use was followed in the case of the Turkish guard tent at Drottningholm, Sweden. This, however, was a much larger construction, as were the tents with copper-tiled roofs at Haga, Sweden, and the Désert de Retz, France. A combination of small-scale tent and a copper roof has been restored at Wotton, Buckinghamshire.

The tent was furnished within, and, as Pyper indicates, there were chairs to provide more comfortable viewing than the wooden benches found in many gardens. The siting of the tent was crucial: it formed an enticing and unusual object in the landscape, and it afforded a particularly fine view, from a height, over a sweep of the pleasure grounds. It was the final point of interest in the gardens, completing the circuit, before the visitor headed for the exit across the parkland. As recreated, the tent stands fifty yards away from its original site but the view is almost identical. Of all the views at Painshill, this is perhaps the most panoramic and satisfying, and Hamilton himself thought so because he considered building a new house there.

Hamilton's Trees and Shrubs

*A*FINE LANDSCAPE GARDEN did not necessarily have to have a wide range of trees and shrubs. The effect was often broad and large scale. 'Capability' Brown's parks were usually composed of a limited number of species, predominantly beech, and the interest was in the overall pattern of the plantings rather than in individual species, though he did make use of shrubberies. But in a few such gardens the arboricultural interest was high, reflecting the passion of the owner for trees and shrubs. This was certainly true of Painshill.

What Hamilton was able to plant was determined by the circumstances of the time and the then available species. Had he lived fifty years earlier Painshill would have looked very different. At the beginning of the century the tree palette was limited – mostly to native species such as oak, elm, lime, beech, ash, chestnut, with one or two that had by then become naturalised, such as the cedar of Lebanon. But by the mid-century the picture had become transformed, with a considerable number of exotics coming in from abroad, in particular from North America. It was these new introductions that especially excited Hamilton and enabled him to create a landscape garden that held great botanical appeal. In effect he made an arboretum of the grounds, although the term was not used till much later.

The cascade of introductions meant that the shape, size and colour of plantings could all be far more varied and subtle than before. Horace Walpole commented on the impact in gardens:

> The introduction of foreign trees and plants, which we owe principally to Archibald duke of Argyle, contributed essentially to the richness of colouring so peculiar to our modern landscape. The mixture of various greens, the contrast of forms between our forest-trees and the northern and West-Indian [=American] firs and pines, are improvements more recent than Kent, or but little known to him. The weeping-willow and every florid shrub, each tree of delicate or bold leaf, are new tints in the composition of our gardens.[1]

LEFT Two swamp cypresses (*Taxodium distichum*), thought to be Hamilton plantings, on the edge of the lake.

The range of new effects was created by both trees and shrubs. In the case of the latter, an expanding interest in the shrubbery meant a great increase in smaller-scale and more intimate floriferous planting. Along with the introduction of many new shrubs came new ways of displaying them, in particular the gradated or 'theatrical' shrubbery, where small species would be grown at the front and progressively taller ones towards the rear, maybe with a backing of trees. In the case of Painshill, different areas were given a different character and appearance, from the formal tiered shrubbery in the 'amphitheatre' to the winding shrubberies below the Gothic Temple. There were open lawns and parkland, screen planting to shut out the River Mole, single trees, clumps and a predominantly evergreen plantation.

Hamilton used plantings for both visual and emotional effect. Sometimes there would be deliberate placing of certain trees and shrubs close to a building to complement the mood or associations evoked by that building. In other cases the plantings themselves would engender a mood which would then affect how the visitor responded to a building therein, such as the dark mainly evergreen wood through which the visitor had to pass before reaching the Hermitage at its very edge. Yet the same wood, viewed from a distance, say from the Gothic Temple, assumed a very different character: it was aesthetically pleasing as a hanging wood on a hill, against which some remote buildings such as the Hermitage or Temple of Bacchus could be seen, and above which the Gothic Tower reared up. Hamilton tended to plant similar species together: as Loudon observed, pines grew with firs and aquatics would be grouped by the lake.[2]

During the 1740s Hamilton started planting in earnest. John Parnell, on his visit in 1769, commented that many exotics and shrubs were planted about 1745, while the cedars near the house date from the late 1740s.[3] From then until about 1760 planting continued at a great pace, but then slackened off as Hamilton turned to buildings from the late 1750s. Although much of the timber, and even many of the shrubs, would take time to grow, an early visitor, Lady Newdigate, was able to comment in 1748 that 'here are a great abundance of uncommon and beautiful Trees and Shrubs'.[4] In 1756 Hamilton built a walled

kitchen garden that survives, consisting of three square bricked enclosures, two of which were joined together. It was hidden by trees. The garden contained a hothouse and 'pine pits', hot beds for growing pineapples. The wall was planted on the outside as well as the inside. Hamilton also had a nursery for raising trees from seed or saplings. By 1759 the nursery had been discontinued, suggesting that Hamilton was turning his main attention elsewhere.

How did Hamilton source his plants? There were quite a few trees already in the grounds when he arrived, such as old oaks (some of them pollarded) in the western gardens, and, as we have seen, the Marquis du Quesne or Bellamy had earlier probably put in place some formal plantings near the house, so it was not a totally blank canvas. But Hamilton was responsible for the exotics, and he would have had to avail himself of the services of London nurserymen. It is not known whom he might have used in the 1740s, but there were several possibilities. The most well known was the Brompton Park nursery, established in 1681, which supplied mainly native species, but those nurserymen with American connections could provide the exciting introductions. Thomas Fairchild at Hoxton had dealings with Mark Catesby, whose experience of North America was extensive; James Gordon, who established a nursery in Mile End in the 1740s, had access to plants from many parts of the world; James Lee joined Lewis Kennedy in about 1745 at the Vineyard, Hammersmith, after working as a gardener at Syon Park and Whitton in Middlesex, thus acquiring knowledge of a great range of plantings; and Christopher Gray, in King's Road, Fulham, had started with the acquisition of many American plants from the collection of Bishop Henry Compton at Fulham Palace.

The principal means of obtaining seeds or plants from North America in Hamilton's time was through the Bartram–Collinson agency. John Bartram was a farmer in Pennsylvania who became deeply involved in the study of botany and the collection of plants, at first from his local region but later from more distant states; and Peter Collinson was a haberdasher and draper in the City of London who had business dealings with the American colonies but who used his contacts to further his love of collecting seeds and plants. The two Quakers

never met, but corresponded and exchanged plants over
a period of thirty-six years or more, from the early 1730s
to Collinson's death in 1768. After the initial contact was
made, Collinson informed Bartram that there were some
of the nobility who might be interested in subscribing
to the material that Bartram could provide, and in 1735
Collinson started to supply Lord Petre, of Thorndon
Hall, Essex, a precocious and brilliant young botanist
and collector, with seeds from across the Atlantic.

The trade built up, and by the early 1740s Collinson
was an agent for quite a number of aristocratic owners
who wished to plant adventurously on their estates,
such as Lord Lincoln at Oatlands; the Duke of Argyll
at Whitton, who had the greatest private nursery of all,
with the possible exception of Thorndon Hall; Sir Francis
Dashwood at West Wycombe; Alderman Beckford at
Fonthill; Norborne Berkeley at Stoke Park, Bristol; the
Duke of Richmond at Goodwood; the Duke of Norfolk
at Worksop, Nottinghamshire (laid out by Lord Petre);
and the Duke of Bedford at Woburn Abbey. In addition,
professional nurserymen soon became interested in the
scheme, so the availability of American species grew ever
wider. As time went on, and Bartram's plant-collecting
expeditions probed deeper into the southerly states,
more species were sent over. It has been estimated that
up to 200 American introductions arrived through the
Bartram–Collinson business.

The boxes supplied to customers generally contained
100–105 items, at five guineas a box. Over the years the
contents would change as Bartram obtained different
specimens, though up to three-quarters of the items
would remain as a standard nucleus. Hamilton became
aware of the scheme in the 1740s, perhaps through
his acquaintance with the Duke of Richmond, and
approached Collinson to ask for one of the boxes. In
March 1747 Collinson communicated this request to
Bartram, and in January 1748 three boxes of 'forest seeds'
were dispatched on the ship *Beulah*, one for Hamilton
and the others for the Duke of Argyll and for Collinson

himself.[5] However, there were considerable delays in
getting the box to Hamilton, for he did not receive it until
the summer, by which time many of the contents were
spoiled. Collinson wrote to Bartram on 6 May 1749 for a
parcel of small magnolia, white and red cedar and spruce
cones for Hamilton in order to make up for the earlier
losses.[6] There was then a gap until Hamilton received a
second box in 1756.

It is clear, however, that the two boxes from Peter
Collinson could have furnished only a small part of
Hamilton's plantings. Not only was Hamilton actively
planting long before the arrival of the first box in 1748,
but the continued expansion of his acquiring trees and
shrubs lasted right through the 1750s and involved other
sources. Some of these sources included plants from
North America, in many cases probably originating
from John Bartram, so the boxes were not Hamilton's
only means of accessing Bartram material. Also, apart
from the formal box trade, there was independent
communication between Hamilton and Collinson, for
instance in a letter of 22 January 1753 Hamilton thanked
Collinson for seeds intended for him.[7] On 28 October
of the same year he thanked Collinson for two presents,
presumably plants, offering in return anything Collinson
wanted from Painshill.[8] Hamilton also conveyed a request
for a box for a neighbour, Colonel Howard.

On 25 July 1754 there is the first of a very long list of
payments to Alexander Eddie.[9] Eddie was a seedsman in

London who established a business (Eddie and Dupin) at 71 Strand by 1768, but was evidently active much earlier. He was engaged by Hamilton for over thirty years, initially presumably as a supplier of seeds but later seemingly in a more general role as steward. His will is dated 15 May 1788 and he is presumed to have died shortly thereafter, not appearing in the rate book for 1790.[10] He was seedsman to Lord Lincoln at Oatlands from 1765 to 1775, which suggests that Lincoln had heard of what service he had been to Hamilton. Two of Eddie's lists for Lincoln are preserved, from which we can see that he supplied some North American material, which was doubtless the case for Hamilton as well.

Initial payments to Eddie were for sums under £100, which suggests they were for seeds and possibly planting. However, from 1758, when there are payments totalling £145 in October and November,[11] the sums suggest that Eddie's role had expanded – perhaps he was now something like a steward or estate manager, responsible for paying labourers and for obtaining materials. From 1758, in any case, plantings were slowing down. In 1772 Eddie paid Hamilton £250, which may suggest that plants and other goods had been sold to him, in a reversal of roles.[12] When he moved to Bath, Hamilton relied more and more on him, the final payment, of £100, being made to him on 12 June 1786 shortly before Hamilton's death.[13] In Hamilton's own accounts there is a reference to Eddie supplying satin and 'old pleating' and a thermometer.[14]

Hamilton's collection received a massive boost in 1755 by an extraordinary piece of luck. He was approached by the Abbé Nolin, who was adviser to Louis XV and Louis XVI on plantings and an ardent collector himself. He was inspector of the royal nurseries. The correspondence between Nolin and Hamilton spanned the years 1755–59,

Pinus rigida.
The rigid, or *American Pitch*, Pine.

Full-grown tree at Pain's Hill, 40 ft. high.
[Scale 1 in. to 12 ft.]

Pinus sylvéstris.
The wood, *or common Scotch*, Pine.

Full-grown tree at Pain's Hill, 60 ft. high; diam. of the head, 40 ft.
[Scale 1 in. to 12 ft.]

OPPOSITE *Pinus resinosa* and *Pinus inops* at Painshill, from AB Lambert, *A Description of the Genus Pinus*, 1803, Vol.1, plates 14 and 13.
LEFT *Pinus rigida* and *Pinus sylvestris* at Painshill, from JC Loudon, *Arboretum et Fruticetum Britannicum*, 1838, Vol.1, plates LXXXIIIO and LXXXIIIA.

most of which coincided with war between England and France. This caused practical problems in exchanging seeds or plants, but did not in any way affect the warmth of the cooperation between the two. The correspondence that has survived is in French and consists of letters from Nolin, with the exception of a copy of one from Hamilton.[15]

The exchanges with Nolin offered a new raft of possibilities. North American sources could be exploited more fully, in a way that complemented Bartram's material, since the French had colonised a large area to the west of the English eastern seaboard colonies and also in Canada. Not only that, but French colonies had spread through Africa, and Nolin also had access, through trade links, to countries such as Spain, Portugal and China. In practice, however, there were some disappointments, sometimes caused by confusion over nomenclature, which led to Nolin sending Hamilton items he already had. Another

problem was transport: for example, on Christmas Day 1755 Nolin wrote that he had received two boxes of trees, shrubs and seeds from Hamilton but the boxes and the pots were shattered and the seeds jumbled.

The war meant that Hamilton and Nolin sometimes had to find indirect ways of sending specimens. Nolin used the nurseryman Gray as an agent in England, and Hamilton was invited to use a number of French addresses. Even when there were no hostilities, packages still had to go through Customs or commissioners who expected some form of remuneration. Gray, incidentally, may have supplied Hamilton as well as Nolin direct.

What was planted at Painshill can be determined by a combination of visitors' descriptions, archival information and field evidence, principally the tree survey of 1982. The range and beauty of the plantings were invariably mentioned by visitors, and appealed equally to the public and to experts. In 1781 a highly distinguished group of botanists visited Painshill, comprising Charles von Linnaeus (Linnaeus's son), Sir Joseph Banks and Dr Daniel Solander. Von Linnaeus exclaimed that 'a greater variety of the fir was to be found on this spot than in any other part of the world which he had ever seen'.[16] It was indeed conifers which had pride of place in the Painshill tree pantheon, causing AB Lambert, author of *A Description of the Genus Pinus* (1803), covering conifers generally, to declare that 'The most remarkable gardens for the cultivation of Pines in this country are at *Pain's Hill*, which are preferable perhaps to any in Europe, both for variety of species, and excellence of growth.'[17] He comments that the gardener used to make a large sum of money each year by selling the cones for seed. This is confirmed in respect of larch by James Malcolm, nurseryman, in *A Compendium of Modern Husbandry* (1805):

> nor was that celebrated man of taste, Mr. Hamilton, when he formed that beautiful place Pains-hill, and

formerly the pride of Surrey, unmindful either of the beauty or the value of Larch, since many of them are still to be seen about the grounds…The tree perfects its seed in the best manner in that neighbourhood, which I can safely assert, having been formerly accustomed to buy large quantities of it annually, that were collected from the trees at Pains-hill.[18]

The most striking of all the conifers is the majestic cedar of Lebanon (*Cedrus libani*), though Hamilton would not have seen any of them reach more than twenty-five years' growth, so they would not have passed beyond their early 'Christmas tree' form. Today, despite many losses, the cedars are the most imposing of the trees, especially the one which is designated 'The Big Cedar', about 130 feet high and 32 feet in girth, supposedly the largest in Europe.

Many other conifers were grown and admired. Hamilton had two other cedars, the white (*Chamaecyparis thyoides*) and the Virginia (*Juniperus virginiana*), many larch (*Larix decidua*), two kinds

LEFT 'The Three Giants' on Grotto Island in 1904.
RIGHT The 'Big Cedar' across the lake.

of thuja (*Thuja orientalis* and *T. occidentalis*), yew (*Taxus baccata*) and the ordinary juniper (*Juniperus communis*). He had the deciduous swamp cypress (*Taxodium distichum*), two of which survive by the lake near the Mausoleum. There was a remarkable collection of pines, including a large number of stone pines (*Pinus pinea*), pinaster (*P. pinaster*), a good many Scots pines (*P. sylvestris*), cluster pine (*P. rigida*) foxtail/pond pine (*P. serotina*), frankincense pine (*P. taeda*), Jersey pine (*P. virginiana*), two-leaved American/pitch pine (*P. resinosa*), Weymouth pine (*P. strobus*), variable-leaved bastard pine (*P. variabilis/P. echinata*) and possibly *P. palustris*. There were also several spruces and firs – the American black spruce (*Picea mariana*), American white spruce (*P. glauca*), Norway spruce (*P. abies*), red spruce (*P. rubra*) and balm of Gilead fir (*Abies balsamea*), together with the hemlock spruce (*Tsuga canadensis*), also known as the Canadian pine. If the garden as a whole could be referred to as an arboretum, the above collection would form a pinetum within it.

Hamilton's favourite deciduous tree was the robinia or false acacia (*Robinia pseudoacacia*). This was grown in clumps in some places and formed one of the most attractive of his plantings, with its slender branches, small yellow-green leaves and bunches of white flowers. More dramatic was the Indian bean tree (*Catalpa bignonioides*), with its large leaves, showy flowers and 'runner bean' pods, while the tulip tree (*Liriodendron tulipifera*) had unusual spatulate leaves, though it would not have flowered in Hamilton's time unless he had managed to obtain a grown specimen. The liquidambar (*Liquidambar styraciflua*) has deeply-lobed leaves that exude a resinous scent when crushed. There were many native species, such as alder, birch, elm, beech, spindle, hornbeam, plane, and sweet chestnut (*Castanea sativa*), together with oaks that ranged from the common English oak (*Quercus robur*) to cork (*Q. suber*), Turkey (*Q. cerris*), willow-leaved (*Q. phellos*) and the evergreen holm oak (*Q. ilex*). Hamilton had both sorts of lime (*Tilia cordata* and *T. platyphyllos*). Some of the native plantings undoubtedly predated him.

Hamilton was equally interested in the more intimate effects of the shrubbery, of which he had several. J C Loudon

claimed he was one of the first to plant rhododendrons and azaleas in England,[19] though the former was probably *Rhododendron maximum* rather than the ubiquitous *R. ponticum*, which was not introduced until 1763. The deciduous azalea, *R. viscosum*, was included in Bartram's boxes, so Hamilton may have had that: the boxes also contained *R. nudiflorum* (now *R. periclymenoides*) and *R. arborescens*, though the latter may well not have taken in English soil. He also grew laurel and laurustinus, magnolia, variegated holly, candleberry myrtle (*Myrica cerifera*) and box. Matthew Boulton pointed out the striking effect of laurel as background to the grotto.[20]

From the above lists it will be seen how much Hamilton owed to North America. While far from dependent on transatlantic imports, he nonetheless deployed them to striking effect, creating the impression that the world of planting at Painshill was new and very different from what it would have been even a few years earlier. It may also be the case that sometimes he wished to create an Italian feeling by using, for example, holm oak in the amphitheatre and near the Temple of Bacchus, and the stone pine, though he seems not to have grown cypress.

Even in the sphere of flowers, Hamilton took more interest than many landowners. Flowers blossomed in the orangery garden near the house, in the lakeside walk leading to the cascade, near the Temple of Bacchus, and even beside the grotto. This, combined with the floriferous shrubs and trees that he cultivated, made for a colourful landscape, not one consisting merely of shades of green and brown as might have been expected. Hamilton's friendship with Richard Bateman of Grove House, Old Windsor, where the garden was filled with flowers and which dated from the 1730s, might have suggested the possibilities of floral colour.

To keep his grounds in good order Hamilton employed a head gardener and up to seven under gardeners. The head gardener was expected to supplement his somewhat meagre wage by tips from the visitors he took round. The most distinguished name was Peter Thoburn, who sold cones and seed from the conifers and who later set up his own nursery in Kensington. Thoburn had a reputation for skill in cultivating pines. Payments to him are recorded

ABOVE Tiered planting in the amphitheatre in winter.

for the years 1772–73, showing that Hamilton engaged him only towards the end of his time at Painshill.[21]

There was a definite rhythm to the plantings which changed and provided contrast as the circuit progressed. At the start of the tour, by the house, there was the orangery garden and parterre. Inside the orangery there were several plants including yuccas and 'a constant succession of flowers'.[22] In the parterre could be seen a multitude of shrubs and many rare American plants, which indicates that botanical interest was at its height in this area, and also that the source of the plants was apparent. Small plantations surrounded the parterre, including orange and lemon trees too large to stay in tubs. A whitethorn hedge protected the garden itself.

The first part of the circuit would take the visitor around and up the amphitheatre hill, through a beech grove, to arrive at the bastion and the ridge overlooking the vineyard. Along the ridge was what was described in 1754 as a botanical walk of varied evergreens, showing that Hamilton was still intent, at this early stage of the tour, on emphasising botanical interest.[23] The path is now lined with different species accordingly. An entrance off the path led into the flat amphitheatre, a formal lawn as Rocque's plan indicates. The present planting is an idea of eighteenth-century design, with the tiered effect of low planting at the front and taller specimens at the back, and the species are those which would have been available to Hamilton. A superb cork oak stands in the amphitheatre, possibly postdating Hamilton. At the time the plantings were recorded as including 'curious hollies', arbutus and laurustinus, with a backing of firs.[24]

A straight walk led from the amphitheatre to the Gothic Temple, whence the panorama would include distant views of blocks of planting, especially the heavily wooded area to the west. Proceeding down the slope from the Temple the visitor would steer a zigzag course through a rich shrubbery which would form a complete contrast to the fir walk and the amphitheatre. John Parnell described the shrubbery as being composed 'of the most rare and beautiful shrubs both English and exotic' and singled out the robinias.[25] Across the 'Chinese' bridge the visitor then moved on to Grotto Island, where the atmosphere was established by the grotto and the 'tufa' eruptions all around but where the plantings played a significant if secondary role. From Woollett's print (see page 120) and Gilpin's sketches (see left and page 98) we can note cedars, firs, pines, robinias and shrubs. Gilpin shows how important the backing of firs was to set off the grotto.

Back on the mainland, the visitor passed along a path between the lake and the river, which was screened off by 'the most elegant trees, full of the lightest greens, and bordered with shrubs and flowers'.[26] A little of that screen can be glimpsed in Woollett. The Mausoleum stood away from the path, and was a fine example of a building and its surrounding plantings working together for a particular effect. The grass was left uncut and yews were planted near the arch to promote feelings of sadness, neglect and some solemnity.

The cascade had its own dendrological accessories, with tree roots and old branches interwoven with the rocks. Beyond, the scenery assumed a wilder, more mountainous character, leading up to the 'Alpine Valley' and entering Walpole's forest or savage garden. Old trees, particularly oak, beech and birch, formed the basis of what Hamilton varied and greatly elaborated by planting pines and other evergreens. Walpole ascribed an alpine character to the wood, in light of his familiarity with the

LEFT ABOVE Exterior of the grotto showing the surrounding plantings, sketch by William Gilpin, 1772.
LEFT BELOW Ornamental beds in the 'Elysian Plains'.
RIGHT View across the park in 1937.

pines on the mountains of the Massif de la Chartreuse, and of his experience of the Alps themselves, though Hamilton would have used mostly American species and Scots pines.[27] It is this wood that gave the Hermitage the dank, dark and gloomy feeling that hung about it.

In total contrast, the nearby open plateau known as the 'Elysian Plains' provided an area of brightness and delight. Once again it was the combination of a building with surrounding plantings that created the effect. The beauty of the light, white Temple of Bacchus was complemented by the colourful beds and shrubberies, containing flowers as well as shrubs, that lay in the lawns in front.

After leaving the pleasure grounds, with a farewell view from the Turkish Tent, the visitor was brought gently and pleasantly back to earth by crossing the parkland back to the house, using if necessary the mown cabriole drive. Even here, however, there were clumps of forest trees and robinias.[28] Walks across the park were marked by close mowing, as they were in the pleasure grounds. Visitors would not normally cross the bridge to the northern part of Hamilton's property, his farm, but, if they did, not only would they have found the second vineyard but a fifteen-acre site which had plantings of conifers and a cultivated area enclosed by a hedge within which was yet another shrubbery. On one side of the hedge was a gravel path, and on the other the vineyard. An orchard occupied much of the land.[29]

Taken all in all, the park and gardens at Painshill demonstrated variety of species; a spectrum of colour, size and shape; different densities of plantings; a balance of tree plantations and shrubberies; use of flowers in addition to floriferous trees and shrubs; contrasts of open lawn and woodland; and above all an enormous love of planting.

A View from the West Side of the Island in the Garden of the Hon.ble Charles Hamilton Esq.r at Painshill near Cobham in Surry.

Veüe dans le Jardin de l'hon.ble Mons.r Charles Hamilton, a Painshill près de Cobham dans la Comté de Surry.

Printed for Roberts Sayer in Fleet Street, John Bowles in Cornhil, Carington Bowles in St Pauls Church Yard, John Bogdell in Cheapside, and Henry Parker in Cornhil.

W. Woollett de.

ABOVE William Woollett's iconic print of the gardens from the west side of Grotto Island, 1760.

Images of Painshill

As PAINSHILL was such a pictorial garden, it is understandable that many artists, both amateur and professional, were impelled to portray it. Furthermore, in an age which did not know photography or digital technology, drawing or painting was the only way to record a garden, along with written description. Such depictions as have survived are immensely important as evidence of how the gardens looked at the time, but equally there are pressures and considerations that sometimes render the images inaccurate in particular details. There are also some surprises: why, for example, were there no engravings of the grotto or the Temple of Bacchus, to name two of the outstanding buildings?

Depictions, of course, often do more than show what was there. The artist's (or patron's) own agenda might determine the choice of scene and how it was to be portrayed. Views might also be intended to aid our interpretation of the owner/designer's purposes. It is consequently dangerous to take all depictions at face value, and if a view is to be used as evidence it should always (if possible) be measured against other evidence such as that from archives or archaeology. One should not, however, lose sight of the possible aesthetic value and appeal that depictions may have as art.

The strong visual culture of the eighteenth century helped to promote the cause of topographical art. At the start of the century literature had the upper hand, with the 'Augustan age' defined by the work of authors such as Pope, but, partly through the effects of the Grand Tour, appreciation of art grew and the status of landscape painting (previously regarded as inferior to religious, portrait or history painting) rose, with the seventeenth-century works of Claude, Poussin, Gaspard Dughet and Salvator Rosa being bought in large numbers and also engraved for wide circulation. The visual arts expanded as the century moved on, and, despite the presence of such literary giants as Dr Johnson and the novelist Henry Fielding, art probably held the greater sway by the middle or later years. Hogarth paved the way for Reynolds and Gainsborough, and the Royal Academy was founded in 1768.

There was a lively art market – buying and selling works of art became big business. We have already seen how entrepreneurs such as Knapton and Pond progressed from being artists to the considerably more lucrative trade of dealers and agents. Once again, it was the Grand Tourists (such as Hamilton) who provided much of the early stimulus. The large sums of money expended on imported art later began to be matched at home after the rise of a native school of art and the establishment of watercolour by Paul Sandby. Reliance on foreign artists – and (usually) French engravers – began to dissolve as English artists and engravers grew increasingly skilled and confident. Paintings, which were unique and would be purchased by one owner although seen by others, could be copied as prints to ensure a wide viewership.

Topographical painting became a genre in its own right. Often a conversation piece or family portrait would be set against a background of the family's gardens, as seen in the work of such painters as Arthur Devis, Edward Haytley and Johan Zoffany. On occasions those backgrounds would be of an imaginary or fantasy landscape, but even so the garden or landscape would form a significant part of the painting, reflecting the taste and status of the owner and the importance of having an estate. More common were the views of a property where the place itself was the centre of interest. The engravings of Kip and Knyff in *Britannia Illustrata* (1707) had shown the possibilities and attractions of bird's-eye views that could encompass an entire estate and much beyond, but this approach was supplanted by views of particular scenes, buildings or vistas within a garden. Artists such as Jacques Rigaud, Pieter Rysbrack, Balthasar Nebot and Peter Tillemans would depict a series of views of well-known gardens like Stowe, Chiswick, Hartwell House and Wrest Park that contained many features of specific interest. In course of time these continental artists, who flourished in the 1730s, were replaced by mostly British painters – Richard Wilson, who, flushed from his sojourn in Italy, painted English gardens such as Wilton and Croome Court in a Mediterranean light, William Tomkins and William Hannan, who painted a series of the gardens at West Wycombe in 1752 and may have been responsible for one or two of the Painshill views.

In the field of prints, native engravers soon sprang up to replace those from Europe. Some initially learned their craft from French engravers, but by the mid-century both artist and engraver were usually British. William Woollett, Luke Sullivan and Anthony Walker engraved their own drawings, leaving us a legacy of sharply detailed (if not a hundred per cent accurate) views. Each also engraved work by others, and Woollett was responsible for more

than one Claude, while Sullivan worked for, and after, Hogarth. Later on, following the success of sets of large garden prints by the three engravers, there were series of small plates of topographical views (usually house and garden), such as William Watts's *The Seats of the Nobility and Gentry* (84 plates from 1779) and William Angus's similar series, *The Seats of the Nobility and Gentry in Great Britain and Wales*, from 1787. Paul Sandby has been mentioned in connection with watercolours, but it should be noted that he also drew for engravings to be made by others, including a magnificent series of views in 1778–81, called *The Virtuosi's Museum*.

The fact that so many visitors drew sketches of Painshill shows it had painterly qualities. While parallels between painting and landscaping cannot be pressed too far, nonetheless the two arts have much in common, as the next chapter demonstrates. But in the case of the eighteenth century there was another element at work that encouraged sketching and painting, namely developments in technique. William Gilpin, in seeking to refine a 'picturesque' way of recording what he saw as picturesque objects, took some time to develop his own method of combining ink and wash over a pencil foundation drawn on the spot.[1] The pencil drawing would give an immediate impression, while the ink and wash treatment would be applied at a later date to allow for recollection, thought and possible adjustment for Gilpin's 'picturesque' purposes.

In the field of painting, the important development was watercolour. Not only was it easier to handle, especially for amateurs, but the softer colours (in comparison with oil) were particularly suitable for conveying the hues of an English garden or park and the light in which it was bathed. Oils could sometimes produce a too lurid effect, which some artists of course would seek, in order to heighten reality. Paul Sandby, originally a military cartographer and surveyor, stands at the head of the English watercolour school, to be followed later in the century by such limners of garden scenes as Thomas Hearne and Humphry Repton.

With regard to prints, the great engravers like Woollett could achieve subtle and delicate effects in what was a laborious and difficult medium by combining the techniques of etching and engraving. So many prints of gardens in the early eighteenth century depict non-specific trees and a certain blandness of surface, but Woollett, Sullivan and François Vivares could bring foregrounds out in an almost three-dimensional way and delineate particular identifiable trees. This greater realism not only had commercial benefit but would spread the essence of the English landscape garden widely at home and abroad.

Perhaps the most well known of the views of Painshill is Woollett's engraving and etching (see page 120), dated 1760 but likely to reflect a site visit of up to a year earlier. This was one of a set of six views of gardens by Woollett: Carlton House (former town house of Frederick, Prince of Wales, see page 35), Foots Cray in Kent, Coombe Bank, also in Kent, two views of Hall Barn, Buckinghamshire, and Painshill. The set was offered by the printsellers of the time as 'Six *delightful Views* of elegant *Gardens*, drawn and engraved from nature by W. Woollet [sic]' for one guinea the set or two guineas hand-coloured.[2] The gardens in question were not all landscape gardens, and both Carlton House and Hall Barn exhibited quite a degree of regularity: but the set, along with other garden views, was placed at the front of the section in the catalogue of sets of prints on all subjects, thus giving priority to gardens. Woollett was an experienced hand at illustrating gardens, starting with apprentice work engraving Donowell's set of views of Chiswick in 1753 when he was seventeen or eighteen. Among his other garden views were several of Kew (drawn by him but engraved by others), two of the Duke of Argyll's gardens at Whitton, and a set of four views of West Wycombe in 1757 after paintings by William Hannan five years earlier.

The print of Painshill raises a number of problems, some of which have been touched on earlier. Broadly speaking, it can be accepted as accurate as regards the plantings, since some of the trees, such as a cedar on Grotto Island, to the right of the picture, survive. The paddle-boat is likewise authentic. The island in the middle distance, however, seems to have been moved to the left or sliced off, in order to reveal a view of the distant bridge which could not have been seen from where the artist was standing. That is likely to be artistic licence,

arranging scenery to display what would otherwise be concealed from view. The bridge in the foreground has some question marks attached – it is neither described nor depicted anywhere else, nor have footings for it been found in that position. However, there certainly was *a* bridge, and Woollett displays it so prominently that it is hard to believe it was fabricated.

It is the buildings which cause the main difficulties. The 'Turkish Tent' looks like an ordinary tent and nothing like what Hamilton erected in 1759, but it might have been in course of construction when Woollett visited, and he portrayed it in the likeness of a tent he was familiar with – the tent on the island at West Wycombe which he had engraved three years earlier. The Temple of Bacchus, which might not have gone up till a year or so later, looks unrealistic and is in any case positioned too low. The Mausoleum might just pass muster, though it is not a true representation and is not set far enough back from the lake. Even the tower, projecting above the trees, looks rather square and chunky.

Woollett's print proved so attractive and popular that it was regularly pirated and reproduced in much poorer quality. It appeared in Le Rouge's French *cahier* of views of English and French gardens (referred to provocatively as 'Les Jardins Anglo-Chinois') with the foreground bridge highlighted and the image in reverse. This is because engraving has to be a mirror image of the original, and a straight copy without the use of a mirror will result in a reverse impression. It was also re-engraved rather crudely in Bond Hopkins's time (see page 124), simplifying the view. This appeared in the topographical publication *The Modern Universal British Traveller* (1779) which included a number of such prints taken from earlier originals. A further copy appeared in the illustrated edition of Whately's *Observations on Modern Gardening* (1801), where it was attributed to Woollett but had obviously been redrawn and engraved by others. The original print was also used as the basis for ceramic reproductions, such as the 'Green Frog' dinner service commissioned by Catherine the Great and, for example, on the lid of a snuff box in the Victoria and Albert Museum.

The print 'A Scene in the Gardens of Painshill' (see page 125) dates from 1761. It accompanied a description

in Vol. V of *London and its Environs Described*, published by R and J Dodsley. There has been confusion over what is supposed to be depicted, but most likely it is a distorted representation of the view from near Cobham Bridge southwards towards Cobham. The water is the River Mole not the lake, and the island was created by Hamilton in about 1742. The building in the background is St Andrew's Church. The artist was Samuel Wale, who was responsible for other views in the same publication, including one of Oatlands which is a risible distortion of reality, with the invention of a mountain in the flat Thames valley. So one should not necessarily look to Wale for accuracy: in the Painshill print, as with Oatlands, there is an invented hill at the back.

Contemporary engravings do not otherwise exist, though one of the sets of small topographical prints, Harrison's *Picturesque Views of the Principal Seats of the Nobility and Gentry* (1787–8) illustrates Bond Hopkins's house from the north-east together with a general grazing area. Hamilton's own house had evidently not yet been demolished. More common are paintings: it is clear from the inventory of Hamilton's collection that far more paintings were produced than have survived, but we are left with a number of views that are both attractive and revealing. Prominent among these is the view from the Turkish Tent, owned by Hamilton (see page 64). The artist may have been any one of three. One is William Hannan, who had been responsible for the views of West Wycombe that Woollett had engraved. Hannan has also been put forward as the artist of two other views of Painshill, below, but he was employed mostly by Sir Francis Dashwood at West Wycombe, where he resided and died around 1775. The second is Elias Martin (1739–1818), who drew three sketches of Painshill but who also exhibited two oils at the Royal Academy in 1777, one of which was titled, 'A View of Pain's Hill, near Cobham, taken from the tent'. Martin was a Swedish artist who visited England in the 1770s and drew and painted several country estates. The third candidate is William Tomkins, who exhibited a pair of views of Painshill in 1772, though details are lacking.[3] These paintings presumably relate to payments to him

OPPOSITE ABOVE Reverse image from Woollett's print by GL Le Rouge, *c.*1780.

OPPOSITE BELOW Pirated version of Woollett's print from *The Modern Universal British Traveller*, 1779.

LEFT The house, bridge and River Mole by Harrison and Co., 1787.

BELOW *A Scene in the Gardens of Pains Hill*, print by Samuel Wale, 1761.

by Hamilton, £50 on 12 January 1774 and again on 12 March.[4] Tomkins was an artist who depicted at least fifty-three views of gardens, notably Audley End, Encombe, Saltram and Mount Edgcumbe.

The painting is dominated in the right foreground by a robinia, appropriately as Hamilton's best-loved tree. It portrays a panorama, incorporating several of the features – the Gothic Temple, the grotto and the 'Chinese' bridge. It is a retrospective view in the sense that it is reached at the end of the circuit, looking back over features that have been seen more closely earlier. The naturalness and openness of the scene are apparent, with the Surrey downs beyond. It is valuable, too, for the only known depiction of the bridge, which, as previously discussed,

may have replaced the Woollett foreground bridge. This was supposedly Hamilton's favourite viewpoint and the spot where he had once hoped to build a new house.

A well-known view is the painting of the Ruined Abbey and vineyard by George Barret the Elder and Sawrey Gilpin, *c.*1780 (see page 146). The scene represents Hamilton's final flourish at Painshill, completed shortly before he left for Bath, though the walk along the left side of the water may be by Bond Hopkins. By the date of the painting the vineyard was actually in decline, though its depiction has proved to be of great help in its restoration. George Barret the Elder (1728/32–84) was a popular artist who presented views of several great landscape gardens, such as Powerscourt in his native Ireland, Chatsworth, Burton Constable, Yorkshire, and a number in Scotland. A romantic in his early days, he turned to more accurate topographical detail later. Sawrey Gilpin was the brother

of William and doubtless learned of Painshill through him. One of his specialties was to add animals and figures to paintings by others, so we may presume that the foreground staffage was executed by him while Barret was responsible for the overall scene.

Also focusing on the vineyard is the painting known as 'La Vendange' (The Grape Harvest), thought to date from about 1780 (see page 147). The vineyard continued to the end of the slope on the right in the previous views and even round the corner, though it then faced east. So this view, which shows the house, must be taken from a position further back and round the hill, though the angle does not correspond with actuality. The artist is unknown, but the work has been attributed to Paul Sandby (1731–1809). This is, however, extremely doubtful, since Sandby as we know worked mainly in watercolour, though oil was a medium he occasionally used in his younger days. He had not done

so, however, for nearly twenty years at the time of this work. The painting may have been commissioned by Bond Hopkins, since the house is that built by Richard Jupp for him, and the painting must therefore postdate 1778.

A painting similar to that by Barret and Gilpin, taken from a slightly different angle, is in a private collection (above left). It confirms the layout of the vineyard and the view along and beyond the lake. It is possibly by Tomkins, though it does not seem stylistically close to his work. If he was indeed the artist of the vineyard painting, the abbey would have been in process of being built or only just completed. Hannan is a second possibility, but Elias Martin must be a strong contender, since his other painting exhibited in 1777 was 'A View of Pain's Hill, taken from the Vineyard'. Also attributed to Tomkins is the oil of the estate and Cobham taken from the north side of the Portsmouth road (above), which may be

OPPOSITE The Ruined Abbey and Vineyard, *c.*1780, artist uncertain.
ABOVE View from the north side of the Portsmouth Road, *c.*1750, artist uncertain.

compared with Wale's print. Neither the kitchen gardens (1756) nor the wooden bridge over the road (pre-1768) feature, however, so if it was by Tomkins it was executed long before his other pair. The painting exists in two versions, one without some of the staffage.

On the following page is a view of the Mausoleum, attributed to Hannan or the 'Irish School', dating from the 1770s. The painting, heavy with craquelure, presents the Mausoleum in a romantic light, rather like Piranesi's atmospheric scenes of ruined buildings in Rome. Unlike the (real) ruined Fountains Abbey, which Gilpin complained

MR HAMILTON'S ELYSIUM

had been spruced up too much, Hamilton's mock ruin, untidy, with signs of neglect, had a powerful emotional and associational appeal, which the painting brings out.[5]

Also possibly by Hannan is the view of the Temple of Bacchus (see opposite), dated 1773. The sense of openness and spirit of cheerfulness are evident, with the temple itself balanced by the flat lawn on which it sits and the varied plantings on each side. The sense of care and order is conveyed by the gardens; the evidence of enjoyment is shown by the visitors pausing or strolling by.

Two paintings of the house from different aspects also show something of the gardens. These works by Theodore de Bruyn (1730–1804) date from 1789 and were exhibited

OPPOSITE ABOVE LEFT The Mausoleum, *c.*1770, artist uncertain.

OPPOSITE ABOVE RIGHT The Temple of Bacchus, 1773, attributed to William Hannan.

OPPOSITE BELOW The house from the park by Theodore de Bruyn, 1789.

BELOW The house from Cobham Bridge by Theodore de Bruyn, 1789.

together at the Royal Academy the following year. De Bruyn was a *grisaille* painter who subsequently studied at the Royal Academy and developed a realistic style of forms and shadows with a strong feeling for atmosphere. He exhibited four paintings of Painshill in all, but the other two have not been traced.

The view of the Jupp house from the bridge over the Mole (see page 128) may be compared with Harrison's print (see page 125). Both show the grazing lawn in front of the house as fairly plain, but the clumped trees are of interest, and the thick massing in the background

on the left invites the spectator to explore the gardens in that direction. The second view, of the house from the park (see page 129), is unusual, depicting something of Hamilton's park which concluded the circuit and which took the visitor to the exit. As we have seen, the park is spacious and used primarily for pasture but there was a mown drive at one side, and specimen trees were dotted about to enliven the scene, as can be seen in the painting.

Drawings are more likely to be spontaneous and done on the spot, though that does not mean that they are always accurate. In one case, a drawing with colour wash attributed to Henry Keene (left), there is a problem inasmuch as it is not known whether it is a drawing of the Turkish Tent as completed or a design for it. The possible connection with Keene has led some to think that he may have had a hand in the design of the Gothic Temple since he worked in rococo-Gothic elsewhere.

Some drawings are intended just to convey the impression of a feature or a view as experienced by the artist, although they may well serve as a record too. The drawings of Elias Martin are good examples. He produced five views of Painshill in all, the three drawings reproduced here plus the two oils mentioned above. The pair of drawings of the interior of the grotto (see below and page 100) are in pen and wash. Although impressionistic, they

ABOVE Turkish Tent by Henry Keene, *c*.1760.
LEFT The interior of the grotto by Elias Martin, *c*.1777.
OPPOSITE The interior of the grotto by FM Pyper, 1779.

have proved accurate and useful in the painstaking process of restoration. They indicate the alcoves, openings, central column, stalactites and rock effects, but they also capture the atmosphere and feeling of a cave of enchantment. The third drawing, with grey wash, is taken from the rear portico of the Temple of Bacchus (see page 24). It shows an oblique distant glimpse of the Gothic Temple (now obscured), thereby illustrating one of Hamilton's many planned linear vistas. The drawing also gives a unique view of the rear of the temple.

A fellow Swede, Fredrik Magnus Pyper (or Piper) (1746–1824), came to England as a young man in 1772 to study architecture with William Chambers, who had Swedish roots and connections. Apart from a visit to Italy in 1776–8 Pyper stayed until 1780, the year in which he sketched the grotto, the water wheel, the Turkish Tent and the cascade at Painshill. Among other gardens he visited and sketched were Stourhead, Stowe and Kew. He travelled round with Whately's *Observations on Modern Gardening*, which he annotated. He then returned to Sweden and

was influential in spreading ideas about the pictorial and naturalistic English Landscape Garden and in encouraging a taste for orientalism, as witness the Turkish Tent at Drottningholm, to say nothing of numerous Chinese buildings at Haga and elsewhere. His drawings of gardens are generally in ink with a monochrome wash.

Pyper's drawing of the cascade (see page 74) supplements and complements a number of written descriptions – it is the only contemporary image. A conglomeration of rocks gave a natural appearance, which was heightened by weeds and even trees growing out of the stones. Pyper also indicates the plantings round about, which give further credence to the idea of a wild and mountainous spot.

His drawing of the Turkish Tent (see page 106) differs in detail from Henry Keene's, which could argue either for Keene's version being a design that was not implemented exactly or for one or other artist not representing accurately what he saw. Pyper's rendition 'shows an impossible state of affairs, structurally speaking', despite his avowed purpose of creating a proper record.[6]

Pyper sketched a number of views of the grotto, of which the most valuable is the plan (see page 100), particularly with regard to the small pump chamber at the top. It is assumed that whatever pump or device was used for lifting water from the lake to sufficient height to feed the water effects inside the cavern it was operated by hand. He was also clearly much taken with the water wheel, devoting fourteen pages of sketches and notes to it. One is reproduced on page 72. He evidently spent much time taking measurements and recording as carefully as he could, down to details of screws and pins, perhaps with a thought of some possible future application of the device in his own land. In August 1779 Henry Hoare wrote to Hamilton (by then in Bath, of course) asking him to permit Pyper to visit his garden at Lansdown House since he had seen Painshill.[7]

William Gilpin will be discussed in relation to Hamilton and the Picturesque, but it may be noted that his sketch-book of Painshill (1772) is probably on the whole accurate though the choice of views was determined largely by his search for the Picturesque.

Friedrich Ludwig von Sckell (1750–1823) was a German landscape designer who was sent to England to study parks and gardens and who returned home, like Pyper, to create gardens which owed something to the English style. His itinerary in England is not fully known, but it is assumed that it must have included Painshill because the sketch of the Hermitage (see page 94) is said to be after an original drawing by him. The copying artist is unknown, though it might have been Samuel Hieronymus Grimm, who drew other gardens like Thomas Goldney's at Bristol.

Designers came from France as well. François-Joseph Bélanger (1744–1818) was an architect who had a special interest in landscape gardens and recorded several in England in the course of repeated visits between 1770 and 1778. Back in France his great achievements were the layouts of Bagatelle and Méréville in an irregular, pictorial style which he must have derived from his tours. He sketched the water wheel (see page 72), with seven spokes rather than the four shown by Pyper, which has been discussed earlier. He also drew the Temple of Bacchus (see page 79), an elevation of the Gothic Temple (see page 84),

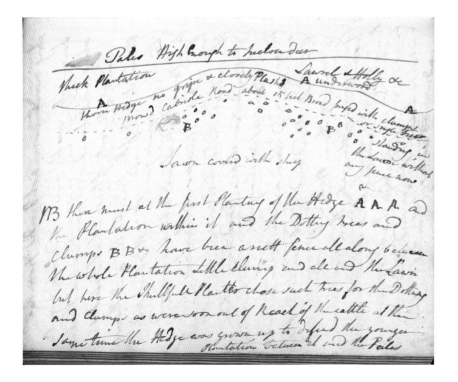

LEFT Sketch and notes on planting round the 'cabriole road' in the park by John Parnell, 1769.
OPPOSITE The Mausoleum depicted on a plate in the Green Frog dinner service of Catherine the Great, 1774.

MR HAMILTON'S ELYSIUM

two views of the bridge crossing the road and one of the Jupp house. All these were reproduced in an article on Bélanger's sketchbook by Kenneth Woodbridge, which reveals that Bélanger, as we would expect of an architect, concentrated on built features in the gardens he saw.[8]

The artist is not always known. An unattributed drawing of the Hermitage, *c*.1752 (see page 94), shows the rear of the building, as Gilpin does, with the thatched roof and a lantern with a bell, though the (shuttered) windows are larger, and set lower, than in Gilpin (see page 143). A third sketch, by Parnell, places the windows at a half-way point between Gilpin and the anonymous sketch, thus crystallising the problems inherent in trying to follow visual evidence.

Quite a number of travellers who wrote descriptions of their visits incorporated rough sketches into the text, suggesting that text and drawings were done together, either on the spot or immediately afterwards when the memory was fresh. The Chinese Seat by Lady Newdigate is a case in point (see page 103), and William Robertson's drawing of Bond Hopkins's water wheels was another. The immediacy of such impressions can be valuable, though it does rely on the draughtsmanship of the author (and most visitors would not aspire to be called artists). Robertson also sketched a lodge gate and a plan of the curve of the wings of Bond Hopkins's house.

John Parnell (1744–1801) incorporated several sketches in his descriptions of gardens. In the case of Hagley, for example, the illustrations of some features are the only ones we have, though with Painshill that is not the case and they are more corroborative. On his first visit in 1763, when he was only nineteen, he sketched the Gothic Temple and the Turkish Tent in a simplified way that is not all that helpful, and he might have been conscious of the fact since he re-drew them on his second visit. Also from 1763 are sketches of the Hermitage, showing the 'tree house' front and the rear entrance, and the tower, which Parnell calls a belvedere. On the 1769 visit he illustrated the Gothic Temple to show two open arches and one with its half-screen and the Turkish Tent, in general confirming Pyper's sketch. He produced a very rough plan of the grounds, which he called 'Something of the Garden of Painshill with

Regard to its Disposition', but as with Gilpin the result of drawing a plan as one goes round is to distort and lose the relation of one feature to another and to the whole. More valuable is a separate plan, an indication of the layout of the mown cabriole road in the park, five metres broad, with a thorn hedge closely planted on one side and a thick plantation behind it and a lawn used as sheep pasture on the other, dotted with clumps. A note says that the trees stand in the lawn without any fence now, implying that they needed protection from livestock as they were growing (see opposite).

One final image should be mentioned, and that is the Green Frog plate with the Mausoleum painted on it (see above). This is separate from the four views taken from the Woollett print and used on other pieces of the dinner service, and presents something of a mystery. The artist is not known: the painting reproduced on page 128 might have served as a model, but there are several differences, such as the angle from which the view is taken, the height of the arch and niches, and the ruined turret rearing up on one side. Given that Wedgwood's artists generally kept fairly closely to the images they copied, the discrepancies suggest a different artist for the original from which the plate painting was taken. Who and when remain unknown.

Hamilton and the Picturesque

WE HAVE SEEN that Painshill is essentially a picture garden, presenting a series of ever-changing views and vistas along a carefully planned circuit. However, there are signs that, particularly as time went on, it also incorporated features that indicate a change or development of sensibility. Those features accord with the 'picturesque' thinking and taste that grew in momentum during the second half of the eighteenth century.

By 'picturesque' is meant the movement, if such it can be called, pioneered by William Gilpin and championed and codified by the two Herefordshire squires Sir Uvedale Price and Richard Payne Knight at the end of the century. In essence it was two things: first, a way of looking at natural scenery and judging it as if it were a painting or series of paintings, and second, the scenery that was to be admired would be varied, broken, irregular and tending to wild. Mountainous and dramatic scenery was, accordingly, particularly prized. The Picturesque related initially, and fundamentally, to natural scenery rather than gardens, but it was embodied in gardens from the middle of the century first by optimising the external views of dramatic scenes where they existed and then by cultivating or creating wildness within the confines of the garden. The natural topography and location of the garden were of course key determinants.

The Picturesque was by no means a constant or fixed system, and tastes changed. Since variety was a keystone of the movement, it became feasible to contrast a degree of formality near the house with a more naturalistic park beyond, as Humphry Repton often did. Where the terrain itself was undramatic, variety of this sort was sometimes the only answer.

In the case of Painshill, the outside scenery – the Surrey downs – was not especially exciting, but it was extensive, and afforded panoramic views from the top of the vineyard and from the Temple of Bacchus plain. Within the estate, however, there were substantial changes in level, some stiff climbing and a steep descent from the Hermitage down to the river. So Hamilton exploited the landform where he could, but his principal means of picturesque expression was through plantings and buildings. A 'wild' feeling was engendered by the plantings in the hilly western part of the grounds – the pine forest and the ancient oaks. This was captured by Horace Walpole in 1770 in his essay *The History of the Modern Taste in Gardening*, in which he creates a category of the forest or savage garden, of which Painshill is the model:

ABOVE The meadow looking towards the Alpine Valley.

I mean that kind of alpine scene, composed almost wholly of pines and firs, a few birch, and such trees as assimilate with a savage and mountainous country. Mr. Charles Hamilton, at Pain's-hill, in my opinion has given a perfect example of this mode in the utmost boundary of his garden. All is great and foreign and rude; the walks seem not designed, but cut through the wood of pines; and the style of the whole is so grand, and conducted with so serious an air of wild and uncultivated extent, that when you look down on this seeming forest, you are amazed to find it contain a very few acres.[1]

This description encapsulates the effect of a picturesque scene, achieved in this case by a combination of the plantings with the illusionistic skill which Hamilton habitually employs.

The wooded area towards the west formed a striking contrast to the elegance and polish of the pleasure grounds, as Thomas Whately (1770) describes:

> it is a wood, which overspreads a large tract of very uneven ground; the glades through it are just cleared of the bushes and plants, which are natural to the soil; sometimes they are closed on both sides with thickets; at other times they are only cut through the fern in the openings; and even the larches and firs, which are mixed with beech on the side of the principal glade, are left in such a state of apparent neglect, that they seem to be the product of the wild, not decorations of the walk.[2]

This shows that some elements of the original heath, such as the fern, remained while planting was added. The Alpine Valley reminded John Parnell of his native Irish

mountain scenery: 'it charmed me it is like a thousand of our little vallies in our woodlands in the county of Wicklow'.[3] The natural appearance was achieved by a mixture of making the most of the existing terrain and judicious planting to enhance it.

The buildings contribute to the Painshill Picturesque too. The Hermitage, both by its primitive construction and by its positioning, perched on a drop down to the river, shows this sort of thinking. It also complements the wild effect of the woodland behind it. Beyond the wood, at the highest point in the grounds, stands the Gothic Tower, which creates a romantic, medieval feeling. Romanticism is certainly part of the Picturesque, and the Romantic Movement can justifiably be claimed to have come out of it, with its birth in the mountains of the Lake District.

The other buildings which can be said to have a picturesque flavour are the ruins (Mausoleum and Ruined Abbey) and the 'exotics' – grotto, 'Chinese' bridge, Turkish Tent. Most of the structures, in fact.

Ruins are indeed a notable feature of picturesque and romantic sensibility. The taste for ruins in a garden actually dates from quite early in the eighteenth century, and by the 1760s it could fairly be said to be a cult. This taste had two well-springs, continental and indigenous. In Europe, the target for those on the Grand Tour was Rome, which of course exhibited a spectacular array of classical ruins. These made a deep impression on the minds and feelings of the young milords who would often later set out to capture something of classical Rome in their gardens. Italian artists and sculptors saw what impact antiquity had on the tourists and quickly

OPPOSITE The Gothic Tower in the woods.

BELOW The woods seen from the Gothic Tower.

of those who came to see them. In some cases a ruined abbey might form a focal point from a landscape garden, the most prominent examples being Fountains Abbey as seen from Studley Royal gardens and Rievaulx Abbey as seen from the great Rievaulx Terrace, both in Yorkshire. Ruined castles might serve a similar purpose and be a chosen part of the view, such as Chepstow Castle seen from Piercefield, Monmouthshire. The taste for ruins should also be seen in the context of a rise in interest in antiquarianism, the investigation of Britain's past.

But, in terms of gardens, sham ruins came to have an even greater presence than real ones. The motivation was partly visual, but also dynastic, in that they would give the impression that the family had lived in the same property for centuries (which might well not have been so) and that the ruin represented a part of their history. This was surely the case with Sanderson Miller's mock castles at Hagley and Wimpole, Cambridgeshire. The earliest ruin seems to have been Alfred's Hall at Cirencester Park, Gloucestershire (1720s–30s), but Stainborough Castle (1731) at Wentworth Castle, Yorkshire, had a complete bailey and towers rather than being ruinous. By the 1740s the Catholic Philip Southcote had erected a ruined chapel at Woburn Farm, which might have had some religious associations – the significance of this is that it was close to Painshill, and some hint of it might have found embodiment in Hamilton's Ruined Abbey.

Ruins were taken very seriously, and writers and philosophers tried to analyse their appeal and effect. The poet William Shenstone, famed for his literary garden of The Leasowes, declared that the appeal was visual, emotional and intellectual: 'A ruin, for instance, may… afford that pleasing melancholy which proceeds from a reflexion on decayed magnificence'[4] and 'Ruinated structures appear to derive their power of pleasing, from the irregularity of surface, which is VARIETY; and the latitude they afford the imagination, to conceive an enlargement of their dimensions, or to recollect any events or circumstances appertaining to their pristine grandeur, so far as concerns grandeur and solemnity.'[5] The philosopher Lord Kames, writing in 1762, concurred that a ruin afforded 'a sort of melancholy pleasure' and drew a distinction between the effect produced by Gothic and

scented the commercial possibilities. Thus, while the sculptors busied themselves with patching together parts of antique statuary for sale to the tourists, paintings of the classical Roman *campagna* by Nicolas Poussin, Claude Lorraine and Gaspard Dughet (though seventeenth-century) became enormously popular, and artists such as Piranesi perhaps rather cynically exploited the market by engraving scenes of Roman antiquities in a heightened and romanticised manner, emphasising their neglect and decay.

In addition to the powerful appeal exerted by the remains of ancient Rome, there was a parallel though different impulse stirring at home. First, there were Britain's own ruins, most prominently in the form of the monasteries dissolved and destroyed by Henry VIII. During the course of the eighteenth century these would often be deliberately presented as tourist attractions, for example Tintern Abbey, thus attesting to the taste by classical ruins.[6] The former announced the triumph of time over strength, which Kames considered a melancholy but not unpleasant thought, while classical ruins suggested the triumph of barbarity over taste, a gloomy and discouraging thought. Since Kames was writing about gardens, it is clear that he had ruined abbeys and castles, mock and real, as well as classical ruins in mind.

Hamilton had both sorts of ruin, in the shape of the Mausoleum and the Ruined Abbey, but for very different purposes. The Mausoleum, constructed as a ruined Roman triumphal arch, was intended for visual and emotional effect, but it was also entirely appropriate because it housed, in its niches, some small busts and fragments which were genuine classical antiques, together with a Roman altar placed nearby. The abbey, however, was a late addition, almost an afterthought, when Hamilton decided to enhance the ornamentation of his estate prior

to sale, and also to mask the site of his earlier brick and tileworks. The effect is suitably Gothic, especially from across the lake, but no great weight of meaning can be attached to it. It does not fit in particularly well with the visitor circuit, which was well established by then, and even today the abbey is something of a detour.

William Gilpin, schoolmaster at Cheam, Surrey, and later vicar at Boldre in the New Forest, is the figure traditionally associated with the early evolution of the

OPPOSITE ABOVE The sham castle at Hagley by Sanderson Miller, 1748.
OPPOSITE BELOW Fountains Abbey viewed from Studley Royal.
BELOW William Gilpin's sketch of the Gothic Tower framed by woods, 1772.

Picturesque. His childhood in the Lake District gave him a lifelong love of nature and wild scenery, to which he returned with increasing feeling later in life. In the same year that he took his MA at Oxford, 1748, he produced *A Dialogue Upon the Gardens…at Stow*, in which Callipholus (presumably Gilpin himself) takes his friend Polypthon round the gardens there, commenting on what they see in terms of visual or art criticism. They admire an 'old Ruin', though Gilpin professed in later years to dislike artificial ruins. A ragged ruin or a rock pleases him more than a regular building (a theme he often returned to). The (irregular) Hermitage at Stowe 'has an exceeding good Effect'.[7]

Gilpin started to make local tours during the summer holidays at Cheam, and then, from 1768, became more adventurous with programmes that lasted from a week upwards. Various regions were explored: East Anglia (1769), the Wye Valley and South Wales (1770), the Lake District (1772), North Wales (1773), the south coast (1774), the west (1775) and the Scottish Highlands (1776). He sketched much of what he saw, furthering his ideas of the Picturesque in the process. In the course of judging scenery as if it were a painting, some scenes fell short of what a 'picturesque' viewer or critic would demand, and Gilpin felt no compunction in adjusting reality in his sketches to accord with the desiderata of light and shade, broken surfaces and edges, and areas that were hidden in shadow. He would later defend himself when readers criticised such illustrations after publication for inaccuracy by pleading that they were not intended to be representational. The publications, starting with his account of the Wye Valley (1782), appeared a good many years after the tours themselves, but they gave considerable impetus to spreading ideas about the Picturesque. His intention to examine landscape 'by the rules of picturesque beauty' was set out in that first book, on the Wye tour. His assessment of, and response to, scenery was always entirely visual, and he is sometimes criticised for lack of a moral or social dimension to his thinking.

Painshill was of particular interest to Gilpin with his 'picturesque' cast of mind. He paid two visits, one on 20 May 1765 (resulting in a written description) and then on 14 August 1772, when the text was no more than notes but was accompanied by a number of sketches. By 1765 his 'picturesque' thoughts were well developed, although the long tours were still to come; and by 1772 his sketching technique, achieved through trial and error, had been perfected. The sketches were drawn on the spot by pencil in a notebook, then later worked up using an ink which was usually a mixture of Indian ink and what Gilpin called 'iron water', producing a brownish tinge. Both grey and brown washes were then added.

Gilpin's sensibility evidently changed, for he liked the Gothic Temple on his first visit, but disparaged it on his second. The view from it, on the other hand, was spoiled on the first visit but 'rich' on the second. The route he took was similar on both occasions, though he did not comment on the abbey despite sketching it. This could have been either because it did not fit into the circuit, as mentioned above, or because the arm of the lake in front of it had not yet been dug and filled.

His sketches, rather than his words, bring out many of the qualities of the gardens at the time. Contrasts, uses of distance, trees, lawn, water, the setting of buildings against slopes – all emerge from the drawings. Gilpin also picks up on Hamilton's subtle circuit, showing distant glimpses early on of buildings that look different when you actually come to them, as witness the Hermitage or the Temple of Bacchus, both of which are approached from the opposite side. Sometimes the sketches contradict the text, showing that his heart and eye did not necessarily concur with his judgment. Thus, he dismisses the 'tufa' facings to the grotto as unnatural, yet devotes two sketches to it, bringing out the contrasts of surface, the balance between stone and the plantings behind, and between light and shadow, with evident delight in these picturesque qualities. Elsewhere, he frames the view up to the Gothic Tower by trees, as if it were a picture, and is alert to the way in which plantings complement buildings, as with the Mausoleum (or Roman Arch, as Gilpin calls it) and the Hermitage in its dark evergreen setting.

Despite his avowed disapproval of artificial ruins, Gilpin praised the Mausoleum, so was evidently happy to accept its picturesque effect. In general he reckoned that no complete building could be picturesque, because it displayed regularity, and said the same about formal gardens.

Although Gilpin was the crusader of the Picturesque, it was left to two argumentative and polemical followers to put the movement, and what they regarded as its principles, on the map. One of these was Sir Uvedale Price, whose influential *Essay on the Picturesque* appeared in 1794. In an attempt to define the term, Price opposed it to harmony, beauty and the polish and order (or monotony, as he saw it) of 'Capability' Brown's parks: 'I am therefore persuaded, that the two opposite qualities of roughness, and of sudden variation, joined to that of irregularity, are the most efficient causes of the

picturesque.'[8] Concomitant with irregularity came the desire for naturalness and the concealment of art. Price spoke glowingly of such effects: 'we have enjoyed the dear delight of getting to some spot where there were no traces of art, and no other walk or communication than a sheep track'.[9]

One of the chief tenets of both Price and Richard Payne Knight was that there should be as little interference with nature as possible, which they endeavoured to put into practice in their own properties. Price talks about how this was achieved in one of the woodland walks at Painshill:

Among many circumstances of more striking effect, I was highly pleased with a walk which leads through a bottom skirted with wood; and I was pleased with it, not from what *had*, but from what had *not*, been

BELOW The Mausoleum by William Gilpin, 1772.

done; it had no edges, no borders, no distinct lines of separation; nothing was done except keeping the ground properly neat, and the communication free from any obstruction; the eye and the footsteps were equally unconfined, and if it is a high commendation to a writer or painter, that he knows when to leave off, it is not less so to an improver.[10]

Price maintained that, in the case of Painshill, the seemingly simple and natural appearance was often the result of hard work that disguised the art involved:

This [the Alpine valley], and other parts of Painshill seem to have been formed on the precept contained in the well-known lines of Tasso, in his description of the garden of Armida:
  "E quell che'l bello e'l caro accresce a l'opre,
  L'arte che tutto fa, nulla si scopre."*
Mr. Hamilton, however, is one of the very few who have profited by it; for although no precept be more generally admitted in theory than that of concealing the art which is employed, none has been less observed in practice.[11]
  *As adapted by Spenser in *The Faerie Queene*: 'And that, which all faire works doth most aggrace,/The art, which all that wrought, appeared in no place.'

Price goes on to contrast Hamilton with certain other contemporaries who are unable to benefit from Tasso: 'nothing of that kind has influenced those of professed improvers; and a style very different from that at Painshill has been exhibited at no very great distance from it, in a place begun I believe by Kent, and finished by Brown [presumably Claremont]'.[12]

Natural appearance did not imply leaving an uninteresting or unattractive site as it was. Price acknowledged Hamilton's Herculean efforts in transforming Painshill, and attributed Hamilton's success to his study of art and his application of the principles of painting:

I have always understood that Mr. Hamilton, who created Painshill, not only had studied pictures, but had studied them for the express purpose of improving real landscape. The place he created (a task of quite another difficulty from correcting, or from adding to natural scenery) fully proves the use of such a study.[13]

In 1801, after disagreement with Payne Knight over distinctions between the Beautiful and the Picturesque, Price framed his further thoughts in the form of a dialogue, or conversation, between three friends, on the grounds that this would be more agreeable and entertaining to the reader. The three friends are a Mr Howard (representing Payne Knight), a Mr Seymour (who has little acquaintance with painting or the application of its principles to gardens or natural scenery) and a Mr Hamilton (representing Price himself).[14] Is it coincidence that Price chose the name of Hamilton for the spokesman for his own views, or is Price in fact aligning himself with what he perceived to be the thinking and practice of the man who created Painshill?

Price was keen to 'prove' the connection between paintings and scenery, and the Picturesque is sometimes characterised, in painting terms, as Salvator Rosa, portrayer of wild, bandit-infested scenes in southern Italy, in contrast to the more ordered world of Claude and Poussin. It has sometimes been claimed that there is a feeling of Rosa in the wooded parts of Painshill, and the idea that the study of paintings had contributed significantly to Hamilton's vision had some currency. However, another contemporary, George Mason, put the matter in a different perspective in response to Price: 'If HAMILTON by studying pictures improved his real landscape, it is to be remembered that he was *previously* a gardener. His thoughts were engaged by their favourite pursuit, which saved them from being cramped and vitiated by painting prejudices.'[15]

In 1858, the Rev. John Mitford, in his edition of the works of Thomas Gray, added a footnote to Gray's letter to Thomas Wharton of 13 August 1754, in which he encouraged Wharton to visit Painshill. The footnote (not present in Mitford's earlier edition of 1816) declared that 'Mr. Hamilton formed many of the beautiful scenes in the grounds of Painshill from the Pictures of Poussin and the Italian Masters'.[16] This was a century after Hamilton, and

it is difficult now to know how much credence to give to this belief. Nonetheless, as has already been shown, Hamilton was unquestionably a visual artist who loved paintings and who approached landscape design with a painter's eye.

In an age when the art of landscape was in any case often compared to that of the seventeenth-century landscape painters, Claude, Poussin and Rosa loom large. The author of *An Essay on the Different Natural Situations of Gardens* (1801) claimed that Poussin and Rosa were the best examples: Rosa was rugged but

> Poussin, on the other hand, added all the beauties of verdure, all the vivacity of water to his great situations: and interspersed amongst them not only living objects, but on the bottoms and sides of the hills, views of temples and palaces of a Babylonish architecture; which by their uncouth appearance correspond to the sentiment he meaned to create. Perhaps the landskips of Poussin are the best instructor, which a gardener of genius and taste can follow for this first branch of the natural division of grounds.[17]

Uvedale Price would readily have agreed, though Poussin was more a model for the pictorial gardens of a previous generation.

Hamilton was perceived by contemporaries as having a feeling for the Picturesque. According to the Rev. Richard Warner, Gilpin's curate at Boldre and a follower of his 'picturesque' principles, Hamilton evolved a 'free and grand manner of gardening' which led away from the building-filled kind of landscape to something much more based just on nature.[18] It is unclear whether Warner meant that in its later years Painshill was more naturalistic than it had been earlier or whether this new manner was the result of his post-Painshill design work, at his ten-acre town garden in Lansdown Road, Bath, or at Bowood and Fonthill, both of which contained striking areas of picturesque naturalness.

Not only was Hamilton's Hermitage, by virtue of its primitive construction, consonant with picturesque thinking, but its precarious positioning was regarded highly in design terms. Henry Hoare, Hamilton's banker, paid him the compliment of taking Hamilton's advice on the siting of his own hermitage at Stourhead, where it had a similarly perilous position on a zigzag path up the steep hill to the Temple of Apollo.[19] This was part of Hoare's own change in later years from a purely classical landscape to one which contained oriental, rustic and Gothic creations.

But it is the use of rockwork which shows most affinity with the Picturesque, combining roughness, irregularity and naturalness. The chief display at Painshill is, of course, on Grotto Island, with its numerous tufa-clad structures supplementing the grotto itself. But the cascade, too, with the various boulders strewn round about, contributes greatly to this impression and paved the way for the more glorious exhibition of rockwork which Hamilton designed at Bowood.

The Picturesque at Painshill, then, manifested itself partly through the forest plantings to the west; through the exploitation of steep landform; through the appearance and positioning of some buildings; through the use of ruins; and through naturalistic rockwork. In many ways Painshill was ahead of its time and demonstrates a wide-ranging and ever-responsive sensibility on Hamilton's part.

The Vineyard

$\mathcal{I}$T IS APPROPRIATE that the creator of the Temple of Bacchus should have experimented with producing wine from his own grapes. The vineyard planted by Hamilton was reckoned in its heyday to be the most successful in the land. It was one of only two in the county, the other having been at Oatlands in the previous century. Situated on the south-facing bank which slopes down to the eastern arm of the lake, it enjoyed the advantage of position but little else: the soil was sandy, with many flints and stones, making the subsoil insufficiently porous, and the English climate was hardly conducive to providing the grapes with the heat and sun they needed. The success of the vineyard in the face of such obstacles is the more remarkable. It was laid out in the 1740s, which means that Hamilton had it early in mind among his horticultural ventures, perhaps prompted by memories of French or Italian vineyards he had seen as a young man. The Barret painting (see page 146) shows the original layout, though by the time of the painting (*c.*1780) it was no longer as productive as formerly.

The vineyard struggled in its early years, and Hamilton realised that he needed expert help. He turned to the best source, a Frenchman with experience of growing grapes in his homeland. This man was David Geneste, who had fled France to escape actual or potential persecution as a Huguenot. Geneste, who hailed from the celebrated wine region of Clairac, was in London by 1739 and became head vine-grower at Painshill from 1748 to 1757.[1] Under Geneste there were many improvements in the cultivation of the vines and in the quality of the wine. He saw that the current methods of cultivation were unsatisfactory, and wrote to his sister in France both for advice and for implements such as pruning knives, which would serve as a model to make others.

A year after Geneste's arrival, Hamilton planted a second vineyard, on the other side of the Portsmouth Road, where his farm stood. Both vineyards were in full swing by 1754, when Richard Pococke confirmed that there were 'ten acres of vineyard here in two places.'[2] The principal site extended further than it does now, around the corner of the south-facing hill, as shown in the painting 'La Vendange', which dates from *c.*1780 (see page 147). It covered about five acres.

Geneste's first letters home indicate that when he took up his appointment in 1748, at a guinea a week, the grapes were very fine, though the vineyard itself was in a poor condition because no one understood how to run it. He

ABOVE The vineyard and Ruined Abbey: compare the painting on page 146.

loved Painshill and hoped that he would be able to stay for a few years. Visitors were generous, and he had already received about £50, a year's wages, in tips. Further letters are spasmodic, but the mixed fortunes of the vineyard can be pieced together. Although in general it flourished, there were disappointing years when rain and early frost prevented ripening. In 1751, for instance, only two barrels were produced, half of which was mere *verjus*, a sour liquid used for vinegar. All English vineyards had been similarly affected that year. Hamilton's enthusiasm was undimmed, however, and he ordered more vines to be planted.

During 1752 Geneste sought assistance in the form of a couple of labourers from France who could help him prune the vines. They were to bring six pruning hooks, six sharpening stones and two trowels for the stony soil. It took a year for them to arrive, but the arrangement seems to have worked well. At the end of 1754 Geneste

noted that there had been four barrels, two of which were to be sold as *vin de Champagne*, and at Easter 1755 he commented that Hamilton had sold the 1753 vintage of white wine at sixty guineas the barrel, the most luxurious wine of its kind ever known.

Geneste's accommodation and expenses in maintaining the vineyard caused him to seek a rise from Hamilton, who responded angrily by sacking him. However, just before his departure, Hamilton sent for him to taste that year's wine, both white and red from the same black grape. In an emotional reconciliation, aided no doubt by copious draughts of the wine, Hamilton proposed better wages plus a house rental, to which Geneste happily agreed. He stayed until 1757, when he was paid £20 on 26 July, but by 1758 his family in France had lost touch with him.[3]

Hamilton's own French contact, the Abbé Nolin, took over as the source for finding French vignerons

MR HAMILTON'S ELYSIUM

OPPOSITE The Ruined Abbey and vineyard by George Barret the Elder and Sawrey Gilpin, *c*.1780.
LEFT 'La Vendange', *c*.1780, artist unknown.

in the summer of 1755. He asked Nolin for his help in obtaining two assistants, and Nolin interviewed thirty candidates. One had gone back on his word, and others were prejudiced by their priests. In September 1755 Nolin wrote that two young men were on their way, but their departure had been delayed by rumour that the French were treated badly in England. But they returned to France within a few weeks, which greatly upset Nolin. He told Hamilton that they had been happy with Hamilton's treatment of them but had made the strange claim that they had been allowed to swear too freely.[4]

Decline set in within the next few years, however, and the problems of climate had more and more effect. In 1766 Dr John Hope observed that the grapes never ripened sufficiently,[5] and in 1782, when the vines were over thirty years old and the weather was particularly cold and wet, the grapes were changing colour only at the end of October and did not ripen properly at all.[6] The situation that year was no better in Portugal, however, where by November the grapes were said to be no more advanced than at Painshill. FX Vispré, author of this account, thought the reasons for the failure of the vineyard were, first, its age, and second, the damp air exuded by the row of horse chestnut trees along the

top of the slope.[7] Survivors, or traces, of the chestnuts are only to be found in a grove on the eastern side of the vineyard, not along the top, however.

By 1795, when William Robertson paid a visit, the vineyard was described as neglected and surviving only in part;[8] early in the nineteenth century Manning and Bray recorded that it was no longer in use;[9] and Loudon in his *Encylopaedia of Gardening* (1830) commented that 'Some of the vines which formed this vineyard may still be seen on the original site, now covered with a grove of Scotch pines.'[10] A nineteenth-century rockery was subsequently formed on the slope, the boulders coming from around the cascade.

According to Geneste, the types of grape grown were *pied rouge, Muscat blanc, Muscat rouge, guillan rouge, guillan blanc* and *sauviot* plus some other quicker-growing varieties of which he did not know the name.[11] Hamilton himself spoke only of two sorts of Burgundy grape, the auvernat, the most delicate in taste but the tenderest, and the miller grape, commonly called the *black cluster*, which was hardier.[12] Presumably after early experiments he settled on these two cultivars, identifiable as *pinot noir* and *pinot meunier* respectively. The varieties currently grown in the restored section of the vineyard (2.5 acres) are one-third *pinot noir*, one-sixth *chardonnay* and one half *seyval blanc*. Although Hamilton's *pinot meunier* is still available, it would not have flourished and so was not considered.

The original spacing of the rows is shown in the two paintings (pages 146, 147). Tending the vines was done by hand but current methods of cultivation render this system impracticable so modern trellising is used except for the three vines at the bottom of each row, which are spaced as formerly. The method employed by Hamilton was clearly based on French practice, as confirmed by William Cobbett, who had seen the vineyard in its prime when he was a boy, and when the vines were planted in rows and tied to stakes.[13] The rows were four feet apart, and the vines were prevented from growing more than four feet in height, as Thomas Kyle, a gardener from Edinburgh, commented in 1761.[14]

Hamilton had in his library a small number of books on viticulture, such as Biddet's *Culture des Vignes* (1752) and *The Art of Cultivating Vines* (1772) by Louis de St Pierre of South Carolina. Vispré's book, mentioned above, was published in Hamilton's home town of Bath in 1786, the year of his death, but he had a copy. The Abbé Nolin said he would keep an eye open for works on the subject, and promised to send one, the *Culture des Vignes*, published in Rheims in 1722, which gave instructions for cultivating a vine and making champagne. This book does not appear in Hamilton's catalogue, however, unless Biddet's work is the same and the wrong date has been ascribed. In addition to the printed word, Nolin gave direct advice to Hamilton: thus, on 4 December 1755, he suggested that a vine should be halted at three or four feet height (as Thomas Kyle later confirmed) and the tendrils carefully removed.

Hamilton gave a long account of his process of making wine to his friend Sir Edward Barry, who published it verbatim in 1775. Barry introduced the subject by saying that Philip Miller had claimed that the soil near London was not conducive to growing vines, but that this was prejudice on Miller's part:

> But had he been acquainted with the success which attended the vineyards of my ingenious friend, the honourable *Charles Hamilton*, who has been long distinguished for his peculiar elegant taste, he would have spoken with more certainty.[15]

Hamilton's description was later reprinted in *The Book of the Household* (*c.*1858) for the benefit of housewives.

Hamilton began by explaining that in his first year he attempted to make red wine in the usual way by treading the grapes and then letting them ferment in a vat, till all the husks and impurities formed a thick crust at the top. The clear wine was drawn off from the bottom, but it was so harsh that **he** despaired of ever making red wine fit to drink: however, through the harshness a slight flavour of French white wine emerged, which gave him the idea of aiming at white wine instead. This was so successful that the very first year it nearly resembled the taste of champagne, and two or three years later, as the vines flourished, the wine improved so much that it had an even finer flavour than champagne. The first draught was as clear as spirits and the second was *oeil de Perdrix*, the colour of light claret, and both runnings sparkled and creamed in the glass like champagne.

Hamilton declared that many connoisseurs were deceived by his wine and thought it superior to any champagne they had ever drunk. Even the Duke of Mirepoix (the French ambassador in London) said he preferred it to any other wine. However, such was the prejudice of most people against anything of English growth that Hamilton found it prudent not to reveal the source until they had passed judgment on it. Given the quality, Hamilton was able to sell it to wine merchants for fifty guineas a hogshead (equal to sixty-three old wine gallons), and one wine merchant had sold the best of it to customers at prices from 7s 6d to 10s 6d a bottle.

Hamilton's final method, arrived at after many years of experiment and experience, was as follows. The grapes were left to hang till as ripe as they would get, and were then cut off with scissors. They were taken to the wine store in small bunches to prevent heat or pressure. Each grape was picked off the stalk and the mouldy or unripe ones discarded. The grapes were pressed a few hours after gathering, and the first running was as clear as water and sweet as syrup. Part of the second pressing continued white, but subsequent pressings grew redder and were not mixed with the best. As the wine ran from the press into a large container it was put into hogsheads and tightly bunged. In a few hours the fermentation began, which would burst the casks if they were not properly hooped and secured in strong wooden frames. Hamilton had frequently seen wine oozing through the pores of the wood at the height of fermentation.

The casks were left all winter in a cold barn, and when fermentation was over (easily determined by the cessation of sound and oozing) the wine was drained into new hogsheads and taken to the vaults before any warmth of weather could start up a second fermentation. In March the hogsheads were examined, and the wine was bottled at about the end of the month. After a further six weeks it would be ready for drinking, and would keep in peak condition for about a year, but after a year the flavour and sweetness would decline. Hamilton said he had kept some bottles for sixteen years, when it became like old hock. The only additive Hamilton employed was three pounds of white sugar candy when the wine was first taken from the press, in order to respond to a passing fad for drinking very sweet champagne.

Hamilton commented that his site was far from ideal, and the soil was not as suitable as could be found elsewhere. The slope was too steep, and too exposed to the south-west wind, and many promising crops had been spoiled by frost in May and by wet summers; 'but one good year balances many disappointments'. Captain St Pierre, mentioned above, who had established vine plantations in South Carolina with a large colony of 300 *vignerons*, spent several days with Hamilton and took plentiful cuttings which he thought would thrive at the latitude in question.[16]

The reception of the wine by visitors swung considerably according to the vintage. Pococke's 1754 visit followed a particularly good year, and he was able to confirm that 'the grape gently press'd makes an excellent champaign, and pressed out, and left on the husk, produces a very good Burgundy: five or six hogsheads have been made in a year, and it sells at the inns here at 7s 6d a bottle'.[17] This was a high price if measured against a labourer's weekly wage of 10s to 15s, but could bear comparison with the prices charged, for example, at Vauxhall Gardens, where in 1762 a bottle of Burgundy cost 6s, champagne 8s and claret 5s.[18] Robert FitzGerald, however, evidently sampled the wine in a bad year (possibly a year or two later than Pococke), for he commented disparagingly that 'the wine has something of the Gout [savour] of champagne but is poor and yet is sold at 6s.a bottle, and by Mr Hamilton at £3 a dozen as our Landlord assured us'.[19]

The restored vineyard is susceptible to the climate, as it was in Hamilton's day, and does not produce wine every year. What has been produced in recent years includes a sparkling white, a rosé and a still white. One or two vintages have been particularly fine, and Hamilton would have been proud of them.

RIGHT Grapes in the recreated vineyard.

Aftermath and Restoration

BY THE TIME Hamilton left, Painshill had become an icon and Hamilton was admired as a progressive and visionary designer. Although subsequent owners effected various alterations, and a considerable amount of planting and replanting was undertaken, nothing radical was done to alter the structure of the landscape, and Hamilton continued to be given credit for its creation. What is striking about the comments and assessments that were made for a century after Hamilton left is that he was not seen as outmoded. There were so many fashions and changing tastes in gardens that a garden or designer would soon be regarded as old-fashioned by succeeding generations, but that did not happen with Painshill. The qualities that appealed in Hamilton's own day were perceived to be above fashion. It was not, indeed, until 1876 that Victorian *hauteur* raised objections: 'It is needless to remark that so elaborately artificial a construction of natural scenery was a mistake in taste.'[1]

There were some visitors who wrote their impressions at the time and then again in subsequent years, informed by later thoughts and the context of the time. George Mason had gone round in the 1760s and published his comments in 1768: however, in the revised edition of 1795 he admitted that he had seen Painshill only once more, in 1770, and never since then.[2] Nonetheless he took the opportunity to consider it in a 'picturesque' light and to correct a criticism he had made earlier, which he said had been due to a defective memory.[3]

John Wesley paid three October visits, the first in 1771, when Hamilton was still owner, when he considered the gardens to be 'inexpressibly pleasant'. The second, in 1779, found him comparing Painshill to Stowe and judging Painshill superior in all respects. On the third occasion, in 1790, Wesley and his companions arrived on the wrong visiting day, but were admitted by Bond Hopkins, when he realised who his distinguished visitor was, and 'spent an hour very agreeably in those lovely walks'.[4]

From 1800 there was a proliferation of topographical histories and gazetteers that kept the reputation of Painshill alive, even though Hamilton's contemporaries were apt to be quoted in support, for instance Manning and Bray in 1809 cite Walpole and Whately.[5] Subsequent writers applaud Hamilton as a pioneer of landscape gardening even though tastes had by then changed:

RIGHT The cleared view from within the restored Gothic Temple.

The demesne of Pains Hill has long been celebrated as one of the earliest and finest examples of the modern style of English landscape gardening. For this reputation it is indebted to the above-mentioned Mr. Charles Hamilton, the first to take advantage of the natural disposition of the grounds, and with an artist's eye and a refined judgment, strengthened by observation in foreign lands, so to distribute his plantations and their artificial accompaniments as both to create and command as rich a succession of picturesque and beautiful views as the situation could possibly afford.[6]

Part of the explanation lies in that word 'picturesque', for as we have seen Painshill was sufficiently well endowed with those qualities to appeal to the next generation (or beyond) which appreciated such things. It was also respected as an early, ambitious and particularly fine exemplar of the landscape garden. Thus, Thomas Moule in 1837 declared: 'As one of the earliest instances of cultivation being applied to the formation of landscape scenery, it is a remarkable spot; all the original features which contributed to its celebrity are still preserved,'[7] while J Weale nearly twenty years later called it 'a grand specimen of modern landscape gardening...[it] may doubtless be inspected again and again with increasing pleasure'.[8]

Painshill continued to be open to the public for some time, with the Earl of Carhampton allowing visitors on Thursdays and Saturdays.[9] Up to the 1830s views continued to be published (Hassell, Prosser) that would have acted as advertisement. Earlier it was noted that in an edition of the works of the poet Thomas Gray (1858) the editor, the Rev. John Mitford, appended a footnote which has continued to have reverberations ever since. This stated that Hamilton had based his landscape on paintings by Poussin and Italian artists,[10] but there is no evidence other than a general impression that such paintings were one of a number of sources of inspiration for Hamilton, which is very different from saying that he copied specific paintings.

From the later nineteenth century, however, Painshill slipped quietly out of view and became something of a Sleeping Beauty, dormant for a century. Yet it was never completely forgotten, and when it did receive attention, as in *Country Life* in 1897 and 1904, its reputation was intact. The 1897 article speaks of the

intelligent care, the artistic mind, and the opulent hand of the Hon. Charles Hamilton...the evidence of whose enthusiasm, love of nature, and discriminating judgment may be seen at this day in the noble domain of Pain's Hill...Mr. Hamilton may be said with truth, as was said of another great landscape gardener, to have worked with the invisible hand of art in the true spirit of nature...Long observation and experience of like work abroad had taught Mr. Hamilton much, and he became a most judicious planter.[11]

By the time of the 1904 article, however, more attention was paid to the Victorian terrace than to the landscape, which had suddenly become out-of-date though still admired: 'It is still the best example that England possesses of the old landscape gardening school.'[12] However, the anonymous author is much more thrilled by the urns and statues on the terrace which are claimed to be unsurpassed anywhere else in England.[13]

In 1925 Elizabeth Wheeler Manwaring gave a general account of the influence of Italian landscape in eighteenth-century England, pinpointing the Mitford quote above on Hamilton following Italian landscape painting.[14] Two years later Christopher Hussey's milestone publication *The Picturesque* naturally picks out Painshill as a garden favoured by the 'picturesque' protagonist Uvedale Price, but rather strangely refers to it as a 'glorified *ferme ornée*'.[15] There were certainly sheep present (though not at the time that Hussey would have seen it), but little sign of a farm, which, as we know, was over the road.

Periodically attempts were made to revive interest in Painshill. One such was Christopher Tunnard's *Gardens in the Modern Landscape* (1938), with its evocative photographs taken at a time when decay had not yet significantly set in. Tunnard accepts the view that the gardens were modelled on paintings by Poussin and others, and draws particular attention to the trees, notably of course the cedars.[16] His section on Painshill forms part of an essay on the landscape garden which in turn forms the background to a discussion of modern garden planning and design. In the same year Alicia Amherst confirmed both the reputation of Painshill and its current condition: 'Pains Hill vies with Stourhead in Wiltshire in its claims to be considered the most unspoiled surviving example of the eighteenth-century picturesque landscape garden.'[17]

A decade later HF Clark's seminal book *The English Landscape Garden* drew attention to its subject almost as if it were new, selecting nine gardens to exemplify the range of the genre, including Painshill and reproducing some of the plates from Tunnard. Clark stressed the 'painting' view even more than Tunnard, considering that Hamilton worked more deliberately and directly than others from Pope's dictum that 'all gardening is landscape painting' and that the 'savage' part of the garden was taken from a scene or scenes by Salvator Rosa.[18] But after the war any interest there might have been was dissipated by the splitting up and neglect of what remained of Hamilton's Painshill.

Osvald Sirén, a post-war visitor, found the grounds poised on the brink of disintegration. The grotto was about to lose its roof, the Temple of Bacchus was propped up by a pole and much of the timber was over-mature. His book *China and Gardens of Europe of the Eighteenth Century* (1950) was written with a deliberate slant to detect Chinese influence, but it is a useful account to show the state of the gardens at the time. For example, he says that the grotto was still intact in 1946 on his first visit (which suggests that the earlier story of munitions exploding during the war is untrue), but the following year he found the roof had collapsed, attributing this nonetheless to the same soldiers who according to him had weakened the roof by removing the lead.[19]

Country Life returned to the scene in 1958. The first article, on 2 January, dealt with the house, but the second, the following week, described Painshill as one of the earliest of the great picturesque landscape gardens, though the author, Gordon Nares, did not expand on what that might mean.[20] But it showed that, even in their forlorn state, the grounds were still recognised and valued. In 1964 the Shell Gardens Book appeared, with signs that the history of the landscape garden was being taken more seriously and analysed: two traditions were detected, one based on the English countryside 'improved' and idealised (e.g. Hagley), and the other the formation of an entirely new landscape with buildings and exotic trees and shrubs (Stourhead and Painshill).[21] Painshill is listed in the gazetteer at the end as a surviving Hamilton landscape in terms of both buildings and timber, though that was to present it through rose-tinted spectacles.

The perceived influence of seventeenth-century painters continued to colour the approach of those who still wrote about Painshill. Edward Malins in *English Landscaping and Literature* 1660–1840 (1966) put forward the influence of Rosa and Gaspard Dughet,[22] while Miles Hadfield in *A History of British Gardening*

RIGHT The Gothic Tower in 1937.

(1969, originally published nine years earlier as *Gardening in Britain*) gave a description of the grounds and then a traditional interpretation:

> Hamilton's aim seems to have been not only to form 'out of a most cursed hill' an idealised landscape after the manner of painters, but, by availing himself on a scale then unprecedented of the exotic trees and shrubs which were now becoming available, to create something that had hitherto not been attempted.[23]

He concluded that Painshill, with its employment of exotics and its appreciative use of their wide range of colour and form, foreshadowed the twentieth century.

Garden history as a subject worthy of serious study and scholarship built up during the 1960s, thanks to the pioneering work of writers such as Hadfield, Christopher Hussey and Peter Hunt. The latter was among those who founded the Garden History Society in 1965. The Society soon turned its attention to Painshill, both in terms of research and a fledgling concern for conservation. At that time it was thought that the first step was to research the history of the garden and that the dissemination of knowledge about it would help in promoting conservation or restoration.

As a result the Society produced, in its journal *Garden History*, a long general article by Alison Hodges in 1973, based on her own research and on information provided by several members of the Society and some others, pooling their knowledge. As well as providing an account of the gardens using the latest scholarship, the article contained a comprehensive bibliography which remains an essential base for any research on Painshill though much has been written (and discovered) since. This article was followed in subsequent issues of the journal by three specialised articles by the same author.

Mrs Hodges' own view was that Hamilton combined the literary–intellectual–pictorial ideas of Pope, who knew his Homer and Virgil but had not seen Italy, with the pictorial interpretation of Italy practised by Kent, who sought to imitate some of the effects he had seen in the gardens of Rome. She claimed that Hamilton intended to evoke the spirit of the classical world. It is doubtful, however, whether much of the literary and intellectual side brushed off on Hamilton in his approach to gardening, and in his varied landscape there is more of a free employment of many styles than a concentration on the classical.

When the February 1975 issue of *House and Garden* reached the letter H in its dictionary of gardens and gardening, it proffered a well-illustrated feature on Hamilton and Painshill, including a rare photograph of the Temple of Bacchus. The garden is described as being now seen as one of the most influential of all landscape gardens. The author, Miles Hadfield, commenting on Hamilton's pioneering work, claims that his originality lay in helping to introduce the *ferme ornée*. This notion may have come from Hussey (see above), but as we have seen it is a rather misleading way to look at Hamilton's achievement.

Geoffrey and Susan Jellicoe, again writing in 1975, have been quoted in relation to Chinese elements at Painshill. They also thought that Hamilton, like Hoare at Stourhead, was influenced by the Italian landscape painters, finding the discipline and the meaning that lay behind the apparent disorder of ruins in those paintings.[24]

In the anthology *The Genius of the Place* (1975) and in *The Figure in the Landscape* (1976) John Dixon Hunt claimed that part of Painshill was specifically designed on the model of some sketches by Rosa, but there appears to be no evidence to substantiate this: the continuing influence of Mitford is detected.

In 1977 Miles Hadfield returned to a favourite topic in *The English Landscape Garden* and once more tempered the aesthetic aspects and considerations with the practical side of Hamilton's interests, i.e. plantings. This balance represents the basis of all modern judgments and assessments.

Restoration

By the mid 1970s the grounds were in an advanced state of neglect and decay. There was rampant overgrowth, views were obscured and many of what were supposed to be paths were blocked by ferns, brambles and nettles. Much of the landscape had reverted to nature, and a wild nature at that. The lake was fished by the Walton Angling Society, but it was fed only by drainage from the A3 and a natural spring. The buildings had either disintegrated or disappeared, and the Gothic Tower was gutted by fire in 1974. The place might well have dropped out of public consciousness altogether had it not been for the passion and belief of, initially, a small number of devotees and then by the formation of the Painshill Park Trust in 1981.

The interest shown by the Garden History Society was echoed by a small group of local enthusiasts who met together as the Friends of Painshill. They conducted research but were also hopeful of reviving Hamilton's lost paradise. The first step towards rescuing the park was to promote public awareness of Painshill and its importance. In the mid-1970s there were two events contributing to this end, an article in the *Guardian* and a documentary feature in the BBC television programme *Nationwide*. Interest was also building up locally, and Elmbridge Borough Council was starting to take notice. A planning application by one of the owners served as a spur to look at the site closely, and notice was served on another of the owners to maintain the listed buildings. A second article in the *Guardian* appeared at a critical moment when the councillors were debating possible acquisition. This was agreed, and the land was purchased in two tranches, totalling 158 acres by 1980. Because of the difficulties posed by multiple ownership of parts and strips of the Hamilton land, it has not been possible to reclaim the entire area – most of the parkland towards the road is still in other hands – but the essential parts, the lake, the wood and the pleasure grounds, were saved. The total purchase price was £195,000, to which Surrey County Council contributed £25,000 and the Countryside Commission £45,000.

It was decided to set up a separate, independent trust to restore and maintain the grounds. The trust would be a charity and be eligible for grant assistance and be able to raise funds in a way that a Council could not. The new trust would be given a ninety-nine year lease of Painshill at a peppercorn rent, and there would be Council representation on the Board of Trustees. The name of the trust was to be the Painshill Park Trust, making it clear to those who were not aware of it that Painshill was a landscape. Historically the name was simply Painshill, and the 'park' appellation was not used before the nineteenth century.

The Trust was set up in 1981 with the purpose of restoring Painshill 'as nearly as possible to Charles Hamilton's original concept of a landscape garden for the benefit of the public, and as a self-financing enterprise'. For the first years the Trust management had to operate from the then Borough offices in Esher, with a timber building and the Gardener's Cottage accommodating personnel in the park. The present 'temporary' office building near the walled garden dates from 1988.

A Painshill Council, consisting of eighteen distinguished names in the architectural, landscape and cultural fields, was set up to present a high public profile. The Trustees, responsible for oversight of the whole programme, included representatives of Elmbridge Council, Surrey County Council, the Royal Horticultural Society, the Garden History Society and Merrist Wood Agricultural College, together with a number of individuals with a strong local interest. HRH The Prince of Wales became Royal Patron in 1986.

With the establishment of a new and independent trust there came the opportunity to do something unprecedented in garden re-creation. Conservation and restoration of gardens were in any case fairly rudimentary in 1980, but the Painshill Park Trust took the chance to re-create and restore with a degree of thoroughness previously unknown. In order to achieve this, the Trust pioneered some techniques, and conducted its investigations, to a depth and on a scale that have now become accepted and applied widely but which were at the time without parallel. A number of honorary panels were set up to investigate and move the project forward on historical lines – an Architects' Panel and Historical Research Panel provided information, interpretation and advice.

However ambitious the plans, successful implementation depended entirely upon the workforce, both skilled and unskilled. A massive amount of clearance, earth-moving, planting and re-establishing of lawns and paths had to be done, particularly in the early years, and labour was a problem, since the Trust had only minimal funding at the outset. Fortunately there was generous Government support through schemes run by the Manpower Services Commission for the long-term unemployed which gave young people training and work experience and a modest wage. Many of the potential candidates were graduates in related academic or vocational fields, and the scheme was hugely influential in laying the foundation of the restoration as well as performing a valuable task of job creation. Other organisations also participated, such as the British Trust for Conservation Volunteers and Merrist Wood, which sent many students as part of their education and training.

Practical surveying was an essential basis for the project, helping to 'read the history from the ground' in view of the dearth of documentary evidence, certainly in the early years, and of the advanced dereliction and decay of the estate. A tree survey was conducted in 1982 to identify not only surviving historic trees but stumps from the Hamilton period. At the time there were reckoned to be about 170 Hamilton trees, but storms and time have since reduced that number to no more than 100. About 700 stumps were located.

Techniques of field archaeology had seldom been applied to gardens before, but at Painshill not only were the foundations of buildings excavated but trenches were dug in selected places to establish the existence of paths, boundaries and other features.

Following the tree survey, which was fundamental to accurate landscape restoration, consultants were sought to assist the Trust with the development of a Masterplan for Painshill. Of the several competitive bids Land Use Consultants were selected. Their plan (1984) coincided with confirmation of the lease, which was linked to the Masterplan, thus protecting Elmbridge Council's interests, and was funded by the National Heritage Memorial Fund. The Fund also supported the day-to-day running of the project. The plan, covering not only restoration but all aspects of the public access and visitor infrastructure, proposed a phased restoration and re-creation over several years, with annual targets. This proved to be essential in making and monitoring progress and in deciding priorities. In subsequent years LUC have periodically reviewed the plan.

Education has always been fundamental to the Painshill project, encouraged at all stages by Surrey County Council, which donated a classroom. As early as 1983 a schools programme was established with a view to encouraging local schools to participate in various activities on site and to use Painshill as a resource in different subject areas. When the national curriculum was introduced, involvement was tailored to suit the requirements of a number of subjects. In addition schools have taken part in such activities as tree-planting in National Tree Week, thereby contributing tangibly to the restoration. A separate body, the Painshill Park Education Trust (later incorporated within the main Trust), was set up to look after what had become an operation on a significant scale, with an education officer. Another development, 'Camp Hamilton', offered educational activities during school holidays on a daily basis, and the park soon became a popular venue for educationally themed birthday parties.

Education has extended to adults as well. From early days there were courses, seminars and study days for adults, which have now developed into regular programmes of talks, ranging from aspects of Painshill itself to related garden history or cultural topics.

Research has also played a significant part in the proceedings. It has focused on the history of Painshill and of Hamilton (and to a lesser extent on subsequent owners), partly for interest but mainly for its value to the restoration programme in terms of knowledge of historical detail and of understanding the landscape. The role of the archivist has ranged from garnering historical information to preparing packs for schools and keeping an archive of photographs as well as documents. The archivist was responsible for the 'Living Memory' project in the mid 1980s, where people who had had earlier connections with Painshill were invited to relate their memories, or those of their families stretching back in time.

Volunteers have made not just a significant but an essential contribution to the programme, as they still do. Undertaking research, supporting management and acting as guides have always been key roles, and over the years a group of skilled and experienced volunteers deeply committed to the cause has evolved. They have assisted a range of visitor management duties too, and have always been integral to the educational activities, giving a boost to the Trust's public relations within the visiting and local communities.

The restoration has been a process of unimaginable scale and complexity. Priority was given to clearance, felling unwanted timber, levelling the ground and reinstating historic views such as the panorama from the Gothic Temple. The tree survey was a good starting-point for replanting, but the problem of the ornamental shrubberies, known to have existed from visitors' descriptions and botanical evidence in the archives, was acute since there was little or no field evidence. In the event planting plans were drawn up based on comparable period designs, enabling plantings to reappear in the amphitheatre, in shrubberies and on the Elysian Plain. As in other respects, this was pioneering work and has encouraged many other restoration schemes to reinstitute shrubberies, for instance at Croome Court and Stowe. Indeed, awareness has grown sharply in the last few years that shrubberies were a normal part of many eighteenth-century gardens large and small.[25]

Paths were originally of sand, gravel, closely-mown grass or just earth. Compromises had to be made to meet the demands of possibly extensive pedestrian traffic and also of heavy machinery. Some paths had to be widened and strengthened accordingly.

The lake required special attention, not least because, lying so close to – and approximately three metres above

– the River Mole, the intervening, retaining 'dam' would need to comply with the Reservoirs Act. Silt was the main problem, with decades of leaf litter from surrounding alders which filled almost its entire depth. The inlet below the Gothic Temple was virtually wooded. Removal of the silt was the priority, carried out in a process of ecological dredging that reflected a sensitive approach to all the earth works. The lake was cleared and cleaned in a way that ensured proper water flow between various features – the wheel and the cascade, the cascade arm of the lake and the main lagoon via the causeway. Some minor islands which were post-Hamilton and which blocked the view across the lake were removed.

Excavation of the cascade revealed that Hamilton's water system for feeding the lake had been severely disrupted by the introduction of the Bramah water wheel. In place of the brick culverts which brought the water from Hamilton's wheel to the lake, an iron pipe conducted the water from the Bramah wheel. Archaeology showed that a reservoir with clay, brick and mortar sides sat behind the cascade, and that the water was discharged in five places through the boulders.

The water wheel of the 1830s was still standing, though the iron blades were heavily rusted. The pump house walls were missing, but, amazingly, the machinery was structurally in place despite the loss of some parts and bearings. It was refurbished and set in working order during 1986. Eight working drawings by the firm of Bramah for the construction of the wheel and its pumping system were discovered in the Science Museum, though not until the works were almost complete. The restoration was found to match the drawings, a considerable tribute to the restorers in bringing this remarkable piece of industrial archaeology so accurately back to life.

Although Hamilton's 'Palladian' bridge in the foreground in Woollett's print has not yet been reconstructed, access from the west side of Grotto Island across to the mainland was essential, and a temporary wooden bridge was laid for the purpose. The archaeological team found the footings of the five-arch bridge (replaced by the present causeway a few yards to the east), and the remains confirmed that the bridge was of wood rendered to simulate stone.

The surviving historic buildings, bridges and their foundations were all in a ruinous state, with those no longer standing requiring complete reconstruction. The differing circumstances and considerations relating to

each of them, and not least the availability of funding, dictated a more flexible programme and varying methodology. This phased approach, whilst it may have some drawbacks, can be beneficial to visitors in that there is nearly always some new progress to see and enjoy.

The Gothic Temple was the first to be restored, starting on the basis of a dilapidated structure held up with scaffolding. Work was completed in 1985. It was possible to reconstruct the temple from what had survived, although it had been 'restored' more than once before, and care had to be taken to get back as far as possible to the original. A problem that particularly exercised the restorers was the original colouring of the interior. Paint scrapings were inconclusive, and the colour scheme adopted represents a consensus of opinions as to what the colours should be. Uncovering the dramatic views to and from the building, together with its restoration, created something of a sensation in the conservation media: it offered, for the first time, a snapshot of what the newly formed, and untested, Painshill Park Trust could achieve. This set in train a gradually evolving success story and continuing media interest, helping greatly with the raising of funds for each successive project.

The Mausoleum presented problems of a different kind. The connecting span had long since collapsed and disappeared, and its restoration was seen as both costly and low priority among the many other candidates for attention. It was stabilised, and the intention is that one day the span should be reinstated, but the building has not been entirely neglected. The archaeologists found about a fifth of the original paving buried, which provided sufficient of the pattern to enable the entire tiled floor to be reconstructed.

The Ruined Abbey was the next project after the Mausoleum and the first full archaeological excavation. What remained standing was most of the façade, supported by the remains of the side walls, and the decision was taken simply to stabilise and restore this structure, leaving any further reconstruction until a later date. The ground was excavated to uncover Hamilton's disastrous tileworks – passages, chambers and kilns. This was then covered up once more for protection to allow work to the abbey walls. It was re-rendered and lime-washed, though not with the scoring of lines to indicate stones as shown in the paintings of the abbey in its original state. The Trust plans to revisit and complete this project,

re-exposing the tileworks, with the protection of some form of roofing, for which there is evidence of a precedent, concealed within the abbey, following reinstatement of more of its structure.

The Gothic Tower was still standing, though with no roof, charred remains of window frames and the interior and stairwell completely burnt out. All missing parts and all four storeys were reconstructed, the spiral staircase simulating (though not replicating, because of exigencies of space) Hamilton's original staircase. The building was of brick, and has remained so in appearance although Hamilton rendered it to look like stone. The tower has been used as a dwelling for a warden and for other staff, and electricity and water are provided. It also serves as exhibition space.

The Turkish Tent presented its own unique difficulty, since it stood mostly on land owned by Heywoods (a Girl Guide Camp), outside the Trust's boundary. It had long since disappeared, but the foundations were still in place. The remains of the floor were uncovered and the area around excavated. Part of a herring-bone patterned brick floor laid on sand emerged, with an outline of the plan of the whole structure. This was in 1985, but it was another few years before reconstruction could begin. Since there was no question of doing so on the Guides' land, the site for the tent was moved to a location just within the Trust's boundary but which gave an equally fine view of the lake and several features of the landscape.

The tent has had to have two reconstructions, for pragmatic reasons. Initially the drapes were made of canvas, as was appropriate, but after a while, in addition to the detrimental effects of acid rain, they occasionally proved a little too tempting to children who enjoyed climbing and sliding down them, causing further damage to the canvas. There was accordingly a second renaissance of the tent with fibreglass drapes, which, though regrettable to the purist, have proved much more durable, particularly with planting to deter the young climbers. This project, typically for Painshill, is a good example of the fruits of collaboration between professionals working on site, in this case the archaeologist, the architect and the archivist, who was able to produce written descriptions and some contemporary illustrations. The background to the use of Turkish Tents in gardens was also researched.[26]

The Hermitage had also disappeared, though vestiges lasted longer than those of the tent. In this instance the new building, of wood, was designed on the basis of the sketch in the Bodleian Library (see page 94). From the front it has the authentic 'tree house' effect shown in the sketch, but the rear has not been restored as it was originally.

The Temple of Bacchus survived till about 1950, though in a perilous condition. The columns of its front portico had been removed to Pains Hill House in the 1920s, and the frieze was disposed of when the temple fell, or was pulled, down. Excavation revealed the foundations and the overall dimensions of the temple, together with a few artefacts like pieces of clay pipe. For many years the site remained with only a sign, but re-creation is now under way (the illustration opposite gives a computer-generated image of what the temple might look like). A wooden board with a picture of the temple, in correct size, was temporarily erected on scaffold where the portico once stood, and this gave a good idea of it. Again, the re-creation is to be based on archaeology, archival material, old images and the restorer's designs.

But the most difficult of all the buildings has proved to be the grotto. Not only was it in a state of complete devastation, with the roof collapsed and most of the ornamentation gone, but it is so large and so labour-intensive that restoration has been spread over many years. Sackfuls of satin spar were gathered from the ground, and the original quarry in Derbyshire was tracked down for supplements of 'blue john'. Seeking out new sources of the decorative minerals has been a considerable challenge, extending as far as Eastern Europe for traditional furnace slag and Morocco for supplies of hand-extracted fibrous gypsum. Reconstructing the stalactites is a slow and painstaking business, and has had to be halted from time to time through lack of labour and funds, and indeed the need to question and perhaps rethink the methodology. Apart from the decoration, the water effects within the grotto – water coming down the niche walls, pools in the floor – had to be reinstated, using an electric pump recycling water from the lake. The exterior cladding of 'tufa' has had to be repaired and augmented from the original quarries, which were still able to provide replacements. This applied furthermore to the other 'tufa' structures on the island, notably the arch, which has been restored while other outcrops have been excavated. The Trust is now planning a substantial new phase of work to complete the grotto.

Other artefacts included the horse-pump machinery near the giant cedar. What was left of the Roman Bath House (slightly post-Hamilton) was examined and may possibly be restored. The Sabine statue had survived on its plinth till about 1950, when it was sold off to a lead merchant for scrap. It was decided to commission the sculptor Ivor Abrahams to produce his own interpretation of the figures, though closely following the original – in this case Giambologna's sculpture in Florence. The result was a bronze group given a special patination to resemble lead (see page 51).

The restoration has had ramifications beyond the gardens. For example, there were problems with the water authorities over taking water from the River Mole when the wheel started operating again. A major problem was the siting of the visitor car park. The gardens were landlocked in the sense that the entrance from the old A3 was restricted to staff and could not be used for public access. There was, nevertheless, considerable local pressure to provide parking within the historic landscape. The Trust, liaising closely with both Surrey County Council and Elmbridge Council planning departments, hoped to keep visitor traffic away from Cobham town centre, with a route clearly visible from the A3. There were three applications to do this, bringing Painshill (A3) traffic, via a small roundabout, through land that had originally been part of the estate, on the other side of the river to reach a car park and a new footbridge across the river into the gardens. All three applications were refused and were appealed, leading to two public inquiries. This cost the Trust a great deal of money and time, though in fact the restoration benefited from restricted public access in the

This was followed in 2001 by a magnificent new Visitor and Education Centre, designed by Feilden Clegg Bradley, funded by the Heritage Lottery Fund and partnership donors. The Centre stands on an axis with the bridge and has won both praise and awards.

Despite a good many vicissitudes over the years, the restoration has continued along the road to its goal. It has received recognition as being both outstanding and innovative. The Trust was awarded the Europa Nostra Medal in 1998, a rare distinction, 'for the exemplary restoration, from a state of extreme neglect, of a most important 18th century landscape park and its extraordinary buildings'. Within the overall programme of works there have been a number of special projects, such as the 'American Roots' exhibition, based in the walled garden, which opened in the summer of 2005. The purpose was to tell the story of the importing of seeds and plants from North America in the eighteenth century and to display specimens, using bed patterns of the period. A secondary purpose was to build up a collection of all such material (not just the plants that Hamilton grew), in collaboration with the Bartram Garden in Philadelphia and working with several organisations in the United Kingdom, such as Kew. It thus represents the Bartram Collection in England.

meantime. Although the Trust won the appeals, it was then denied the land, leading to a compromise solution further along the riverside, bringing Painshill traffic nearer the town and giving visitors a winding approach and further to walk before reaching the footbridge and park entrance.

Although the Trust had welcomed visitors throughout the project under the twenty-eight day planning restriction, supplemented by pre-arranged group and school party visits, full public access was not achieved until the car park and modern access bridge were in place, with temporary ticket and tea-room provision,

Funding has, of course, been crucial at every stage of the project, and purchase of the land was only the start.

In order to implement all aspects of the Masterplan a substantial fund-raising programme was needed to meet capital costs, along with significant running costs over an extended period until such time as the park was fully open to visitors and able to pay its own way, which was the ultimate goal. With an early brief input of excellent professional fund-raising advice, the Trust has been able, for more than twenty years, to keep the annual fund-raising costs down while maximising the benefit of grants and donations to the project. The National Heritage Memorial Fund (now the Heritage Lottery Fund) has been a very important, long-term supporter, as has been English Heritage (formerly the Historic Buildings Council) and the Monuments Trust. The staffing provision through the former Manpower Services Commission, referred to earlier, represented a gift of great value to the project. Surrey County Council has given consistent and valued advice throughout the life of the Trust, and, especially latterly, Elmbridge Borough Council has given significant support. Generous funding, over many years, has also been given by private donors, together with a great number of grant-making trusts both large and small, and welcome support has come from the corporate sector. Painshill's appeal for capital funds will be ongoing until the completion of the full restoration and no doubt thereafter to fund more modest projects for the further benefit of visitors and the Trust's educational programme.

At the time of writing the restoration programme still has some way to go, and thus is still a story in progress. The unique history of the restoration is a subject that will require separate and more detailed treatment, and it is hoped that it will be told one day. In the short account here it would have been invidious to name one or two individuals and not countless others who have contributed significantly to this massive project, but that does not imply lack of awareness or appreciation.

OPPOSITE ABOVE AND BELOW The grotto in process of restoration.

RIGHT ABOVE The new entrance bridge.

RIGHT CENTRE Some of the produce from the vineyard on sale in the shop.

RIGHT BELOW The Visitor Centre.

Conclusion

Since 1980 writings on Hamilton and Painshill have been affected by the process of restoration and also encouraged by it. Research has continued into Hamilton's life and financial transactions and into visitors' accounts of Painshill during the eighteenth century. Some valuable descriptions by foreign visitors have come to light, such as those of the German architect FW von Erdmannsdorff in 1764, Zinzendorf in 1768, the Russian Princess Ekaterina Dashkova in 1770, the Hungarian Count Ferenc Szechenyi in 1787 and the Dutch Biljoen in 1791.[27] In addition to providing details which might not otherwise be known, such accounts convey the perceptions of visitors who not only came to England with different expectations and experiences of gardens but came to learn about them, often with a view to creating something similar back home.

It may still be too early to arrive at a definitive assessment of Hamilton and his achievements. While he has been rescued from comparative obscurity, his reputation stands well below that of such familiar figures as Brown or Kent. He should be thought of not only as an originator but that rarity: the originator who also brings a particular concept to the zenith of its expression. His ideas, though based on some things that had gone before, were new in extent and application, his planting was certainly new, and the fulfilment of his notion of controlled variety meant that, after Painshill, there was nothing better that could be created in the same genre. The balance between nature and art is finely and sensitively observed. Trees, parkland, contours, thickets and winding water are so ordered that their impact is maximised within the control of the points from which they are seen; and special visual effects not to be achieved by nature alone are brought about by means of the garden buildings. Art therefore creates a focus of interest and heightens mood.

On the one hand Hamilton achieved a liberation of nature while at the same time presenting it in an ideal pictorial form, the effect being enhanced by the judicious use of artefacts. Nature itself suggested different moods, and by the density or openness of planting and by the choice of different kinds of trees (dark conifers massed together, for instance) the visitor could be made to experience many kinds of thoughts and feelings.

Hamilton is important for leading from the still rather stylised landscape work of Kent to a freer and more open manner as well as developing the picture garden to its uttermost. As a horticulturist he paved the way for the explosion of interest in exotics, particularly in the nineteenth century, and it is a tribute to his choice and taste (one might say foresight) that the very trees and shrubs he helped to introduce from America – rhododendrons, azaleas and many kinds of fir and pine – have become ubiquitous in popularity and well and truly naturalised.

As John Wilkes wrote at the time, Hamilton created a veritable paradise.

References

THE GARDENS OF PAINSHILL *pages 6-13*

1 Joseph Warton, *An Essay on the Genius and Writings of Pope* (Dublin, 1782), II, p.244.
2 Emily J Climenson, *Elizabeth Montagu, The Queen of the Bluestockings: Her Correspondence from 1720 to 1761* (London, 1906), II, pp.75-6.
3 (Daniel Defoe), *A Tour through the Island of Great Britain* (Dublin, 1779, ninth edition), II, pp.206-7.
4 Rev S Duck, *Caesar's Camp: A Poem* (London, 1755), pp.17-18.
5 Thomas Whately, *Observations on Modern Gardening* (London: T Payne, 1793, fifth edition), pp.190-1, 192.
6 William Shenstone, *The Works in Verse and Prose* (London: R&J Dodsley, 1764), II, p.131.
7 Quoted in Dianne Barre, 'Sir Samuel Hellier (1736-84) and his Garden Buildings: Part of the Midlands "Garden Circuit" in the 1760s-70s?', *Garden History* 36:2, 2008, p.310.
8 *Ibid.*, p.125n.
9 Henry Home, Lord Kames, *Elements of Criticism* (Edinburgh, 1774), II, p.432.
10 *Ibid.*, p.437.
11 John Parnell, quoted in James Sambrook, 'Painshill Park in the 1760s', *Garden History* 8:1, 1980, p.97.
12 'A Gentleman', *A Tour thro' the Whole Island of Great Britain* (London: 1762, sixth edition), I, p.227.
13 Joseph Spence, *Observations, Anecdotes, and Characters of Books and Men*, ed. JM Osborn (Oxford: The Clarendon Press, 1966), I, §1137, p.426.
14 *Ibid.*, §1144a, p.427.
15 *Ibid.*, §1130, p.425.
16 *Ibid.*, §1104, p.419.
17 Richard Warner, *An Historical and Descriptive Account of Bath and its Environs* (Bath, 1802), p.107.
18 George Mason, *An Essay on Design in Gardening* (London, 1795 edition), p.102.
19 Arthur Young, *A Six Weeks Tour Through the Southern Counties of England and Wales* (London, 1768), p.192.
20 Spence, *Observations*, II, pp.646-50.

A BRIEF HISTORY OF THE ESTATE *pages 18-29*

1 The account given here is based on information contained in: a report by Land Use Consultants, 1982; Norman and Beryl Kitz, *Pains Hill Park: Hamilton and his picturesque landscape* (Cobham: Norman Kitz, 1984); research by David Taylor held in the Surrey History Centre, Painshill Park Archive, PPT/4/2/16/1; and typed mss by the late George Greenwood including notes in PPT/4/2/1/3.
2 Thomas Ruggles, 'On Planting and the Use of Trees', *Annals of Agriculture*, collected and published by Arthur Young (London, 1786), V, p.182.
3 N Salmon, *Antiquities of Surrey* (London, 1736), p.181.
4 John Parnell, 1763, quoted in James Sambrook, 'Painshill Park in the 1760s', *Garden History* 8:1, 1980, p.91.
5 Surrey History Centre, PPT/4/2/3/47.
6 *London and its Environs Described* (London: R&J Dodsley, 1761), V, p.101.
7 Henry Skrine, *A General Account of All the Rivers of Note in Great Britain* (London, 1801), p.373.
8 British Library, Holland House papers, Add Mss 51408, ff.152-3 and Add Mss 51426.
9 British Library, The Bowood (Lansdowne) Papers (Deposit 9516), B35 no.37, no date but not earlier than 1784.
10 Arthur Young, *A Course of Experimental Agriculture* (London, 1770), II, Book 5, pp.4-15.
11 *The Letters of Horace Walpole, Fourth Earl of Orford*, ed. Mrs P Toynbee

(Oxford, 1903), II, p.332.
12 Dr Richard Pococke, *Travels Through England*, ed. JJ Cartwright (London: Camden Society, 1889), II, p.166.
13 John Parnell, *Journal of a tour thro' England and Wales, Anno 1769*, London School of Economics and Political Science, ms Coll. Misc. 38, I, f.163.
14 Thomas Moule, *The English Counties Delineated* (London: George Virtue 1837), I, p.104.
15 Surrey History Centre, PPT/4/2/3/47.

THE HON. CHARLES HAMILTON *pages 30-49*

1 Horace Walpole, *The Yale Edition of Horace Walpole's Correspondence*, ed. WS Lewis (New Haven and Oxford: Yale University Press and Oxford University Press, 1980), 42, pp.88-90.
2 Lt. Col. George Hamilton, *A History of the House of Hamilton* (Edinburgh: J Skinner & Co., 1933), p.42.
3 Joseph Spence, *Observations, Anecdotes, and Characters of Books and Men*, ed. JM Osborn (Oxford: Clarendon Press, 1966), I, §1103, p.417.
4 Surrey History Centre, Painshill Park Archive, PPT/4/2/2.
5 Spence, *Observations*, I, §1103, p.417.
6 British Library, Bentinck papers, Egerton mss. 1711.
7 *Ibid.*
8 Lucy Moore, *Amphibious Thing: The Life of Lord Hervey* (Harmondsworth: Viking/Penguin, 2000), p.88.
9 Letter from Lord Hervey to Stephen Fox, 23 August 1731, quoted in *Lord Hervey and his Friends 1726-38*, ed. Earl of Ilchester (London: John Murray, 1950), p.78.
10 Spence, *Anecdotes*, I, §1103, p.417.
11 Joseph Spence, *Letters from the Grand Tour*, ed. S Klima (Montreal and London: McGill-Queen's University Press, 1975), pp.419-20.
12 British Library, Holland House papers, Add Mss 51408, f.101.
13 See George Clarke, 'The Gardens of Stowe', *Apollo*, June 1973, p.568.
14 Moore, *Amphibious Thing*, p.208.
15 AN Newman, 'The Political Patronage of Frederick Lewis, Prince of Wales', *The Historical Journal*, 1:1. 1958, pp.68-9.
16 Lord Edmond Fitzmaurice, *Life of William, Earl of Shelburne* (London: Macmillan & Co., 1875), I, p.60.
17 *Ibid.*, pp.61-2.
18 *Ibid.*, p.63.
19 *Ibid.*
20 Spence, *Anecdotes*, I, §1103, p.418.
21 Dorset Record Office, Ilchester papers, D124, Box 240.
22 British Library, Holland House papers, Add Mss 51417.
23 *Ibid.*
24 Sussex Record Office, correspondence, Duke of Richmond to the Duke of Newcastle, 7 June 1745.
25 Dorset Record Office, Ilchester papers, D124, Box 240.
26 British Library, Holland House papers, Add Mss 51418.
27 Letter from Elizabeth Wyndham to Hester Grenville, 13 November 1746, The National Archives, Chatham, 30/8/34, f.104.
28 British Library, Collinson papers, Add Mss 28727.
29 British Library, Holland House papers, Add Mss 51419.
30 British Library, Add Mss 48218, f.1.
31 *Ibid.*, f.2.
32 British Library, Holland House papers, Add Mss 51403, f.177.
33 Letter of Lady Luxborough to William Shenstone, cited in Surrey History Centre, PPT/4/2/2/73.
34 Joseph Farington, *The Farington Diary*, ed. J Greig (London: Hutchinson & Co., 1924), III, p.222.
35 Thomas Faulkner, *History and Antiquities of Kensington* (London: T Egerton & Co., 1820), p.121.

36 *Mrs Montagu, 'Queen of the Blues', Her Letters and Friendships from 1762 to 1800*, ed. R Blunt (London: Constable, 1923), I, p.123.
37 British Library, Collinson papers, Add Mss 28727, f.20.
38 British Library, Holland House papers, Add Mss 51408, f.98.
39 *Ibid.*, f.99.
40 Earl of Ilchester, *Henry Fox, First Lord Holland* (London: John Murray, 1920), I, p.60.
41 *Ibid.*
42 Public Record Office of Northern Ireland, Abercorn papers, T2541.
43 *Ibid.*
44 Dorset Record Office, Ilchester papers, D124, Box 240.
45 *Ibid.*
46 British Library, Holland House papers, Add Mss 51408, ff.100-1.
47 Fitzmaurice, *Shelburne*, II, p.15.
48 British Library, Holland House papers, Add Mss 51420.
49 Fitzmaurice, *Shelburne*, II, p.15.
50 British Library, Holland House papers, Add Mss 51408, f.104.
51 *Ibid.*, f.105.
52 *Ibid.*, Add Mss 51420.
53 *Ibid.*, Add Mss 51408, f.106.
54 *Ibid.*, ff.108 and 109 verso.
55 British Library, Bute papers, Ms 570 6.D, f.84.
56 See Michael Cousins, '"As for Paradise, which is but another Name for Kingsgate"', *Follies* 12:2, 2000, p.8.
57 British Library, Holland House papers, Add Mss 51408, f.114.
58 *Ibid.*, f.116 verso.
59 *Ibid.*, f.118.
60 *Ibid.*, f.119 verso.
61 PRONI, Abercorn papers, T2541.
62 British Library, Collinson papers, Add Mss 28727, f.109.
63 British Library, Holland House papers, Add Mss 51408, ff.130-4.
64 *Ibid.*, f.125.
65 Hoare's Bank Archives, Mortgages 1743-73 (1766).
66 *Ibid.*, f.139 and verso.
67 The National Archives, Chatham papers, 30/8/39, f.63.
68 *Ibid.*, f.65.
69 British Library, Holland House papers, Add Mss 51413, ff.109, 114, 132, 138, 144, 163, 186, 199, 206 and 209.
70 Michael Blackman, *A Short History of Walton-on-Thames* (Walton and Weybridge Local History Society, 1989), p.24.
71 See Kenneth Woodbridge, *The Stourhead Landscape* (National Trust, 1982), p.27.
72 PRONI, Abercorn papers, D623/A/9.
73 British Library, Holland House papers, Add Mss 51408, ff.142 and 143 verso.
74 *Ibid.*, f.144 verso.
75 *Ibid.*, f.146.
76 Letter from Molly Hood to Lady Chatham, 30 May 1773, cited in Mike Cousins, 'The Grotto, Ascot Place, Berkshire:- another Lane grotto?', *Follies*, 67, 2007, p.11.
77 British Library, Holland House papers, Add Mss 51408, f.146 verso..
78 *Letters and Diaries of Mary Hamilton*, ed. E and F Anson (London: John Murray, 1925), p.27.
79 PRONI, Abercorn papers, T2541.
80 *Ibid.*, D623/A/10/2.
81 Bath Council Minutes, 22 September 1777.
82 *Ibid.*, 4 October 1779, 27 March 1780, 5 January 1781.
83 Personal communication from Rosemary Harriott.
84 Richard Warner, *An Historical and Descriptive Account of Bath and its Environs* (Bath, 1802), p.106.
85 Hamilton Papers, quoted in JW Oliver, *The Life of William Beckford* (London: Oxford University Press, 1932), p.74.
86 Cyrus Redding, *Memoirs of William Beckford of Fonthill, Author of*

'*Vathek*' (London: Skeet, 1859), II, p.148.
87 PRONI, Abercorn papers, T2541/EA2/2.
88 Warner, *Account of Bath*, p.107.
89 Surrey History Centre, correspondence from Hamilton to Beckford, PPT/4/2/2/73.
90 Bodleian Library, Shelburne papers (microfilm), 49, ff.10-12.
91 R.G., 'Bowood, the Seat of the Marquis of Lansdowne', *The Gardeners Chronicle*, 1845, p.755.
92 See Michael Symes, 'Charles Hamilton at Bowood', *Garden History* 34:2, 2006, pp.210-11.
93 British Library, Add Mss 33539, f.206.
94 Richard Warner, *Excursions from Bath* (London, 1801), p.210.
95 Edward Edwards, *Anecdotes of Painting* (London, 1808), p.v.
96 Walpole, *Correspondence*, 33, p.527.

HAMILTON THE COLLECTOR *pages 50-61*
1 Louise Lippincott, *Selling Art in Georgian London: The Rise of Arthur Pond* (New Haven and London: Yale University Press, 1983).
2 *Ibid.*, p.40.
3 *Ibid.*, p.44.
4 British Library, Add Mss 23724, f.49.
5 *Ibid.*, f.30.
6 *Ibid.*, ff.67,69.
7 *Ibid.*, f.74.
8 Lippincott, *Selling Art*, p.112.
9 Richard Pococke, *Travels Through England*, ed. JJ Cartwright (London: Camden Society, 1889), II, p.166.
10 List attached to letter of 17 November 1765 to Henry Fox, British Library, Holland House papers, Add MS 51408, ff.132-3.
11 Michael Symes, *William Gilpin at Painshill* (Cobham: Painshill Park Trust, 1994), p.32.
12 The Royal Bank of Scotland Group Archives, Box 48 (1764).
13 Joseph Spence, *Observations, Anecdotes, and Characters of Books and Men*, ed. JM Osborn (Oxford: Clarendon Press, 1966), §1103, p.418.
14 Allan Cunningham, *The Lives of the Most Eminent British Painters, Sculptors, and Architects* (London: John Murray, 1830), III, pp.78-9.
15 Alastair Laing, 'Bacchus the Wanderer', *Apollo* National Trust supplement: Historic Houses and Collections, 2008, p.25.
16 *Ibid.*, p.27.
17 *Ibid.*, p.25.
18 Jan Clark, 'The Travails of Bacchus', *Talking Heads: Garden Statuary in the Eighteenth Century* (Buckinghamshire Gardens Trust, 2007), p.22.
19 *Ibid.*, p.23.
20 Laing, 'Bacchus the Wanderer', p.29.

THE LAKE *pages 62-75*
1 Count Frederick Kielmansegge, *Diary of a Journey to England in the years 1761-1762*, trans. Countess Kielmansegge (London: Longmans & Co., 1902), p.56.
2 Quoted in John Fleming, *Robert Adam and his Circle in Edinburgh and Rome* (London: John Murray, 1962), p.265.
3 George Mason, *An Essay on Design in Gardening* (London, 1795), p.17.
4 Thomas Whately, *Observations on Modern Gardening* (London: T Payne, 1793, fifth edition), p.191.
5 EW Brayley, *A Topographical History of Surrey* (London: Virtue & Co., 1878–81), II, p.122n.
6 Whately, *Observations*, p.63.
7 Kielmansegge, *Diary*, pp.55-6.
8 Whately, *Observations*, p.196.
9 J Trusler, *Elements of Modern Gardening* (London, 1784), p.39.
10 *Ibid.*, p.43.
11 Michael Symes, *William Gilpin at Painshill* (Cobham: Painshill Park Trust, 1994), p.30.

12 See James Sambrook, 'Painshill park in the 1760's', *Garden History* 8:1, 1980, p.92.

13 Whately, *Observations*, p.196.

14 Michael Symes, 'Robert FitzGerald's tour of Surrey gardens', *Journal of Garden History* 6:4, 1986, pp.323-4.

15 William Bray, diary entry for 4 May 1755, transcribed by Mavis Collier, Surrey History Centre, Painshill Park Archive, PPT/4/2/3/29.

16 R&J Dodsley, *London and its Environs* (London, 1761), V, p.101.

17 Richard Pococke, *Travels through England*, ed. JJ Cartwright (London: Camden Society, 1889), II, p.166.

18 British Library, Holland House papers, Add MSS 51408, ff.151 and verso.

19 Symes, 'Robert FitzGerald', p.323.

20 Joseph Spence, *Observations, Anecdotes, and Characters of Books and Men*, ed. JM Osborn (Oxford: Clarendon Press, 1966), I, §1102, pp.417-8. The wheel at Marly on the Seine, constructed 1681-7, raised water 200 feet to an aqueduct.

21 Kielmansegge, *Diary*, p.56.

22 *Surrey Archaeological Collections* (London: Surrey Archaeological Society), 58, 1961, p.63.

23 *Gentleman's Magazine*, February 1771, p.57.

24 The Royal Bank of Scotland Group Archives, Boxes 60 (1770), f.575, and 62 (1771), f.140.

25 Birmingham Archives and Heritage Service, Matthew Boulton papers, Ms 3782/12/108/7, Notebook 8, 1772, p.17.

26 Translated from Bélanger's French caption to the sketch of the water-wheel in Kenneth Woodbridge, 'Bélanger en Angleterre: son carnet de voyage', *Architectural History* 25, 1982, p.17.

27 William Robertson, 'Travel Diary', National Library of Ireland, ms 248, ff.106-7.

28 Brayley, *History of Surrey*, II, p.124.

29 Drummonds Bank Archives, Box 38 (1759).

30 University of Nottingham, Newcastle Archives, NeC 4317a-4318b.

31 Arthur Young, *A Six Weeks' tour through the Southern Counties of England and Wales* (London, 1768), pp.189-90.

32 Kielmansegge, *Diary*, p.56.

33 Robertson, 'Travel Diary', p.104.

THE BUILDINGS *pages 76-95*

1 William Robertson, Travel Diary, National Library of Ireland, ms 248, f.108.

2 Thomas Whately, *Observations on Modern Gardening* (London: T Payne, 1793, fifth edition), pp.196-7.

3 *Thomas Jefferson's Garden Book 1766-1824*, ed. EM Betts (Philadelphia: American Philosophical Society, 1944), p.112.

4 EW Brayley, *A Topographical History of Surrey* (London: Virtue & Co., 1878-81), II, p.124.

5 Letter of Henry Hoare to his daughter Susanna, 23 October 1762, quoted in Kenneth Woodbridge, *Landscape and Antiquity: Aspects of English Culture at Stourhead 1718 to 1838* (Oxford: Clarendon Press, 1970), p.52.

6 J Hassell, *Picturesque Rides and Walks* (London, 1818), II, p.268.

7 Tessa Murdoch, 'The Huguenots and English Rococo', *The Rococo in England: A Symposium* (London: Victoria and Albert Museum, 1986), pp.76-7.

8 The Royal Bank of Scotland Group Archives, Boxes 31 (1752), 32 (1753) and 33 (1754).

9 Horace Walpole, 'Journals of Visits to Country Seats, &c.', *The Walpole Society*, 16, 1928, p.37.

10 Brayley, *History of Surrey*, II, p.123.

11 Arthur Young, *A Six Weeks Tour through the Southern Counties of England and Wales* (London: W Nicoll, 1768), p.189.

12 Batty Langley, *New Principles of Gardening* (London, 1728), Plate XX.

13 J Hassell, *Picturesque Rides*, II, p.267.

14 L Collison-Morley, *Companion into Surrey* (London: Methuen & Co., 1938, revised 1949), p.145.

15 Michael Symes, *William Gilpin at Painshill* (Cobham: Painshill Park Trust, 1994), pp.30 and 34.

16 *Walpole Society* 16, pp.36-7.

17 William Keene, *The Beauties of Surrey* (London, 1849), p.36.

18 Hassell, Picturesque Rides, II, p.268.

19 Whately, *Observations*, p.190.

20 Robertson, Travel Diary, f.107.

21 John Vanbrugh to the Earl of Manchester, 18 July 1707, quoted in Geoffrey Beard, *The Work of John Vanbrugh* (London: Batsford, 1986), p.51.

22 Alistair Rowan, *Garden Buildings* (Feltham: Country Life, 1968), p.49.

23 Horace Walpole, *The History of the Modern Taste in Gardening* (New York: Ursus Press, 1995, orig. 1770), p.53.

24 Joseph Spence, *Observations, Anecdotes, and Characters of Books and Men*, ed. JM Osborn (Oxford: Clarendon Press, 1966), I, §1101, p.417.

25 Whately, *Observations*, p.194.

26 Spence, *Observations*, I, p.417, §1101.

27 John Seward, *The Spirit of Anecdote and Wit* (London, 1823), II, p.309.

28 JT Smith, *A Book for a Rainy Day*, ed. W Whitten (London, 1905, orig. 1845), p.289n.

THE EXOTIC AND ORIENTAL *pages 96-107*

1 See James Sambrook, 'Painshill park in the 1760's', *Garden History*, 8:1, 1980, pp.92-3.

2 The Royal Bank of Scotland Group Archives, Box 48 (1764).

3 *Ibid.*, Boxes 50 (1765) and 52 (1766).

4 *Ibid.*, Box 58 (1769).

5 *Ibid.*, Boxes 58 (1769), 60 (1770) and 64 (1772).

6 *Ibid.*, Box 64 (1772).

7 For an account of the Fuller White saga at Clumber, see Michael Symes, 'The Garden Designs of Stephen Wright', *Garden History* 20:1, 1992, pp.21-2.

8 The Royal Bank of Scotland Group Archives, Boxes 56 (1768) and 58 (1769).

9 Nottingham University Library, Newcastle Archives, NeA 690/100a.

10 Quoted by Osvald Sirén in *China and Gardens of Europe of the Eighteenth Century* (Washington: Dumbarton Oaks, 1990, reprint from 1950), p.46.

11 Lady Newdigate, 'Travel Journal' ms., Warwickshire County Record Office, CR 1841/7, f.23.

12 For the arguments, see, for example, the summary provided by David Jacques, 'On the Supposed Chineseness of the English Landscape Garden', *Garden History* 18:2, 1990, pp.180-91.

13 Lord Macartney, *An Embassy to China*, introduction by Jonathan Spence and edited by JL Cranmer-Byng (London: Folio Society, 2004), p.73.

14 Jean-Baptiste Du Halde, *Description Geographique, Historique, Chronologique De L'Empire de la Chine, et de la Tartarie Chinoise* (Paris: PG Le Mercier, 1735), I, pp.74 and 243.

15 William Robertson, 'Travel Journal', National Library of Ireland, ms 248, ff.104, 106.

16 Barbara Jones, *Follies & Grottoes* (London: Constable, 1974), p.40n1.

17 Sirén, *China and Gardens of Europe*, p.8.

18 Maggie Keswick, *The Chinese Garden: History, Art and Architecture* (London: Frances Lincoln, 2003, revised ed.), pp.24-32. See in particular illustrations on pp.86, 168 and 182.

19 Quoted in Sirén, *China and Gardens of Europe*, p.46.

20 Geoffrey and Susan Jellicoe, *The Landscape of Man: Shaping the Environment from Prehistory to the Present Day* (London: Thames & Hudson, 1975), p.243.

HAMILTON'S TREES AND SHRUBS *pages 108-119*

1 Horace Walpole, *The History of the Modern Taste in Gardening* (New York: Ursus Press, 1995, orig. 1770), p.46.

2 JC Loudon, *Encyclopedia of Gardening* (London, 1830), p.1667, §7527.

3 John Parnell, *Journal of a tour thro' England and Wales, Anno 1769*, London School of Economics and Political Science, ms. Coll. Misc. 38, I, ff.150-1.

4 Lady Newdigate, 'Travel Journal' ms., Warwickshire County Record Office, CR 1841/7, f.23.

5 *The Correspondence of John Bartram 1734-1777*, ed. Edmund Berkeley and Dorothy Smith Berkeley (Florida: University of Florida Press, 1992), pp.285, 291.

6 *Ibid.*, p.299.

7 Letter from Hamilton to Peter Collinson, American Philosophical Society, Philadelphia, ms., B C 692.1.

8 *Ibid.*

9 The Royal Bank of Scotland Group Archives, Box 33 (1754).

10 Information on Alexander Eddie from Kath Clark.

11 The Royal Bank of Scotland Group Archives, Box 37 (1758).

12 Hoare's Bank Archives, Ledger 84 (1771-2).

13 The Royal Bank of Scotland Group Archives, Box 109 (1786).

14 Public Record Office of Northern Ireland, Abercorn papers, D.623/A/10/1.

15 *Ibid.*, D.623/A/8/1-23.

16 Thomas Moule, *The English Counties Delineated* (London, 1837), I, p.104.

17 AB Lambert, *A Description of the Genus Pinus* (London, 1803), I, p.i.

18 James Malcolm, *A Compendium of Modern Husbandry* (London, 1805), p.257.

19 JC Loudon, *Arboretum et Fruticetum Britannicum* (London, 1838), I, p.71.

20 Birmingham Archives and Heritage Sevice, Matthew Boulton papers, Ms 3782/12/108/7, Notebook 8, 1772, p.16.

21 The Royal Bank of Scotland Group Archives, Boxes 64 (1772) and 66 (1773).

22 Thomas Whately, *Observations on Modern Gardening* (London: T Payne, 1793, fifth edition), p.189.

23 Richard Pococke, *Travels Through England*, ed. JJ Cartwright (London: Camden Society, 1889), II, p.166.

24 James Sambrook, 'Painshill Park in the 1760's', *Garden History* 8:1, 1980, p.92.

25 *Ibid.*

26 Whately, *Observations*, p.193.

27 Walpole, *History*, p.52.

28 Sambrook, 'Painshill Park', p.95.

29 Parnell, *Journal*, I, f.163.

IMAGES OF PAINSHILL *pages 120-133*

1 See Michael Symes, *William Gilpin at Painshill* (Cobham: Painshill Park Trust, 1994), pp.20-4.

2 *Sayer and Bennett's Catalogue of Prints for 1775* (London: Holland Press, 1970, facsimile reprint), p.35.

3 John Harris, *The Artist and the Country House* (London: Sotheby Parke Bernet, 1979), p.254.

4 The Royal Bank of Scotland Group Archives, Box 68 (1774).

5 David R Coffin, *The English Garden: Meditation and Memorial* (Princeton, New Jersey: Princeton University Press, 1994), p.32.

6 Mavis Collier and David Wrightson, 'The Re-Creation of the Turkish Tent at Painshill', *Garden History* 21:1, 1993, p.52.

7 Public Record Office of Northern Ireland, Abercorn papers, D.623/A/10/6.

8 Kenneth Woodbridge, 'Bélanger en Angleterre: Son carnet de voyage', *Architectural History* 25, 1982, pp.8-19.

HAMILTON AND THE PICTURESQUE *pages 134-143*

1 Horace Walpole, *The History of the Modern Taste in Gardening* (New York: Ursus Press, 1995, orig. 1770), pp.52-3, orig.1770.

2 Thomas Whately, *Observations on Modern Gardening* (London: T Payne, fifth edition, 1793), pp.193-4.

3 John Parnell, *Journal of a tour thro' England and Wales, Anno 1769*, London School of Economics and Political Science, Ms Coll. Misc.38, I.f.161.

4 *The Works in Verse and Prose of William Shenstone, Esq.* (London: R&J Dodsley, 1764), II, p.126.

5 *Ibid.*, p.137.

6 Lord Kames (Henry Home), *Elements of Criticism* (Edinburgh, fifth edition, 1774), p.437.

7 [William Gilpin], *A Dialogue Upon the Gardens...at Stow* (London: B Seeley, 1748), p.6.

8 Uvedale Price, *An Essay on the Picturesque* (London: J Robson, 1794), pp.44-5.

9 (ed.) Sir Thomas Dick Lauder, *Sir U. Price on the Picturesque* (Edinburgh, 1842), p.231.

10 Price, *Essay*, p.277.

11 Lauder, *Price*, p.230.

12 *Ibid.*, p.232.

13 *Ibid.*, p.230.

14 Uvedale Price, Esq., *A Dialogue on the Distinct Characters of the Picturesque and the Beautiful* (London: J Robson, 1801), pp.104ff.

15 George Mason, *An Essay on Design in Gardening* (London: B&J White, 1795), p.206.

16 Thomas Gray, *Works*, ed. John Mitford (London, 1858), III, p.120n.

17 [S Ward], 'An Essay on the Different Natural Situations of Gardens', contained in Thomas Whately, *Observations on Modern Gardening* (London: 'new edition', 1801), p.148.

18 Richard Warner, *An Historical and Descriptive Account of Bath and its Environs* (Bath, 1802), p.107.

19 Letter from Henry Hoare to his grand-daughter Harriot, November 1771, quoted in Kenneth Woodbridge, *The Stourhead Landscape* (London: The National Trust, 1982), p.27.

THE VINEYARD *pages 144-149*

1 For all the information concerning David Geneste, see Claude Martin, 'David Geneste – a Huguenot Vine Grower at Cobham', *Surrey Archaeological Collections* LXVIII, 1971, pp.153-60.

2 Dr Richard Pococke, *Travels Through England*, ed. JJ Cartwright (London: Camden Society, 1889), II, p.166.

3 The Royal Bank of Scotland Group Archives, Box 36 (1757).

4 See Michael Symes, *Fresh Woods and Pastures New: The Plantings at Painshill* (Wallington: author, 2006), pp.44-5.

5 John H Harvey, 'A Scottish Botanist in London in 1766', *Garden History* 9:1, 1981, p.62.

6 FX Vispré, *A Dissertation on the Growth of Wine in England* (Bath, 1786), p.51.

7 *Ibid.*, p.51n.

8 William Robertson, 'Travel Diary', National Library of Ireland, ms 248, f.96.

9 Rev. O Manning and W Bray, *The History and Antiquities of Surrey* (London, 1809), II, p.769.

10 JC Loudon, *Encyclopaedia of Gardening* (London, 1830), §216, p.949.

11 Martin, 'Geneste', p.156.

12 Sir Edward Barry, *Observations Historical, Critical, and Medical on the Wines of the Ancients and the Analogy between them and Modern Wines* (London: Cadell, 1775), p.471.

13 William Cobbett, *The English Gardener* (London, 1829), §285.

14 Journal of a journey by Thomas Kyle, ms., East Riding Archives and Local Studies, DDCC/150/294.

15 Barry, *Observations*, p.471.

16 *Ibid.*, pp.471-6.

17 Pococke, *Travels*, p.166.

18 Warwick Wroth, *The London Pleasure Gardens of the Eighteenth Century* (London: Macmillan, 1896), pp.298-9.

19 Michael Symes, 'Robert FitzGerald's tour of Surrey gardens', *Journal of Garden History* 6:4, 1986, p.324.

AFTERMATH AND RESTORATION *pages 150-163*

1 James Thorne, *Handbook to the Environs of London* (Bath: Adams and Dart, 1970, orig. 2 vols, 1876), p.113.

2 George Mason, *An Essay on Design in Gardening* (London: B&J White, 1795), p.viii.

3 *Ibid.*, p.53n.

4 The three visits are listed in Surrey History Centre, Painshill Park Archive, PPT/4/2/3/C31.

5 Rev. O Manning and W Bray, *The History and Antiquities of Surrey* (London: J White, 1809), II, pp.768-9.

6 EW Brayley, *A Topographical History of Surrey*, rev. and ed. E Walford (London: Virtue & Co., 1878–81), II, pp.120-1.

7 Thomas Moule, *The English Counties Delineated* (London, 1837), I, p.104.

8 J Weale (ed.), *The Pictorial Handbook of London* (London: HG Bohn, 1854), p.528.

9 J Hassell, *Picturesque Rides and Walks* (London, 1818), II, p.265.

10 *The Works of Thomas Gray*, ed. Rev. J Mitford (London, 1858), III, p.120n.

11 *Country Life*, I, 6 March 1897, pp.239-40.

12 *Country Life*, XV, 19 March 1904, p.414.

13 *Ibid.*, p.420.

14 Elizabeth Wheeler Manwaring, *Italian Landscape in Eighteenth Century England* (London: Frank Cass, 1965, orig. 1925), p.155.

15 Christopher Hussey, *The Picturesque: Studies in a Point of View* (London and New York: GP Putnam's Sons, 1927), p.134.

16 Christopher Tunnard, *Gardens in the Modern Landscape* (London: The Architectural Press, 1938), pp.25-32.

17 Hon. Alicia Amherst, *Historic Gardens of England* (London: Country Life, 1938), p.176.

18 HF Clark, *The English Landscape Garden* (Gloucester: Alan Sutton, 1980, orig. 1948), pp.55-7.

19 Osvald Sirén, *China and Gardens of Europe of the Eighteenth Century* (Washington, DC: Dumbarton Oaks, 1990, orig. 1950), p.44.

20 *Country Life*, 9 January 1958, p.63.

21 *The Shell Gardens Book*, ed. Peter Hunt (London: Phoenix Rainbird, 1964), p.24.

22 Edward Malins, *English Landscaping and Literature 1660-1840* (London: Oxford University Press, 1966), p.121.

23 Miles Hadfield, *A History of British Gardening* (Feltham: Spring Books, 1969), p.207.

24 Geoffrey and Susan Jellicoe, *The Landscape of Man: Shaping the Environment from Prehistory to the Present Day* (London: Thames & Hudson, 1975), p.242.

25 See Mark Laird, *The Flowering of the Landscape Garden: English Pleasure Grounds, 1720-1800* (Philadelphia: University of Pennsylvania Press, 1999).

26 Mavis Collier and David Wrightson, 'The Re-creation of the Turkish Tent at Painshill', *Garden History* 21:1, 1993, pp.46-59.

27 See *For the Friends of Nature and Art* (Wörlitz: Institut für Auslandsbeziehungen, Kulturstiftung Dessau Wörlitz, 1997), pp.52-3; Géza Hajós, 'The gardens of the British Isles in the diary of the Austrian Count Karl von Zinzendorf in the year 1768', *Journal of Garden History* 9:1, 1989, p.43; Anthony Cross, 'The English garden in Catherine the Great's Russia', *Journal of Garden History* 13:3, 1993, p.173; Jozsef Sisa, 'Count Ferenc Széchényi's visit to English parks and gardens in 1787', *Garden History* 22:1, 1994, p.65; and Heimerick Tromp, 'A Dutchman's Visits to Some English Gardens in 1791', *Journal of Garden History* 2:1, 1982, p.46.

Select Bibliography

ARCHIVES CONSULTED

Birmingham Archives and Heritage Service, Matthew Boulton papers

Bodleian Library, Shelburne papers (microfilm)

British Library, Holland House papers; Bentinck papers (Egerton mss); Collinson papers; Arthur Pond, 'Journal of Receipts and Expenses From 1743-1750'

British Library of Political and Economic Science, London School of Economics and Political Science, John Parnell, 'Journal of a tour thro' England and Wales, Anno 1769'

Dorset Record Office, Ilchester papers

The Royal Bank of Scotland Group Archives

East Riding Record Office, report of a journey by Thomas Kyle, 1761

Folger Shakespeare Library, Washington, DC, John Parnell, 'An Account of the many fine Seats of Nobles I have seen, with other Observations made during my Residence in England in 1763'

Hoare's Bank Archives, Mortgages 1743-73

National Archives, Chatham papers

National Library of Ireland, 'A Journal by Wm Robertson, Archt 1795'

Public Record Office of Northern Ireland, Abercorn papers

Surrey History Centre, Painshill Park Trust Archives

Warwickshire County Record Office, 'Travel Journal of Lady Newdigate, wife of Sir Roger Newdigate of Arbury, 1748'

Precise references are to be found in the References.

BOOKS

A Tour through the Island of Great Britain [orig. by Daniel Defoe], 8th edition, 1778

Sir Edward Barry, *Observations Historical, Critical, and Medical on the Wines of the Ancients and the Analogy between them and Modern Wines*, Cadell, London, 1775

EW Brayley, rev. and ed. E Walford, *A Topographical History of Surrey, Vol II*, Virtue & Co., London, 1878–81

HF Clark, *The English Landscape Garden,* Alan Sutton, Gloucester, 1980 (orig. 1948)

Lord Edmond Fitzmaurice, *Life of William, Earl of Shelburne, Vol I*, Macmillan & Co., London, 1875

Miles Hadfield, *A History of British Gardening*, Spring Books, London, 1963

Lt Col George Hamilton, *A History of the House of Hamilton*, J. Skinner & Co., Edinburgh, 1933

J Hassell, *Picturesque Rides and Walks*, Vol II, London, 1818

Christopher Hussey, *The Picturesque: Studies in a Point of View*, GP Putnam's Sons, London and New York, 1927

Ed. Earl of Ilchester, *Lord Hervey and his Friends 1726-38*, John Murray, London, 1950

David Jacques, *Georgian Gardens: The Reign of Nature*, Batsford, London, 1983

Geoffrey and Susan Jellicoe, *The Landscape of Man: Shaping the Environment from Prehistory to the Present Day*, Thames & Hudson, London, 1975

William Keane, *The Beauties of Surrey*, London, 1849

Count Frederick Kielmansegge, trans. Countess Kielmansegg, *Diary of a Journey to England in the years 1761-1762*, Longmans & Co., London, 1902

Norman and Beryl Kitz, *Pains Hill Park: Hamilton and his picturesque landscape*, N Kitz, Cobham, 1984

Mark Laird, *The Flowering of the Landscape Garden: English Pleasure Grounds, 1720-1800*, University of Pennsylvania Press, Philadelphia, 1999

AB Lambert, *A Description of the Genus Pinus,* Vol I, London, 1803

Louise Lippincott, *Selling Art in Georgian London: The Rise of Arthur Pond*, Yale University Press, London, 1983

London and its Environs Described, Vol V, R & J Dodsley, London, 1761

Revd O Manning and W Bray, *The History and Antiquities of Surrey*, Vol II, J White, London, 1809

Elizabeth Wheeler Manwaring, *Italian Landscape in Eighteenth Century England*, Frank Cass & Co., London, 1965 (orig. 1925)

George Mason, *An Essay on Design in Gardening*, London, 1768 and 1795 (revised ed.)

Thomas Moule, *The English Counties Delineated*, Vol I, George Virtue, London, 1837

GF Prosser, *Select Illustrations of the County of Surrey*, C & J Rivington, London, 1828

Tim Richardson, *The Arcadian Friends: Inventing the English Landscape Garden*, Bantam Press, London, 2007

Osvald Sirén, *China and Gardens of Europe of the Eighteenth Century*, Dumbarton Oaks, Washington DC, 1990 (orig. 1950)

Joseph Spence, ed. JM Osborn, *Observations, Anecdotes, and Characters of Books and Men*, Vol I, Clarendon Press, Oxford, 1966

Michael Symes, *William Gilpin at Painshill*, Painshill Park Trust, Cobham, 1994

Michael Symes, *Fresh Woods and Pastures New: The Plantings at Painshill*, Michael Symes, Wallington 2006

Christopher Tunnard, *Gardens in the Modern Landscape*, The Architectural Press, London, 1938

Horace Walpole, *The History of the Modern Taste in Gardening* [1770], Ursus Press, New York, 1995

GA Walpoole, *The New British Traveller*, London, 1784

Thomas Weiss and Ursula Bode, *For the Friends of Nature and Art*, Kulturstiftung Dessau Wörlitz, Gerd Hatje, Ostfildern-Ruit, 1997

Thomas Whately, *Observations on Modern Gardening*, published for T Payne, London, 1770

Arthur Young, *A Six Weeks Tour Through the Southern Counties of England and Wales*, W Nicoll, London, 1768

Tim Richardson, 'Painshill, Surrey', *Country Life*, 4 January 2001

Tim Richardson, 'Lights Fantastic' [Painshill at night], *Country Life*, 9 December 2004

James Sambrook, 'Painshill Park in the 1760's', *Garden History* 8:1, 1980

Joseph Sisa, 'Count Ferenc Széchényi's visit to English parks and gardens in 1787', *Garden History* 22:1, 1994

Michael Symes, 'Charles Hamilton's Plantings at Painshill', *Garden History* 11:2, 1983

Michael Symes, 'The Hon. Charles Hamilton at Holland Park', *Journal of Garden History* 3:2, 1983

Michael Symes, 'Nature as the Bride of Art: The Design and Structure of Painshill', *British and American Gardens in the Eighteenth Century*, ed. Robert P Maccubbin and Peter Martin, The Colonial Williamsburg Foundation, 1984

Michael Symes, 'Preparation of a Landscape Garden: Charles Hamilton's Sowing of Grass at Painshill', *Garden History* 13:1, 1985

Michael Symes, 'Robert FitzGerald's tour of Surrey gardens', *Journal of Garden History* 6:4, 1986

Michael Symes, 'A. B. Lambert and the Conifers at Painshill', *Garden History* 16:1, 1988

Michael Symes, 'Benjamin Bond Hopkins at Painshill', *Garden History* 27:2, 1999

Michael Symes, 'Charles Hamilton at Bowood', *Garden History* 34:2, 2006

Heimerick Tromp, 'A Dutchman's Visits to Some English Gardens in 1791', *Journal of Garden History* 2:1, 1982

Horace Walpole, 'Journals of visits to Country Seats, &c', *The Walpole Society* 16, 1928

Kenneth Woodbridge, 'Bélanger en Angleterre: Son carnet de voyage', *Architectural History* 25, 1982

Other sources are cited in the References.

ESSAYS AND ARTICLES

Jan Clark, 'The Travails of Bacchus', *Talking Heads: Garden Statuary in the Eighteenth Century*, Buckinghamshire Gardens Trust, 2007

Mavis Collier and David Wrightson, 'The Re-Creation of the Turkish Tent at Painshill', *Garden History* 21:1, 1993

Country Life, 6 March 1897, 19 March 1904 and 9 January 1958 (article by Gordon Nares)

Anthony Cross, 'The English garden in Catherine the Great's Russia', *Journal of Garden History* 13:3, 1993

Géza Hajós, 'The gardens of the British Isles in the diary of the Austrian Count Karl von Zinzendorf in the year 1768', *Journal of Garden History* 9:1, 1989

John Harris, 'Return to Eden', *Landscape*, June-August 1988

Lesley Howes and Jane Ward, 'Temple of Bacchus – 1762: Age of elegance restored', *Popular Archaeology*, February 1984

Alison Hodges, 'Painshill Park, Cobham, Surrey (1700–1800)', *Garden History* 2:2, 1973

Alison Hodges, 'Further notes on Painshill, Cobham, Surrey: Charles Hamilton's vineyard' [also notes on the water wheels], *Garden History* 3:1, 1974

Alison Hodges, 'Painshill, Cobham, Surrey: The grotto', *Garden History* 3:2, 1974

Roger Hunt, 'Painshill Paradise', *Surrey County magazine*, August 1991

Alastair Laing, 'Bacchus the Wanderer', *Apollo* [National Trust supplement], 2008

Claude Martin, 'David Geneste – a Huguenot Vine Grower at Cobham', *Surrey Archaeological Collections* LXVIII, 1971

Index

Acknowledgements

It would be impossible to thank everyone who has contributed to my knowledge and understanding of Painshill over a period of more than thirty-five years. However, particular mention must be made of the help provided by Karen Bridgman, Jan Clark, Kath Clark, Mark Ebdon, Lesley Howes, Pamela Hunter, Sally Jeffery, Caroline Jones, Norman and Beryl Kitz, Mark Laird, Cherrill Sands, David Taylor, Bill Tomlins, Philip Winterbottom and David Wrightson. The late Mavis Collier, formerly archivist to the Painshill Park Trust, furnished me with a great deal of material over the years, and I always profited from discussions of Painshill matters with her. In the early days I owed much to the late Alison Hodges, one of the 'pioneers' of the Garden History Society's drive to secure the restoration of the gardens, and she and Mavis Batey always gave encouragement.

Special mention must be made of Janie Burford, for so long Director of the Trust. Over the years her enthusiasm and support have been invaluable, together with her recognition of the importance of historical research, and in the case of this book she has contributed substantially to the account of the restoration.

The book would not have been possible without the active support of Mike Gove and the Painshill Park Trust in providing material, particularly in the form of illustrations. I am greatly indebted to all involved. The Trust has made a truly remarkable job of this large-scale and complex restoration.

Permission to quote from manuscript sources has been kindly granted as follows: Birmingham Archives and Heritage Service, The British Library Board, The Dorset History Centre, C Hoare & Co, The London School of Economics and Political Science, The National Archives, The National Library of Ireland, The Deputy Keeper of the Records of the Public Record Office of Northern Ireland, The Royal Bank of Scotland Group Archives and Warwickshire County Record Office.

Picture credits are recorded separately. In some instances it has not proved possible to identify the copyright owner, but the publishers would be glad to know if any such identifications can be made.

Picture credits

Images are reproduced by courtesy of the following:
Bodleian Library, University of Oxford, p.94 (bottom): Gough Maps 30, f.59v, item c.
The Bray family, p.28: 685/2/1/2/46.
British Library Board, p.69 (bottom): CRACH 1 Tab 1.b.1, Vol XVI, after p768; p.112 (left): 173518 Tab 14; p.112 (right): 173518 Tab 13; p.113 (left): 1609/2456, p.329 fig. LXXXIIIO; p.113 (right): 1609/2456, p.312 fig. LXXXIIIA; p.124 (top): CRACH 1 Tab 1.b.1, Vol. XVI, after p.768; p.125 (top): 34.f.11 Plate 3.
Trustees of the British Museum, pp.39, 53.
Kathleen Clark, p.118.
Ecole des Beaux-Arts, Paris, p.72 (top): EBA 1762/78; p.79: EBA 1762/94; p.84 (top): EBA 1762/92.
Elmbridge Museum (part of Elmbridge Borough Council's The Evelyn Estate, p.27: 6330/plan 6.
Leisure and Cultural Services Division), p.90: 108.1972/24.
Fitzwilliam Museum, Cambridge, p.26: PD6.-1953.
Fred Holmes, cover; pp.2, 4-5, 6, 17-18, 43, 59, 63, 66-7, 73, 75, 88-9, 91, 93, 95-6, 105, 106 (bottom), 107-8, 117, 135-7, 145, 156, 160, 162 (bottom), 165.
London School of Economics and Political Science, pp.84 (bottom), 106 (top right), 132: Ms Coll Misc 38 vol.I, ff.166, 160 and 158.
The National Archives, p.22: MR1/294.
The Nationalmuseum, Stockholm, p.24: NMH 201/1977; p.100 (bottom): NMH 446/1884; p.130 (bottom): NMH 51/1921.
Painshill Park Trust, pp.23, 51, 77, 85, 115, 151, 153, 157, 158 (left and right), 159, 161 (left), 162 (top), 163 (bottom).
Royal Academy of Art, Stockholm, pp.72 (bottom), 74, 100 (top), 106 (top left),131.
The Trustees of Sir John Soane's Museum, p.78 (both).
Sotheby's, p.94 (top).
State Hermitage Museum, St Petersburg, p.133.
Surrey History Centre, p.20: 7015/6b.
Townely Hall Art Gallery and Museum, Burnley, Lancashire/The Bridgeman Art Library, p.52.
V&A Images/Victoria and Albert Museum, p.3: E916-1921, p.130 (top): CT73592.
Warwickshire County Record Office, p.103: CR1841/7, f23.
David Wrightson, p.161 (right).

All other illustrations are from private collections.